# About This Book

## Why is this book important?

This is a book about a new instructional design approach that I call "scenario-based e-learning." You may have heard other names, such as immersive learning, problem-based learning, or whole-task instruction. What's important is not the name—but how you design, develop, and deploy a learner-centered instructional environment that can accelerate expertise, build critical thinking skills, and promote transfer of learning. In this book you will learn the what, when, why, and how of scenario-based e-learning lessons, ranging from simple branched scenarios to complex simulated environments.

You can apply the guidelines in this book to design of e-learning lessons intended to be self-study or self-study with online collaboration, or to instructor-led settings that use the scenario-based e-learning lessons as case study resources.

## What can you achieve with this book?

The guidelines and examples in this book will help you:

- Distinguish between scenario-based e-learning and traditional instructional approaches
- Identify the benefits of a scenario-based e-learning design for your learners and instructional goals
- Determine when scenario-based e-learning is appropriate in your context
- Identify specific outcomes of scenario-based e-learning relevant to your organizational goals
- Classify your instructional goals into one or more of eight learning domains that are good candidates for scenario-based e-learning
- Apply a design model to your own content and learning objectives
- Evaluate outcomes from your scenario-based e-learning course
- Apply current research on scenario-based e-learning to your own courses
- Identify tacit expert knowledge using cognitive task analysis techniques
- Make a business case for scenario-based e-learning in your organization

To help you achieve these goals, each chapter ends with a worksheet in which you can apply the guidelines and examples in that chapter to your own projects. You can find the worksheets online at www.pfeiffer/go/scenario. The password is Professional.

## How is the book organized?

The first two chapters focus on the what, why, and when of scenario-based e-learning. Based on examples from diverse scenario-based multimedia lessons, you will see the unique features and benefits of this approach and identify situations in your organization that could profit from it. As you start to consider potential candidates for scenario-based e-learning in your organization, you can review eight knowledge and skill objectives, along with eight learning domains that represent the most common applications and will guide your design process.

Chapters 3 through 8 make up the heart of the book and focus on a design model for a scenario-based e-learning lesson, starting with an overview in Chapter 3 and proceeding with detailed guidelines and examples for each of the seven components of the design. In these chapters you will define the following key elements: general and specific intended outcomes, trigger events, case data, guidance and instructional resources, and feedback-reflection components.

In the last third of the book I summarize strategies to evaluate outcomes from scenario-based e-learning with an emphasis on testing to assess the instructional quality of and learning from your lessons. Although scenario-based e-learning is relatively new, in Chapter 10 I summarize recent research evidence followed by a chapter on supplementing your traditional job analysis with cognitive task analysis. In the final chapter you will find a brief discussion of how to make a business case for a scenario-based e-learning design project to include cost-benefit analysis.

## Appendices

Please take a look at Appendices A and B, as they will guide your understanding of the examples in the book. Appendix A introduces the main samples used throughout the book, giving you a little background on each lesson. Appendix B is a repeat of all of the screen-capture figures in the sequence shown throughout the book. Because of space limitations, I refer back to many figures appearing in previous chapters. To make your access of these easier, you can bookmark Appendix B and look there to quickly find a specific figure. Note that all screen capture figures also appear online at www.pfeiffer.com/go/scenario.

Appendix C is adjunct information related to Chapter 9. It summarizes guidelines on ways to evaluate your scenario-based e-learning project. To measure learning outcomes, you will need to construct reliable and valid tests. In Appendix C you will find a review of test reliability and validity, essential concepts to any test development process. Review Appendix C if you plan to develop tests to assess knowledge and skill gains from your scenario-based e-learning course *and if you need a refresher on these concepts.*

## What's Online

To supplement the book, you can find the following at www.pfeiffer.com/go/scenario. Password: Professional:

1. Screen Captures in Book Figure Sequence. Because books are limited regarding the number, size, and color of figures, I have put all screen capture figures online in the sequence in which they appear in the book. Consider keeping your smart phone or tablet next to the book while reading in order to easily view the screen shots in color.
2. Sample Storyboards from Seven Scenario-Based eLearning Lessons. I have drawn primarily upon seven lessons to illustrate the concepts and guidelines in this book. However, in the book they do not appear in an organized instructional sequence. Therefore, online you will find storyboards from these courses arranged in a logical instructional flow. Here you will see additional screens beyond those displayed in the book.
3. Planning Worksheets. At the end of each chapter is a section titled "Scenario-Based e-Learning and You" that contains a worksheet for applying chapter ideas to your own projects. You can access these online for adaptation to your own environment.
4. Instructor Guide. For anyone who would like to use the book as a course text, you can contact your Pfeiffer representative to access an instructor guide to include a syllabus and slides.

# About Pfeiffer

Pfeiffer serves the professional development and hands-on resource needs of training and human resource practaitioners and gives them products to do their jobs better. We deliver proven ideas and solutions from experts in HR development and HR management, and we offer effective and customizable tools to improve workplace performance. From novice to seasoned professional, Pfeiffer is the source you can trust to make yourself and your organization more successful.

**Essential Knowledge**  Pfeiffer produces insightful, practical, and comprehensive materials on topics that matter the most to training and HR professionals. Our Essential Knowledge resources translate the expertise of seasoned professionals into practical, how-to guidance on critical workplace issues and problems. These resources are supported by case studies, worksheets, and job aids and are frequently supplemented with CD-ROMs, websites, and other means of making the content easier to read, understand, and use.

**Essential Tools**  Pfeiffer's Essential Tools resources save time and expense by offering proven, ready-to-use materials—including exercises, activities, games, instruments, and assessments—for use during a training or team-learning event. These resources are frequently offered in looseleaf or CD-ROM format to facilitate copying and customization of the material.

Pfeiffer also recognizes the remarkable power of new technologies in expanding the reach and effectiveness of training. While e-hype has often created whizbang solutions in search of a problem, we are dedicated to bringing convenience and enhancements to proven training solutions. All our e-tools comply with rigorous functionality standards. The most appropriate technology wrapped around essential content yields the perfect solution for today's on-the-go trainers and human resource professionals.

www.pfeiffer.com

*Essential resources for training and HR professionals*

# SCENARIO-BASED e-LEARNING

## Evidence-Based Guidelines for Online Workforce Learning

### RUTH COLVIN CLARK

Pfeiffer

A Wiley Imprint
www.pfeiffer.com

Published by Pfeiffer
An Imprint of Wiley
One Montgomery Street, Suite 1200, San Francisco, CA 94104-4594 www.pfeiffer.com
Cover art: Photo ephemera | Getty

For additional copies/bulk purchases of this book in the U.S. please contact 800–274–4434.

Pfeiffer books and products are available through most bookstores. To contact Pfeiffer directly call our Customer Care Department within the U.S. at 800-274-4434, outside the U.S. at 317-572-3985, fax 317-572-4002, or visit www.pfeiffer.com.

Pfeiffer publishes in a variety of print and electronic formats and by print-on-demand. Some material included with standard print versions of this book may not be included in e-books or in print-on-demand. If this book refers to media such as a CD or DVD that is not included in the version you purchased, you may download this material at http://booksupport.wiley.com. For more information about Wiley products, visit www.wiley.com.

**Library of Congress Cataloging-in-Publication Data**
Clark, Ruth Colvin, author.
    Scenario-based e-learning: evidence-based guidelines for online workforce learning / Ruth Colvin Clark.
    pages cm
    Includes bibliographical references and index.
    ISBN 978-1-118-12725-4 (pbk.); 978-1-118-41645-7 (ebook); 978-1-118-41900-7 (ebook); 978-1-118-43370-6 (ebook)
        1. Employees—Training of—Computer-assisted instruction.  2. Problem-based learning.  3. Instructional systems—Design.  I. Title.
    HF5549.5.T7C58824  2013
    658.3'124—dc23

                                                                                    2012032814

| | |
|---|---|
| Acquiring Editor: | Matthew Davis |
| Director of Development: | Kathleen Dolan Davies |
| Production Editor: | Dawn Kilgore |
| Editor: | Rebecca Taff |
| Manufacturing Supervisor: | Becky Morgan |

Printed in the United States of America

*PB Printing*      10  9  8  7  6  5  4

# CONTENTS

# FOREWORD

To young adults across the world, learning to drive a car is a rite of passage. A long-awaited milestone to be celebrated. A ticket to independence and freedom.

To those tasked with teaching a young adult to drive, it is a burden to be feared. A milestone to be avoided at all costs. A test of patience and fortitude.

Driving a car is among the most complex activities that human beings learn in their lifetime, as it involves the simultaneous physical mastery of vehicle handling, intellectual mastery of traffic rules, and emotional mastery of everyone who stands between you and your destination. Anyone who has ever survived the ritual of driver education has likely started out by breaking down this mind-bogglingly complex activity into a series of simple steps. For example, anytime you enter a vehicle, one driver education resource suggests following the procedure:

1. Adjust the driver's seat.

2. Fasten your seatbelt.

3. Secure loose items in the passenger compartment.

4. Adjust the rearview and side mirrors.

5. Verify visibility through the windshield.

6. Adjust ventilation.

7. Adjust head restraints.

8. Wear any prescription glasses or contact lenses.

9. Lock your doors.

Let's be honest with each other: How many times have you followed these steps above (or a procedure like it) when getting into the car for your morning commute or quick trip to the corner market? One hundred times, ten, once, perhaps never?

As in the case of this driving procedure, instructional design 101 has traditionally taught us to break down tasks into learning objectives, decompose complex objectives into smaller ones, chunk them, sequence, and simplify. We must first teach learners requisite facts and concepts. We should offer them a small, manageable number of basic procedures and processes: the ten steps to quit smoking, seven habits of successful people, five phases of developing training, or nine steps to drive a car.

The reality is that providing simplified steps like these is indeed useful when we first endeavor to master a complex activity. However, as we build expertise, two things become clear: (1) procedures that helped make us proficient as learners aren't always comprehensive or even correct and (2) it's not always easy or possible to decompose certain behaviors into steps or a simple checklist.

As we gain mastery within a domain, we also develop the ability to identify steps that are truly necessary, ones that can be reordered, steps that are just situational, and the tasks that can be skipped entirely. In short, we begin to question whether the best practices that were bestowed upon us are really . . . well, the best. For example, adjusting the seat and mirrors in a car is really only necessary after someone else has recently borrowed your vehicle. Perhaps it's best to secure loose items in the back seat before buckling in rather than afterward. Prescription glasses may only be useful when it's dark out, adjusting the air conditioning only when it's hot. On a day-to-day basis, it's only necessary to fasten your seat-belt and then race to enter the crawl of rush-hour traffic.

In addition, we encounter situations in which different approaches to the same problem can lead to the same outcome. For example, if you provide two cab drivers with the same destination address, it's possible that one may take a longer route via the freeway while the other takes a shorter route using surface streets, and both could arrive at the same time. One salesman may prefer to use a consultative approach while another is a master of the "hard sell," but both could ultimately be successful at closing a deal with a treasured client. Two instructional designers given the same performance problem will likely design and develop learning solutions that are markedly different. In short, many problems that we encounter are difficult to deconstruct and simplify, as the right and wrong way to do something is not always black and white.

Enter scenario-based e-learning.

Scenario-based e-learning (SBeL) acknowledges that the world is not black and white but rather shades of gray. It enables learning professionals to design training that accommodates the fact that there may not be a wrong way of doing something, but there may in fact be good, better, and best ways. It allows us to immerse learners in real problems, provide them with guidelines and principles to deal with those problems, and show them the consequences of their choices in a safe, efficient manner.

SBeL is not at all new. In fact, proponents of scenario-based and, more broadly, problem-based learning (PBL) have been actively espousing its benefits for almost thirty years. However, we have entered an exciting period that makes scenario-based e-learning both timely and relevant.

Just a dozen years ago, it would have been cost and time-prohibitive (but not impossible) to build an e-learning course that presented the learner with real problems, adapted to their choices, and gave them targeted feedback on their performance. This has changed over the years, and now several rapid e-learning tools have emerged on the market that make the creation of robust scenario-based e-learning courses as simple as building a presentation. The upside is that, more so than at any point in the training industry, it is easy for learning professionals to design and develop scenario-based e-learning that is effective and efficient. The downside is that it is now easy for learning professionals to design and develop SBeL that is neither effective nor efficient.

The other reason that this is an exciting time for us is that Ruth Clark has added to her tremendous legacy in the learning industry with her latest contribution *Scenario-Based e-Learning.* I can attest first-hand that Ruth has a tremendous and unique gift. She is unparalleled in her ability to consume volumes of published research, see patterns and trends across the research, and distill these into concepts and guidelines that are easy for you and me to apply when solving our learning problems. In the book that you now hold in your hands, Ruth helps you to identify situations in which SBeL should be applied, to design effective scenario-based e-learning, to best provide guidance and feedback, and to evaluate and assess learning.

For those who know me, it is no secret that I like cars. It would come as no surprise then that I recently decided to take a class on high-performance driving. In short, after driving an automobile for about two decades, I decided to go back to school and relearn how to drive.

In many ways, this book is like making a very similar choice. You may be a seasoned learning professional who has designed hundreds if not thousands of courses. You may be new to the field with some recent introduction to instructional design. Whatever the case may be, I challenge you to let go of your existing paradigms and relearn how to design effective and interactive learning.

Frank Nguyen

# ACKNOWLEDGMENTS

A book like this one demands plenty of diverse examples to make it meaningful. I could not have written the book without the lesson samples generously provided by many instructional colleagues. Here is a list of contributors and the examples they provided:

| *Contributor* | *Organization* | *Example(s)* |
| --- | --- | --- |
| Dale Bambrick | Raytheon Professional Services | Automotive troubleshooting Optical lab |
| Andrew Corbett | Veterinary Information Network | Cat anesthesia Dog blood loss |
| Gary Klein | Klein Associates | Cognitive task analysis example |
| Susanne Lajoie | McGill University | Bioworld |
| Nancy Michael | Moody's Analytics | Bank loan underwriter lesson |
| Mark A. Palmer | Mapgraphs | Graphic design for Bridezilla and pharmaceutical sales |
| Sharon Sloane | WILL Interactive | Gator 6 Beyond the Front |
| Carol Wideman | VCOM 3D | Customer service demonstration |

What you are about to read is clearer and better organized thanks to the advice of reviewers who dedicated the time to read through an unedited manuscript and make detailed and helpful suggestions for improvement. My thanks to:

*Reviewers*

Dale Bambrick

Marjan Bradesko

Rob Foshay

Frank Nguyen

Tanya Pang

Ken Silber

### *Editors*

Matt Davis for initial and continued support of the book

Leslie Stephen for expert developmental guidance

Rebecca Taff, whose copyedits have made the book consistent and more readable

# CHAPTER

1

# WHAT IS SCENARIO-BASED e-LEARNING?

Imagine Corey, an apprentice automotive technician. He's had basic training in the fundamentals. He's completed a year on the job. Still, when an unusual work order shows up, he can't help feeling a little uneasy. He sees the confidence and efficiency of the journeymen technicians and wishes he could get there faster. . . .

Next consider the situation of a new combat officer. He's been on several deployments, but this is his first time in charge of the entire company in a combat situation. He looks forward to the challenge but also realizes that he will be making life-and-death decisions. Everyone has to start somewhere, he thinks. But he wishes he had a little more experience to fall back on.

Finally, consider Linda. As a software development team lead, she spends a lot of time with customers, team members, and contractors. Linda groans as she sees all tomorrow morning blocked out for the annual mandatory compliance training. Just like last year—staff from legal and HR lecture on everything from taking gifts from clients to insider information laws and penalties. And this year there is a new policy—NO mobile devices on during the training! *I really could use the time to review the latest project plan revision! How can I get around this time-waster?*

If any of these situations sound familiar, you may find a solution in scenario-based e-learning.

The complexity of 21st century work is rooted in expertise. And as the word implies, expertise grows out of experience. In fact, psychologists who studied experts in sports, music, and strategy games like chess have found that people require about ten years of sustained and focused practice to reach the highest levels of competency in any domain. However, today's organizations don't have ten years to grow expertise. And some skills such as reacting to emergencies demand practice before the situation arises. Are there some ways to accelerate expertise outside of normal job experience? Are there some training techniques to turn a compliance meeting into a more relevant and engaging experience? One answer is scenario-based e-learning.

## SCENARIO-BASED e-LEARNING: A FIRST LOOK

Let's begin with a couple of examples. I will draw on seven main lesson examples throughout the book and you can see an orientation to these lessons in Appendix A. In addition, you can find color screen shots from these lessons at www.pfeiffer.com/go/scenario. One set of online screen shots is organized in the sequence in which they appear in the book. You can refer to these as you read the book. A second set shows multiple screen shots from several of the main lessons in their logical instructional sequence to illustrate how an intact lesson might flow.

Figure 1.1 illustrates a virtual automotive repair bay. After reviewing a work order, the student technician can access the various on-screen shop tools to run virtual diagnostic tests. The results are saved on his virtual clipboard. As he works

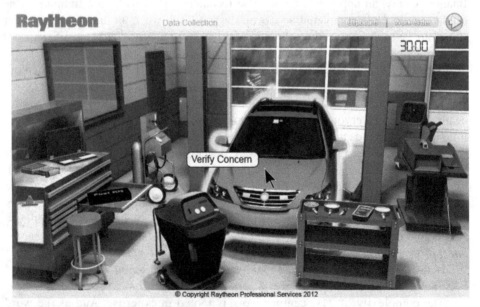

**FIGURE 1.1.** *A Virtual Automotive Shop.*
With permission from Raytheon Professional Services.

through the problem, he can access the company technical reference guides on the online shop computer as well as expert advice through the telephone. When he is ready, he can select the appropriate failure and repair from a list of ten failures. After making a selection, the automobile functions normally or continues to show symptoms associated with the failure. At the end of the lesson, he can review his sequence of testing activities, which have been tracked by the program. He can compare his decisions, shown in Figure 1.2 on the right, with an expert solution shown on the left.

For contrast, let's take an introductory look at a second example from a demonstration lesson called Bridezilla that Mark Palmer and I designed for newly hired wedding planners. This course uses tabs to navigate to each of four main resources: (1) worksheets where client data is entered and stored, (2) an album that includes examples with financial data for different types of weddings, (3) advisors, and (4) a notes section. In Figure 1.3 I show the menu to access advice on religion, design, negotiation skills, and finances—each a major knowledge and skill domain required for successful wedding planning. Each advisor provides basic information with additional links to various reference sources. Unlike the troubleshooting scenario, the goal

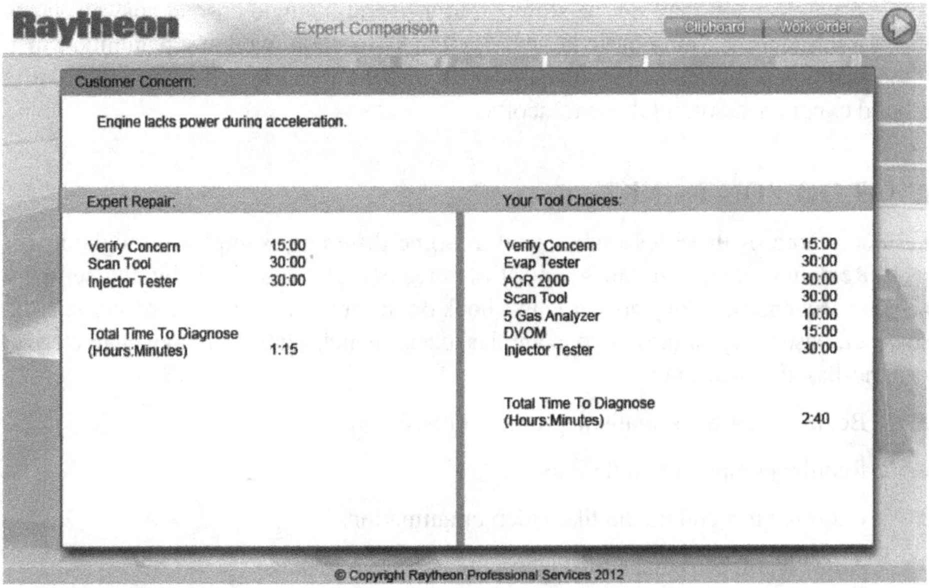

**FIGURE 1.2.** *Learner Actions (on Right) Compared with Expert Actions (on Left).*
With permission from Raytheon Professional Services.

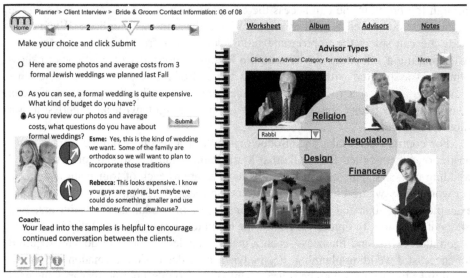

**FIGURE 1.3.** *The Learner Can Access Virtual Advisors for Wedding Planning.*

of this type of lesson may not be so much to arrive at a single correct answer but to offer a context for learning basic knowledge and skills about wedding planning. Most of the wedding solutions will involve tradeoffs, and the scenarios offer the opportunity to build experience around those tradeoffs.

## WHAT DO YOU THINK?

We'll see more of these lessons as well as some different examples throughout the book. Remember that you can see a set of screens organized either by course or in the same sequence that they appear in this book online at www.pfeiffer.com/go/scenario. However, based on just these two examples, check which features below characterize scenario-based e- learning:

❑   1. Begin with a work-realistic problem or assignment.

❑   2. Require computer simulations.

❑   3. Require high-end media like video or animations.

❑   4. Allow learners to make mistakes and learn from mistakes.

❑   5. Provide immediate feedback when an incorrect option is selected.

❑   6. Use a structured rule-example-practice sequence.

You can see my answers at the end of the chapter. Take a look now if you can't wait—or find most of the answers by reading the next few pages.

## SCENARIO-BASED e-LEARNING DEFINED

I know it's not too exciting to start a discussion with a definition. However, our training field actually needs more definitions because we routinely use the same words to mean different things and different words to mean the same thing. No point in moving forward until we make a good attempt at a common understanding. Here's my definition:

> Scenario-based e-learning is a preplanned guided inductive learning environment designed to accelerate expertise in which the learner assumes the role of an actor responding to a work-realistic assignment or challenge, which in turn responds to reflect the learner's choices.

Let's look at this definition in more detail.

### *The Learner Is an Actor Responding to a Job-Realistic Situation*

By actor, I mean that the learner is placed in a realistic work role and takes on-screen actions to complete a work assignment or respond to a work challenge. Because the environment is highly learner-centric, a key feature of scenario-based e-learning is high engagement learning. In traditional instructional environments such as a slide-based presentation, the learner is an observer and listener—primarily playing the role of a passive receiver. I call these learning environments receptive or "show and tell."

In directive environments, the learner observes and listens and periodically responds to some questions or a short exercise based on what she has heard and seen. In these moderately engaging environments, the learner is a receiver and an occasional responder to highly structured questions. Procedural software training often reflects this type of design. In contrast, in scenario-based e-learning, the learner assumes the role of an active respondent from the beginning and continues in that mode throughout the lesson.

### *The Environment Is Preplanned*

Like any well-designed training, there are defined learning objectives and desired knowledge and skill outcomes which are the focus of the lesson design. For example, in the automotive technician training, the objective requires the learner to follow an efficient and accurate process to perform and interpret diagnostic tests in order to identify the correct failure and repair action. In Bridezilla, there is no single "correct" answer. Instead, the objective is to help learners make decisions during wedding planning consultation that reflect the religious, financial, aesthetic, and social values of the clients. As the learner works with different virtual clients, she has the opportunity to learn about diverse cultural, religious, aesthetic, and financial aspects of weddings as well as to apply problem-solving skills in negotiating discrepancies in client resources or opinions.

### Learning Is Inductive Rather Than Instructive

In inductive environments, the emphasis is on learning from a series of progressively complex experiences by taking actions, reviewing responses to those actions, and reflecting on the consequences. For example, the automotive technician student has the opportunity to try a diverse sequence of tests (some more relevant than others) and to learn from the results of his choices. Contrast this approach with a directive design that emphasizes learning from a structured series of explanations and short practice exercises. For example, a traditional course design teaches the five stages of a trouble-shooting process along with associated tools by presenting steps, giving examples, and assigning structured practice activities.

### The Instruction Is Guided

One of the most important success factors in scenario-based e-learning is sufficient guidance to minimize the flounder factor. A recent meta-analysis summarizing more than five hundred studies that compared a discovery approach with either directive or guided discovery, found significantly better learning among the more guided versions (Alfieri, Brooks, Aldrich, & Tenebaum, 2011). There are a number of ways you can provide guidance, ranging from case complexity progression (low to high), amount of support provided (high to low), and interface and navigation design. Chapter 6 is devoted solely to techniques and examples for guidance in scenario-based e-learning environments.

### Scenarios Incorporate Instructional Resources

Unlike most games that rely solely on inductive learning, scenario-based e-learning environments embed a number of resources for explicit learning, including virtual coaches, model answers, and even traditional tutorials. As illustrated in Figure 1.3, the scenario offers a number of virtual coaches as sources for diverse perspectives on wedding planning. Like a game, scenario-based e-learning presents a challenge. However, competition to achieve a particular score or out-play others is not an essential feature and can even be counterproductive. In Chapter 7 I will illustrate different approaches you can use to embed instructional opportunities in your learning environments.

### The Goal Is to Accelerate Workplace Expertise

By working through a series of job scenarios that could take months or years to complete in the work environment, experience is compressed. At its core, scenario-based e-learning is job experience in a box—designed to be unpackaged and stored in the learner's brain. Unlike real-world experience, scenario-based e-learning scenarios not only compress time but also offer a sequence and structure of events designed to guide learning in a controlled manner. The automotive technician and the wedding consultant would most likely eventually learn the skills needed on the job. However, rather than months and years, the multimedia compressed experiential environment shrinks the learning experience into a matter of hours.

You will discover a wide range of design options that reflect these six features that I designate as key elements of scenario-based e-learning. One of my goals is to help you adapt these features to meet the specific goals, learners, and resources available in your organization.

### What's in a Name?

Before we leave this section on definitions, as I mentioned previously, in our profession, we have few consistent terms. What I am calling scenario-based e-learning has also been labeled problem-based learning, whole-task learning, guided discovery, immersive and goal-based learning, to name just a few. Almost every time I do a workshop, I hear a new term. I know that some experts have precise definitions for these various instructional designs. And if your organization has a different term, feel free to stick with it. For consistency I'm going to use scenario-based e-learning. However, my goal in this book is to provide some guidelines and examples to help you to design learning environments that are task-centered, engaging, and designed to accelerate expertise, regardless of what you want to call them.

## SCENARIO-BASED VS. DIRECTIVE TRAINING ENVIRONMENTS

Let's contrast a scenario-based e-learning design to a more traditional approach, known as a directive or part-task design. In Table 1.1 and the discussion to follow I summarize some of the main differences.

If you have designed, taught, or taken a beginning software course, you are familiar with a directive design. Traditional procedural training, also known as *part-task* or *directive,* typically follows a "rule-example-practice-feedback" sequence. Directive training based on behaviorist learning psychology emphasizes learning based on stimulus (question)-response (response to the question) and feedback (immediate knowledge of results). Typically, the job role is parsed into a number of small tasks, each to be taught in a lesson that states and demonstrates steps, assigns practice, and gives immediate corrective feedback.

Take an Excel class, for example. The goal of using a spreadsheet is broken into a number of small tasks, each with associated key knowledge topics. For example, topics such as *What is a cell? What are cell references?* or *What are formulas?* are explained and demonstrated by the instructor using a simple spreadsheet. Next the students practice constructing and inputting several formulas following step-by-step directions. When they make a mistake, they receive immediate feedback and correct their responses. After completing several lessons, a small business case study gives students the opportunity to consolidate and practice the component skills in a holistic context.

In contrast, in scenario-based e-learning, the lesson kicks off with a case assignment. For example, in an Excel lesson, the learner is given a simple spreadsheet for a small business and asked to calculate weekly sales totals. Rather than receiving a series of structured lessons and demonstrations, the learners are free to try different

TABLE 1.1. **Scenario-Based e-Learning vs. Directive Training Environments**

| Feature | Scenario-Based | Directive |
|---|---|---|
| Role of Case Study | Lesson begins with the case The case serves as a context for learning | Lesson ends with the case The case serves as culminating application for learning |
| Lesson Organization | Holistic—Variable chunks Knowledge and skill components integrated into the case assignment | Hierarchical—Small Chunks Knowledge and skill components build from simple to more complex culminating in case assignment |
| Role of Learner | An actor to resolve challenges and tasks in the scenario | A responder to frequent and structured questions designed to build knowledge and skills |
| Role of Instruction | Provide a realistic engaging scenario accompanied by resources to support learning | Provide highly structured content, examples, and practice with feedback to support learning |
| Instructional Approach | Inductive—Learning from experience and reflection on the consequences of actions taken or decisions made | Instructive—Learning from a structured, organized sequence of exposition, examples, and frequent content-specific practice exercises |
| Interactivity | High overt learner activity in an environment of moderate to high levels of learner control over actions | Moderate overt learner activity during periodic structured interactions |
| Feedback | Consequential in which the learner takes actions, makes decisions and experiences the outcomes as well as corrective in which the learner is told whether the response is accurate and why | Corrective, in which the learner responds to structured questions and is told (usually immediately) whether a response is accurate or not and why |

| Feature | Scenario-Based | Directive |
|---|---|---|
| Best Uses | Building critical thinking skills and experience in strategic tasks<br>Accelerating expertise when on-the-job training is unsafe, impractical, or too slow<br>Motivating learners through job-relevant scenarios | Building procedural skills to learn relatively routine tasks<br>Offering efficient paths to learning knowledge and skills associated with procedural tasks |
| Target Audience | Often best suited for apprentice workers who already have relevant work background experience | Often best suited for learners who are new to the knowledge and skills included in the training |

actions and also to access reference and guidance resources as they proceed. Learning and reference resources are embedded or linked into the scenario environment.

## Learning from Mistakes

Compared to directive designs, scenario-based e-learning assumes quite a different attitude toward mistakes. Rather than viewing errors as negatives to be hopefully avoided or at least immediately corrected, in scenario-based e-learning mistakes are seen as learning opportunities. As Neils Bohr said: "An expert is someone who has made all of the mistakes that can be made in a limited domain." In some scenario-based e-learning designs, as in the real world, learners may not realize they've made some poor decisions until they are near the end of the case. In the automotive example, only after the learner selects the correct failure and repair activity, does he see the consequences of his choices by comparing his process with that of an expert. In other scenario-based e-learning lessons, feedback is provided with each step. In Chapter 8, you can review much more detail about the what, when, and where of feedback in scenario-based e-learning.

## Scenarios to Lead or to Culminate?

Purists will argue that true scenario-based learning leads with the scenario, which serves as the engine for learning. Various learning resources are linked into stages of scenario resolution. However, I've seen several clients switch from using the scenario as a lead-off event to preceding it with a structured series of lessons. I'm not sure of all the reasons, but I suspect that, in some situations, the mental load imposed by learning while resolving a problem was too heavy for many learners. Instead, they have found it more effective to use the scenario as a culminating learning experience. The best solution no doubt depends on the prior knowledge of your learners and the complexity of your instructional goals.

In Chapter 10, which summarizes research evidence related to scenario-based e-learning, I will describe some experiments showing benefits of starting with a scenario followed by directive training and others showing benefits of preceding a scenario-based simulation with directive training. Whether your scenario initiates or follows directive instruction, the guidelines in this book are applicable to your scenario design.

## *Target Audience*

Because learning new knowledge and skills while solving a job-realistic problem can impose quite a bit of mental load, in general scenario-based e-learning is best suited to learners who already have some job experience. For example, the automotive trouble shooting lesson would likely be quite overwhelming for learners unfamiliar with common testing equipment in a service bay. In contrast, a directive approach is well suited for workers with new job roles or assignments. Because the directive approach offers small chunks in a hierarchical sequence, the learner is spared excessive mental overload.

## WHAT SCENARIO-BASED e-LEARNING IS *NOT*

It might be helpful to clarify what scenario-based e-learning is by looking at a few examples that could be misclassified as scenario-based e-learning. Here are some of my favorites:

### *Not a Game*

Clark and Mayer (2011) define games as a competitive activity with a challenge to achieve a goal, a set of rules and constraints, and a specific context. How is scenario-based e-learning different? Like a game, scenario-based e-learning does pose a challenge, and there may also be rules and constraints. However, an element of competition is not the essential feature that it is in games. Second, an essential feature of scenario-based e-learning is a specific context—the context of the workplace. Some games may embed a work context, but many do not.

Although scenario-based e-learning could have a game overlay—say by tracking and showing progress "scores," there is no solid evidence that a competitive element will lead to better learning. In fact, if you want to wrap your scenario-based e-learning in a game shell, you need to be careful that the activities and rewards associated with game progress are aligned to your learning goals. In summary, while some scenario-based e-learning could be designed with gaming elements, I view scenario-based e-learning and serious games as two separate approaches to learning.

### *Not a Scenario with Questions*

I have seen lessons called scenario-based e-learning that consisted of a work scenario followed by a series of multiple-choice or open-ended questions about the scenario.

For example, learners view a customer service interaction. Then they respond to questions such as: *How could the customer service representative have responded more effectively? Which of the following principles did the customer service representative apply when she. . .?*

While these kinds of scenario-driven exercises have learning value, they fail to incorporate all of the features of a scenario-based e-learning environment. In particular, the learner does not become an actor in the scenario. Rather, he or she is more of an observer reflecting on and analyzing it. Often these types of lessons approximate a directive design more than scenario-based e-learning.

### Not a Simulation

Although scenario-based e-learning can be based on a simulation, simulation is not an essential element. I define a simulation as a dynamic model of a real-world phenomena or process often simplified to reflect core principles. Neither the automotive troubleshooting nor the Bridezilla examples I introduced in this chapter are based on a truly dynamic simulation. In contrast, in Figure 1.4 I show a scenario-based e-learning lesson on emergency treatment for blood loss in dogs. In this simulation, the learner has a choice of different treatments for a dog with blood loss. As treatment decisions are made, the student can review dynamic changes in the dog's status reflected in

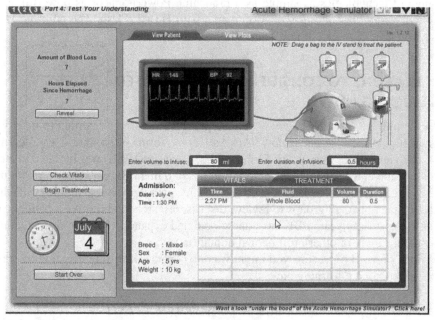

**FIGURE 1.4.** *A Scenario-Based e-Learning Simulation of Treatment of a Dog for Blood Loss.*
With permission from the Veterinary Information Network.

the on-screen EKG. The EKG responses are programmed with a mathematical model based on known physiological responses.

### Not About a Delivery Mode or Media

You could present your scenario entirely in text—although evidence is accumulating that, at least for tasks that rely on discrimination and interpretation of sights and sounds, some visualization of the case promotes learning. A scenario-based e-learning lesson could be "delivered" as a stand-alone self-study digital resource either on the Internet or on a CD. Alternatively, it could serve as a resource in an instructor-led training (ILT) environment—in either a face-to-face or virtual classroom. In an instructor-led environment, learners could review the case as prework or as an initial learning exercise at the first meeting. Then, depending on the outcome goals, the instructor can provide learning resources, assign teams to select and discuss scenario actions and resolutions, and offer teams opportunities to present and debrief their solutions. A recent meta-analysis reports that blended learning environments that incorporate both synchronous and asynchronous events result in better learning than either instructor-led or self-study alone (U.S. Department of Education, 2010).

### Not About Specific Technology

Scenario-based e-learning is an instructional design approach that can be realized with a range of technologies as simple as a branching PowerPoint or as powerful as the automotive troubleshooting scenario created with HTML/Flash. The point is: Don't think you need high-end or new technologies to implement it.

## SIX REASONS TO CONSIDER SCENARIO-BASED E-LEARNING NOW

Why should you consider how you can adopt scenario-based e-learning to meet your organizational learning needs now? After all, some forms of scenario-based learning have been around for forty years. Problem-based learning (PBL) was initiated in medical education at McMasters University in the 1970s. In a PBL curriculum, rather than taking a series of science classes, such as anatomy, pathology, or bacteriology, medical students meet in small groups to review, discuss, research, and resolve a patient case. Over the past forty years PBL has gone global and expanded beyond medical education into a variety of other professional domains.

Here's my list of reasons you might want to consider investing time and resources in scenario-based e-learning now:

### 1. Scenario-Based e-Learning Can Accelerate Expertise

There is no substitute for experience as the basis for job competence, and scenario-based e-learning offers opportunities to gain experience in a safe and controlled manner. The world of work often includes tasks that occur infrequently. For example, some automotive failures are relatively rare. Scenario-based e-learning can focus specifically on those scarce opportunities.

Second, the world of work does not usually present learning opportunities in the best sequence for learning. But in scenario-based e-learning a series of simulated work challenges can be organized from simple to complex, thus assuring a smoother learning curve.

Third, responding to high-risk tasks such as emergencies cannot be readily practiced in a real-world environment. Scenario-based e-learning can build cases from records of actual incidents to help learners gain expertise before it's needed.

### 2. Scenario-Based e-Learning Can Offer Return on Investment

Most likely before you begin a major training initiative, you need to present a business case. In situations in which on-the-job experience is rare, dangerous, or impractical, scenario-based e-learning can provide a cost-effective option. For example, the automotive troubleshooting lessons could be learned on the job or in a teaching shop using cars with various failures. However, a cost-comparison of these three alternatives found that a scenario-based e-learning approach offered the best return on investment. See Chapter 12 for more details on making a business case for scenario-based e-learning.

### 3. Learners Like Scenario-Based e-Learning

Evaluation of PBL in medical education finds that most medical students like it better than the traditional science-based curriculum. Why? I think the answer is relevance. Because medical students have patient-care career goals, they find learning in the context of a patient case more motivating than learning science facts in a decontextualized manner. A second satisfier is engagement. In scenario-based environments, the learner is the main actor and spends most of his or her time interacting in the scenario world.

Remember Linda, who was dreading taking the annual compliance training consisting of a series of lectures on company policies? Imagine her reaction to being told that she can take the required course any time in the next quarter on the intranet in approximately two hours. Further, once logged in, she finds herself in the position of having to immediately make a decision about accepting an offer of some game tickets from a client. Before she knows it, she's not only physically but also mentally engaged in the experience and starting to consider how corporate policies apply to her work.

### 4. Scenario-Based e-Learning Has Better Transfer Potential

How often have you taken a class but never really used the skills back on the job? The class may have contained some useful knowledge, but it was not presented in a way that could be readily applied to your work setting. Scenario-based e-learning provides a solution to transfer failure. Because scenario-based e-learning is all about context, you learn in an environment that mirrors the job or something similar to it. Rather than attending lectures on compliance policies and laws, you apply those policies by resolving compliance dilemmas. Your new knowledge is contextualized and indexed in your brain in a manner more likely to be retrieved when needed on the job.

### 5. Scenario-Based e-Learning Can Build Critical Thinking Skills

While directive designs are effective for learning procedures, they are often limited when it comes to building knowledge and skills for more strategic tasks that do not have a simple

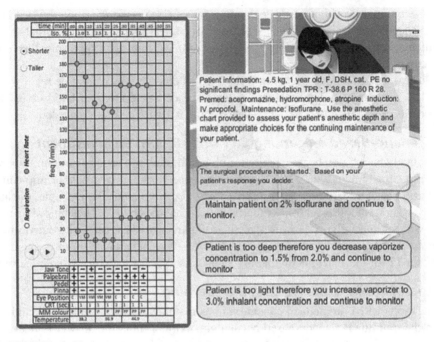

**FIGURE 1.5.** *A Branched Scenario Can Be Based on Links in Presentation Software.*
With permission from Veterinary Information Network.

correct or incorrect answer. In the next chapter we will look in greater detail into the types of tasks, outcome skills, and learners who benefit most from scenario-based e-learning.

### 6. Technology Can Facilitate Scenario-Based e-Learning Development

Recent advances in authoring resources make it much easier to construct a scenario-based e-learning lesson than has been the case in the past. In fact, some authoring programs are designed specifically for that purpose. But you don't need a huge arsenal of authoring expertise either. For example, some lessons, such as the anesthesiology lesson shown in Figure 1.5, could be developed using basic presentation software with feedback links from the on-screen options selected.

### WHAT DO YOU THINK? REVISITED

In the beginning of the chapter, you had the opportunity to select which features below characterize scenario-based e-learning:

❑   1. They begin with a work-realistic problem or assignment.

❑   2. They require computer simulation capabilities.

❑   3. They require high-end media like video or animations.

❑   4. They allow learners to make mistakes and learn from mistakes.

❑   5. They provide immediate feedback when an incorrect option is selected.

❑   6. They use a structured rule-example-practice sequence.

My answers are Items 1 and 4. Regarding Options 2 and 3, while simulations and high-end media may characterize some scenario-based e-learning, they are not essential. The blood loss emergency treatment lesson is based on a simulation. In contrast, the Bridezilla and anesthesiology examples use branching logic and rely on text with static graphics to support the scenario. Options 5 and 6 apply more to directive designs than to scenario-based e-learning.

## COMING NEXT

I ended this chapter with six reasons to consider scenario-based e-learning now. But there are multiple issues to consider. With every new instructional approach and technology, there are those enthusiasts who believe the new should totally replace the old. I don't agree. Instead, I believe that there is a time and place for older as well as for newer designs. Furthermore, learning can be blends of different design approaches. In the next chapter I focus on the when and for whom of scenario-based e-learning. My goal in that chapter is to help you further pinpoint opportunities for scenario-based e-learning in your organization.

At the end of each chapter, I will present a short worksheet or questions to help you apply the guidelines to your own instructional goals. Naturally, you can review these—or bypass them for now. All of the worksheets and checklists can be found online at www.pfeiffer.com/go/scenario. Password: Professional.

## ADDITIONAL RESOURCES

Task-centered design models—what I'm calling scenario-based e-learning—have been described in several recent books. Two I have used as resources are

Merrill, M.D. (2012). *First principles of instruction.* San Francisco: Jossey-Bass.
   A very comprehensive text that describes common design principles for all effective instructional environments with an emphasis on scenario-based learning designs.

Van Merrienboer, J.J.G., & Kirschner, P.A. (2007). *Ten steps to complex learning.* New York: Routledge.
   Based on their research, the authors of this book describe a model for designing task-centered instruction including scenario-based e-learning.

# SCENARIO-BASED e-LEARNING AND YOU: WHY NOW?

As a start, review the following reasons to consider scenario-based e-learning, checking all that might apply to your instructional goals: Write down several potential instructional goals that might be a good fit for scenario-based e-learning in your organization.

## Reasons to Consider Scenario-Based e-Learning

- ☐ Accelerate expertise
- ☐ Build critical thinking skills
- ☐ Build skills impossible/impractical to gain on the job
- ☐ Promote learning transfer
- ☐ Gain a return-on-investment
- ☐ Motivate learning
- ☐ Exploit technological resources effectively
- ☐ Engage a target audience that already has basic job familiarity

## My Instructional Goals

# CHAPTER

## 2

# WHEN TO USE SCENARIO-BASED e-LEARNING

When it comes to designing learning environments, there is no yellow brick road. By that I mean there is no single path that is best for all purposes and all learners. Perhaps after reviewing the six reasons that scenario-based e-learning might work for you now listed in Chapter 1, you are starting to think about how you have used or might apply this approach to your own training needs. In this chapter I will describe the types of tasks, learning outcomes, and learners who are good candidates for scenario-based e-learning designs. I also introduce four navigation/interface designs for scenario-based e-learning. Specifically, as you read this chapter, you will see how scenario-based e-learning applies to:

- Strategic versus procedural learning goals

- Features specific to tasks and learners

- Eight knowledge and skill objectives

- Eight learning domains

- Four navigation and interface designs

## CONSIDER SCENARIO-BASED e-LEARNING
## FOR STRATEGIC TASKS

I divide learning goals that require skill building into two main categories: procedural tasks and strategic tasks. Procedural tasks are routine work activities that pretty much follow the same sequence each time they are performed. Logging into e-mail and completing an online timesheet are two common examples. Procedures can be broken down into steps and are trained most efficiently by the directive approach I described in Chapter 1.

Scenario-based e-learning is generally better suited to strategic tasks that require judgment and tailoring to each new workplace situation. Unlike procedures, strategic tasks cannot be decomposed into a series of invariant steps. Instead, strategic tasks require a deeper understanding of the concepts and rationale underlying performance in order to adapt task guidelines to diverse situations. Some common examples of strategic tasks include making a sale, designing a website, or evaluating a loan application. The experienced sales person adjusts her approach with each engagement, depending on the client, the product, and the sales context.

## WHAT DO YOU THINK?

Put a checkmark next to each task below that you think is a strategic task:

- ❏  1. Completing a routine customer order form
- ❏  2. Building a marketing plan
- ❏  3. Responding to an upset customer in a call center
- ❏  4. Troubleshooting an unusual mechanical failure
- ❏  5. Preparing a meatloaf

Your answers will depend on your experience with and assumptions about those tasks. Here are my thoughts. Task 1 is most likely a procedural task and would be best trained by a demonstration, practice and a job aid following a directive training plan. In fact, if the order form is simple enough, a performance aid alone may suffice. Tasks 2 through 4, however, I categorize as strategic tasks because they require judgment and/or problem solving, and there is rarely a single right answer. For example, there may be a flow chart for troubleshooting many routine failures. Something unusual, however—say two simultaneous failures—might not be captured on a flow chart. It would be just about impossible as well as cost-ineffective to document all possible combinations of failures. Instead, an individual with a deeper understanding of the equipment and a rich bed of experience would draw on her mental index of failures and rules of thumb to isolate and resolve the problem.

How about meatloaf? What kind of cook are you? Do you pull out your cookbooks and follow a recipe? If yes, you are a procedural cook. Or do you construct your own creations using your past experience and a pinch of instinct? Fast-food organizations definitely apply a procedural approach. Their goal is a consistent product produced by a high turnover of relatively low skilled workers. In contrast, the culinary school I visited in Hawaii focuses on the principles and economics of cooking—not just the procedures. In one culinary class, for example, learners might make five cakes, leaving out a key ingredient each time. In that way the budding chefs experience directly the effects of the salt, flour, sugar, and baking powder on the final product.

The point of the meatloaf digression? Some tasks such as cooking can sometimes be treated as procedures and other times as strategic tasks. Whether a task is treated as procedural or as strategic may depend on the business model and constraints of the organization. For fast-food preparation, the emphasis may be procedural; for a culinary professional, a deeper level of understanding is needed. Therefore, you will need to consider the context of your organization as you define the best approach.

## SITUATIONS THAT CALL FOR SCENARIO-BASED e-LEARNING

In addition to focusing on a strategic task, there are a number of other contextual factors that could point you toward a scenario-based e-learning design. These relate to the frequency, criticality, timeline, and goals for the task, as well as to the prior experience level of the learners. Here I summarize some of the more common indicators:

### Rare Occurrence Tasks

Some situations that require problem solving simply don't pop up that often on the job. In Chapter 1 I mentioned research showing that most experts require a solid ten years of sustained practice to reach highest proficiency levels. One reason is that the real world rarely serves up scenarios in an ideal learning sequence. Take troubleshooting. You are likely to see plenty of certain kinds of failures. However, other failures may be much more infrequent. If you identify those infrequent tasks, you can package them in scenario format and offer virtual opportunities to build expertise in their resolution. Another example is supervisory challenges. For example, a new supervisor may not have to hire a new employee or initiate disciplinary action for months. By embedding hiring or discipline scenarios in a scenario-based e-learning course for new supervisors, they can gain initial experience not otherwise feasible.

### Critical Thinking Skills Training

Most strategic tasks will require critical thinking skills to enable workers to adapt their experience to new situations. Research on the reasoning skills of experts shows that critical thinking skills are domain-specific. By that I mean that the facts, concepts, rules of thumb, and rationale that a military commander would consider when responding to a situation are quite different than those of a physician. Training on very general thinking skills such as "brainstorm alternatives" or "break the problem into smaller parts" will have limited transfer to real work decisions. Instead, for successful learning, you need to identify and teach critical thinking skills that are unique to the work domain.

You may be familiar with Bloom's Taxonomy. Initially published in 1956, recent revisions have updated the original (Anderson et al., 2001). Other psychologists have put forth slightly different classifications of knowledge and skills involved in critical thinking (Leighton, 2011). As of now there is no single agreed-on classification system. Drawing on the commonalities among several of these taxonomies, in Table 2.1 I summarize eight knowledge and skill categories associated with many problem-solving tasks in the workplace.

Most problems of any degree of complexity will involve several of these knowledge and skills. However, in different problem domains, some may be more critical than others. For example, troubleshooting will draw heavily on the following knowledge and skills: facts and mental models of the target equipment; the analysis of failures, including gathering and interpreting data; the application of rules of thumb specific to the domain; and the ability to monitor progress and adjust as needed. As you frame your desired learning outcomes and supporting knowledge, you can adapt many of these knowledge and skill categories to the target domain of your training.

### Compliance-Mandated Training

I mentioned compliance training in Chapter 1. Most large organizations have regular training required of many workers for compliance with legal mandates or corporate policy. Typical topics involve information security, safety, ethical conduct, or HR issues such as sexual harassment. Frequently, these classes consist of policy lectures with a few war stories thrown in. As an alternative, consider scenario-based e-learning to immerse learners in a situation requiring them to make a decision in a context related to application of policies and then experience the consequences of their decision.

### Learner Expertise and Scenario-Based e-Learning

In many cases scenario-based e-learning designs are best matched to more experienced workers already familiar with the basics of the environment—the equipment, the terminology, the context. For a novice worker, a scenario-based e-learning lesson may be overwhelming, with visual interfaces that offer too many choices and not enough structure. Therefore you might target scenario-based e-learning for apprentice level workers or for post-introductory levels of training.

### Lengthy Timeline Tasks

In some situations, actions and decisions in the workplace can unfold over a period of weeks or even months. Even a relatively simple troubleshooting dilemma could require tests that take hours, ordering new parts that requires days, and so on. In a scenario-based e-learning environment you can compress time. Want to execute a troubleshooting test? Click on the test equipment and the test is "run." Want to replace a part? Click on a part on the screen and it is replaced. The consequences of these decisions and actions can be seen immediately. The result is a much closer alignment of actions to consequences and the opportunity to resolve many situations in a short period of time.

TABLE 2.1. **Common Knowledge and Skills Required in Workplace Tasks Involving Critical Thinking**

| Knowledge/ Skill | Learner Is Able to | Examples |
|---|---|---|
| 1. Remember or Access Facts | Recall or look up relevant discrete information | Describe product features and benefits<br>Name object (equipment, anatomy) parts<br>Identify relevant policy |
| 2. Apply Concepts | Classify data, objects, events, or symbols into categories | Select the circuit with the correct resistance<br>Distinguish abnormal breathing patterns |
| 3. Perform Procedures | Complete a task that is performed the same way each time | Close a valve<br>Log into the system<br>Enter data into the correct fields |
| 4. Apply Mental Models | Demonstrate an understanding of how systems behave | Draw a model of heart circulation<br>Select what would happen next in the equipment start-up phase |
| 5. Analyze Situations | Define the problem, identify and prioritize relevant data, interpret data | Verify an equipment failure<br>Identify and conduct appropriate tests<br>Assess the validity of data<br>Interpret graphs and charts |
| 6. Apply Rules of Thumb | Make decisions or take actions based on domain-specific problem-solving guidelines | Use split-half testing approach<br>Ask open-ended questions |
| 7. Create a Product | Build, write, or produce a deliverable that optimizes situation constraints and goals | Write a report<br>Create a marketing plan<br>Build a prototype<br>Respond in a role play |
| 8. Monitor Progress | Assess the current status of a situation against constraints and desired outcomes and take actions to readjust as needed | When system does not respond as anticipated, evaluate and change parameters<br>If the prototype does not meet specifications, readjust relevant features |

**FIGURE 2.1.** *Unnecessary Causalities Result from Poor Leadership Decisions.*
With permission from Will Interactive.

### Risk-Adverse Tasks

Some tasks simply cannot be learned through normal work experience. The consequences of errors are too high. Tasks with injury consequences are one example. The new military commander faces his first combat assignment as team lead. Inappropriate responses to multiple unknown and unanticipated problems can result in lethal consequences. For example, a scenario-based e-learning course for military officers called Gator 6 starts off with a failed military operation in which soldiers and civilians die unnecessarily. Figure 2.1 shows a screen shot from the introduction to this program. The learner assumes the role of the commander and goes back in time with the opportunity to make decisions that will result in a better outcome. The anesthetics lesson illustrated in Figure 1.5 is another example of a high-risk task.

Failing to interact effectively with an important person is yet another example. In the real world you may not get a second chance to make a good impression. For example, a soldier meets a village elder. What should he say? How should he act? How should he interpret the responses of the elder in a specific cultural setting? While scenario-based e-learning may never replace the real thing, even some basic exposure to a new environment can translate into a performance booster.

## EIGHT SCENARIO-BASED LEARNING DOMAINS

So far I've reviewed some general situations that lend themselves to use of scenario-based e-learning. Now let's zoom into some specific workplace domains that will benefit. In Table 2.2 I summarize eight domains that reflect the most common applications of scenario-based e-learning. These domains are not mutually exclusive and do not reflect all potential applications of scenario-based e-learning. But they do provide a starting place for planning. Here I describe each in a bit more detail:

**TABLE 2.2.  Eight Scenario Learning Domains in Workforce Training**

| Domain | Desired Outcome | Examples |
|---|---|---|
| 1. Interpersonal Skills | Communicate effectively to achieve operational goals | Customer service Sales |
| 2. Compliance: Policies and Procedures | Select actions or responses that best comply with legal and organizational policy guidelines | Supervisor tasks Information security Safety |
| 3. Diagnosis and Repair | Access and interpret relevant data, diagnose problem, perform repair or prescribe treatment | Equipment troubleshooting Allied health professionals |
| 4. Research, Analysis, and Rationale | Identify and assess data sources; make optimal decisions or recommendations based on rationale | Bank loan analysis Journalism |
| 5. Tradeoffs | Apply knowledge to take actions or make decisions for which there may be multiple solution paths or solutions | Project planning Making ethical decisions |
| 6. Operational Decisions and Actions | Take actions in simulated production or operational environments to optimize performance | Production control adjustment Aircraft navigation |
| 7. Design | Create an original product to meet scenario constraints—no single correct solution | Design a website Conduct a needs assessment Develop a project plan |
| 8. Team Coordination | Communicate and coordinate activities among specialists to achieve an objective | Deploy resources to respond to a disaster situation such as a hurricane |

## 1. Interpersonal Skills

In this category I include communication tasks such as those involved in customer service, sales, management, or teaching. Interpersonal scenarios typically follow a linear sequence of "he says . . . she responds." You can design highly structured scenario environments with limited choices for entry-level lessons and evolve to open role-play environments for more advanced lessons. For example, in Figure 1.3 you can view a segment from a client interview led by the wedding consultant. Regarding knowledge and skills, interpersonal domains will often require remembering or accessing factual information such as product knowledge, applying concepts such as open-ended questions or empathy, analyzing situations such as a client's requirements, applying rules of thumb such as start with open-ended questions, and monitoring progress, including making adjustments based on body language of the respondent.

## 2. Compliance Policies and Procedures

Here I incorporate actions and decisions made by leaders such as supervisors, managers, and military officers as well as staff actions or decisions that reflect application of policies. Management work certainly involves interpersonal skills but also requires knowledge of organizational policy or legal issues. In this scenario-based e-learning domain, the major emphasis is on appropriate application of these policies. Relevant knowledge and skills include remembering or accessing factual information such as policy references, applying concepts such as recognizing a compliance violation, analyzing situations that involve compliance issues, and applying rules of thumb such as taking organizationally approved action when confronting a policy violation.

## 3. Diagnosis and Repair

Work in this domain typically involves verifying, researching, and resolving failures. The typical scenario is initiated by a failure, be it a sick cat for a veterinarian or an automotive failure for a technician. Most flavors of system troubleshooting fall into this category as well as medical diagnostics and treatment decisions. One important element of these scenario-based e-lessons is an emphasis not only on individual actions or decisions but on the entire sequence of decisions made. For example, in automotive troubleshooting, the technician could take an inefficient random approach to tests. Eventually she may resolve the problem but waste a great deal of time in the process. Therefore the scenario-based e-learning design should allow learners multiple solution paths and provide instruction and feedback on those paths. In other words, the focus is not only on a correct answer but also on the process for deriving the answer.

Related knowledge and skills include remembering or accessing factual information such as a schematic diagram for equipment, applying concepts such as a functional circuit, performing procedures such as using test equipment, applying mental models such as understanding how the equipment works, analyzing failures, applying rules of thumb for testing, interpreting test data, and analyzing repair alternatives as well as monitoring progress. Although this domain incorporates multiple knowledge and skills, often the problems are relatively structured. By that I mean, there is typically a correct answer that leads to appropriate functioning of the system.

### 4. Research, Analysis, and Rationale

Many workplace contexts require the worker to achieve a goal by identifying and gathering relevant data, evaluating that data, and making decisions or taking actions based on a rational synthesis of information available. The diagnostics worker discussed in the previous paragraph is also engaged in research and analysis. However, the difference here is that the trigger event need not be a failure or problem. For example, when evaluating a new loan candidate, the underwriter must access and evaluate a number of data resources about the applicant. Similar to the diagnostic cases mentioned previously, there is usually an efficient sequence to follow. Likewise, when a decision is made, often a rationale for that decision is an important element.

Related knowledge and skills can include any of the eight listed in Table 2.1, but typically rely heavily on applying concepts, analyzing situations, and creating a product such as a loan justification form.

### 5. Tradeoffs

At times there really is no single "best" answer or resolution to a work dilemma. Your instructional goal in a tradeoff scenario-based e-learning design is not to derive a correct answer. Rather, the focus is an engaging context for learners to review multiple perspectives or applicable policies or laws as they make a decision or take an action. The feedback may show consequences of decisions made; however, all decisions will have positive and negative consequences. For example, in the Bridezilla lesson, learners have an opportunity to seek input from diverse sources of expertise, including clergy, designers, finance, and negotiations experts. In a project planning lesson, decisions will need to weigh the tradeoffs among budget, schedule, resources, and politics, to name a few.

Tradeoff lessons at an introductory level may focus on remembering or accessing factual information such as average costs for formal wedding receptions, applying concepts such as formal versus informal weddings, analyzing situations, and creating a product such as a project plan and budget. Monitoring progress will be another important element for the wedding planner since the project will play out over an extended period of time and involve coordination of multiple elements.

### 6. Operational Decisions and Actions

The goal of these scenarios is to offer opportunities for operators or technicians to make decisions and take actions in the context of a (usually simulated) operational environment. Training for power plant operators or medical procedures such as laparoscopy are two examples. Typically, large-scale operational environments with major safety consequences use realistic 3D simulators. However, such simulators are expensive and may be supplemented with a lower-fidelity multimedia version. In addition, some operational decisions must be made quickly and thus rely on a degree of automatic performance by decision-makers. Automaticity can be built by using scenarios as a context for drill and practice.

Operational decisions and actions will depend heavily on remembering or accessing factual information, applying concepts, performing procedures, applying mental models, analyzing situations, applying rules of thumb, and monitoring progress.

### 7. Design

Most of the domains I've reviewed so far are relatively structured. That is, they assume there are some defined outcome decisions or action paths. Design scenarios, however, focus on creation of a product that could have multiple effective solutions. Some common examples include developing a website to meet a client's constraints or designing a marketing plan for a new product. Design goals will require a much more open-ended environment as well as a checklist of desired end-product features to evaluate outcomes. Because design decisions of any complexity typically reflect multiple subtle factors, often human feedback (from an instructor, peers, or expert) will be needed. For this reason, design lessons will be best mediated in an environment of high social presence such as an instructor-led virtual or in-person class.

Among all of the knowledge and skills, design will rest heavily on analyzing a situation, creating a product, and monitoring progress.

### 8. Team Coordination

In some work settings, success depends on rapid and accurate communication and coordination among multiple specialist workers. Some examples include emergency room medical staff, a combat team, or aircraft crews. Studies of aircraft crews have derived best practices in cockpit resource management that are being adopted by other skilled teams such as medical specialists in operating or emergency rooms.

Some key knowledge and skills especially relevant to team coordination include situation analysis, applying rules of thumb, and monitoring progress.

## SCENARIO-BASED MULTIMEDIA INTERFACES

So far I've mentioned a number of workplace factors that point toward using a scenario-based e-learning design. In Table 2.3 I introduce four interface-navigation designs commonly used to present scenarios and to support navigation. These interfaces can be mixed and matched to best fit your scenario domain, learner profile, and available technological resources.

The four options vary primarily on the type of structure and navigation options offered. Lower levels of learner control that restrict learner choices are most effective for more novice staff and for tasks with relatively defined outcomes. In contrast, more flexible designs are better for more advanced lessons and for tasks with multiple paths or outcomes.

## TABLE 2.3.  **Scenario-Based e-Learning Interface-Navigation Options**

| Interface | Description | Example | When to Use |
|---|---|---|---|
| Branched Scenario | Learner responds to situations by selecting from three or four text choices | Cat anesthesia Gator 6 officer training | For high to moderate structured scenarios resolvable with linear response paths |
| Menu-Driven | Learner selects scenario elements from a persistent on-screen menu | Bridezilla Bank loan analysis | For moderately structured scenarios in which learner can select from a menu of scenario elements |
| Full Screen Active Object | Learner selects on-screen objects to access scenario elements | Automotive troubleshooting | For less structured scenarios; when instructional goals focus on process as well as solutions |
| Virtual Worlds | Learners are free to interact with environment or with others | Sales role play Emergency response | For open-ended learning opportunities; for coordination among multiple players in a 3D virtual environment |

### Branched Scenarios

In a branched scenario, the learner is exposed to a brief episode and is offered three or four alternative responses, usually via a text link. For example, the cat anesthetic scenario shown in Figure 1.5 illustrates a typical branched scenario. Patient information is provided in text in the upper right corner and in the left-hand chart. After responding, corrective instructional feedback is given and the learner has the opportunity to select a different option or is presented with a new set of options.

Likewise, the Gator 6 military officer training is based on a branched scenario design. Following the opening video shown in Figure 2.1, the learner goes back in time and has the opportunity to make multiple decisions to improve the final outcomes. For example in Figure 2.2, the learner has time only to respond to one among several demands. As you can see by comparing the anesthesia and military examples, the media can vary from relatively simple still images to video. Branched scenarios lend themselves to tasks with linear progressions such as interpersonal skills and

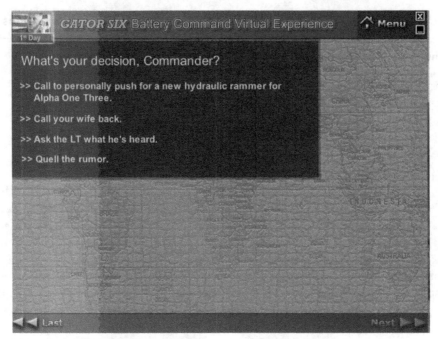

**FIGURE 2.2.** *There Is Time Only to Select a Single Action.*
With permission from Will Interactive.

tasks that would unfold over time. Situations in which learners need opportunities to make multiple decisions at a single point in time in order to learn the most appropriate action sequence would not lend themselves as well to a branched scenario approach. Branched scenarios are useful for entry-level lessons because of the degree of structure imposed. Unlike the designs to follow, the learner faces only three or four choices with each transaction.

### Menu-Driven

In Figure 1.3 I showed an example of a menu-driven scenario-based e-learning lesson for newly hired wedding counselors. Here the learner has a defined set of options displayed as tabs in the upper right portion of the screen that she can select in any order. A second helpful example, shown in Figure 2.3, is a menu-based design for an underwriter loan analysis scenario. Across the top of the screen are six high-level menu options, including overview, introduction, data, analysis, facility structure/price, and recommendations. These menu options represent the main stages in the analysis workflow. When one of these high-level tabs is selected, the submenus on the left side of the screen appear. For example, in Figure 2.3 a high-level "data" tab has been selected and the learner can then select subordinate left tabs linking to different sources of data such as the financial data shown in this screen shot.

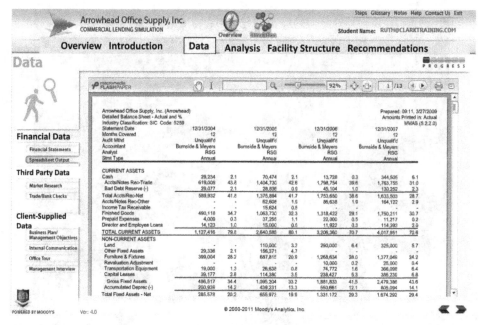

**FIGURE 2.3.**   *A Menu-Driven Interface for Bank Loan Analysis.*
With permission from Moody's Analytics.

A menu-driven approach could be useful when multiple resources or scenario perspectives are available and you want to allow the learner the freedom to select from among those before making a decision or taking action. Menus offer an intermediate level of learner control—more than the branched scenario but less than the full-screen design described in the next paragraph.

### Full Screen Active Object

In Figures 1.1 and 1.2 I showed troubleshooting training situated in a virtual automobile repair shop. This approach has a game-like interface with multiple on-screen objects for the learner to explore. The active object interface potentially offers a high degree of learner control and in fact could lead to confusion and mental overload for an entry-level worker. However, if your instructional outcome involves learning an optimal (efficient or logical) sequence of activities, learners will need an interface that gives them freedom to enact different sequences. This interface could work well for some compliance, diagnostic, research, tradeoffs, and operational goals.

**FIGURE 2.4.**  *A Virtual World Sales Training Environment.*
Credit: Mark Palmer.

### Virtual Worlds

In Figure 2.4, I show a virtual world interface for a sales training class. Just as in in-person classes, the learner in the form of an avatar is free to generate her own responses and move around the 3D space at will. In contrast to the branched scenario, which offers limited choices, or the menu design, which offers several defined choices, here the learner exercises much higher degrees of freedom. Virtual worlds could offer a useful alternative to a face-to-face classroom for role plays or for design projects—especially for designs that involve manipulation of three-dimensional objects. From a visual perspective, obviously the virtual world provides opportunities to engage with three dimensional objects. However, many skills could be learned as effectively in a two-dimensional environment such as the automotive shop described in the previous paragraph. You will need to consider when the extra fidelity of a third dimension along with high levels of learner freedom will best serve your desired learning outcomes.

Although technology may overcome current limits, three-dimensional learning environments require specialized technical skills and digital resources. Based on an informal survey of my colleagues, as of the writing of this book, virtual worlds are not predominant learning environments. For example, one colleague has found two main barriers to implementing virtual worlds, including the high cost of development due to expensive technology and, secondly, the majority of learners (unfamiliar with 3D worlds) are challenged with the additional mental load of navigating and responding in a new environment.

## MEET THE SCENARIO-BASED e-LEARNING SAMPLES

I am very grateful to my colleagues who have given permission to include screen shots from their excellent courses to illustrate this book, as well as to Mark Palmer, who worked with me to design the Bridezilla lesson. Although I have included quite a few examples throughout the book, I have relied primarily on seven courses. You can see an orientation to each course in the back of this book in Appendix A. In addition, you can find screen shots from these courses organized in the sequence in which they appear in the book as well as organized by course in a logical learning sequence online at Pfeiffer.com/go/scenario. Password: Professional.

## COMING NEXT

By this stage you should be forming some ideas as to the kinds of instructional challenges you face that might benefit from scenario-based e-learning. Now it's time to consider your design. In the next chapter I offer a bird's eye view of a design plan for a scenario-based e-learning lesson to be followed by expanded discussions of each component in the chapters to follow.

## ADDITIONAL RESOURCES

Kapp, K.M., & O'Driscoll, T. (2010). *Learning in 3D*. San Francisco: Pfeiffer.
 This book focuses on effective use of virtual world technology for learning and instruction.

Leighton, J.P. (2011). A cognitive model for the assessment of higher order thinking in students. In G. Schraw & D.R. Robinson (Eds.), *Assessment of higher order thinking skills*. Charlotte, NC: Information Age.
 See this chapter for a more detailed and technical discussion of a taxonomy of the critical thinking skills I summarize in Table 2.1.

## SCENARIO-BASED e-LEARNING AND YOU: YOUR SCENARIO-BASED e-LEARNING OPPORTUNITIES

By now you should be ready to pinpoint some learning opportunities in your organization that could profit from a scenario-based e-learning approach and even consider which interface designs might be best. In the space below, briefly describe a task and potential learning audience for a scenario-based e-learning lesson. Then use the checklists to identify the related knowledge and skills as well as the learning domain and interface features you might consider. In the next chapters you will be able to use your example to plan the core elements of your scenario-based e-learning lesson.

1. Your Task(s):

2. Your Learners:

3. Task and Learner Features: Check all that apply.

- ☐ The task is strategic, not a procedure.
- ☐ The task occurs infrequently.
- ☐ The task can take long periods of time to resolve on the job.
- ☐ The task has high risk-adverse consequences.
- ☐ The task involves critical thinking skills.
- ☐ The task involves compliance issues.
- ☐ The task requires rapid responses based on automatic skills.
- ☐ Learners have some related work experience.
- ☐ Other relevant factors:

4. Knowledge and Skills Associated with Expertise in the Task: Check all that apply. Circle two or three that are the *most aligned to your desired learning outcomes.*

- ☐ Remember or access facts
- ☐ Apply concepts
- ☐ Perform procedures
- ☐ Apply mental models
- ☐ Analyze situations
- ☐ Apply rules of thumb
- ☐ Create a product
- ☐ Monitor progress
- ☐ Other:

5. Learning Domains: Check all that apply.

- ☐ Interpersonal skills
- ☐ Compliance
- ☐ Diagnosis and repair
- ☐ Research, analysis, and rationale
- ☐ Tradeoffs
- ☐ Operations
- ☐ Design
- ☐ Team coordination
- ☐ Other:

6. Possible Interface/Navigation Design: Check all that apply.

- ☐ Branched scenario
- ☐ Menu
- ☐ Full screen active object
- ☐ Virtual world

# CHAPTER

## 3

# DESIGN OF SCENARIO-BASED e-LEARNING

By this point you may have identified one or more good candidates for a scenario-based e-learning lesson or course. All good training begins with a blueprint and in this chapter I overview a design model to guide your planning. I will introduce six elements that make up the core of a scenario-based e-learning lesson. In chapters to follow I will define each of these elements in more detail.

## OVERVIEW OF A SCENARIO-BASED e-LEARNING DESIGN MODEL

The scenario-based e-learning design model illustrated in Figure 3.1 specifies each of the following core components: task deliverable, trigger event, case data, guidance/instruction, feedback, and reflection. While some components, such as the task deliverable, trigger event, and feedback, are required elements, others may vary according to your learning domain and context. In the following paragraphs I introduce each core feature. In the chapters to follow I provide detailed guidelines on each component.

### Component 1: The Task Deliverable

All good instruction starts with the end in sight. The "end" is the goal of your training effort, which is typically specified by one or more learning objectives. By task deliverable I mean the actions taken, decisions made, or products produced to resolve or complete the scenario. The task deliverable should be specific to the learning domain. For example, a scenario-based e-learning focused on interpersonal skills might use a branched scenario design with a task deliverable of selecting an optimal set of

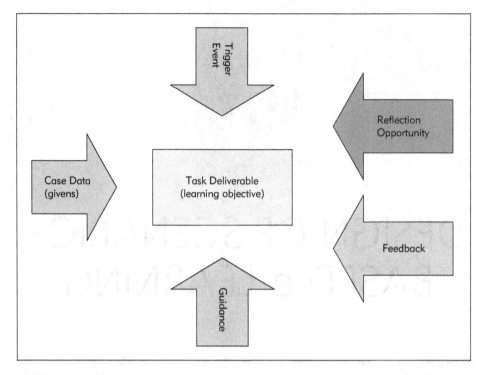

**FIGURE 3.1.**  *A Design Model for Scenario-Based e-Learning Lessons.*
© 2012, Ruth Clark.

responses proven to lead to customer satisfaction and/or close of a sale. A trouble-shooting lesson might use a full-screen active object such as the auto shop in Figure 1.1. One task deliverable for the troubleshooting lesson is to select the correct fault and/or repair action. The second major deliverable is to select and interpret the appropriate tests in a logical and efficient sequence to identify the fault. In Table 3.1 I list some typical end-task deliverables, along with sample learning objectives for each of the learning domains introduced in Chapter 2.

Some experts recommend omitting learning objectives in scenario-based learning. I disagree. I see scenario-based e-learning as an alternative design that, like any other training resource, should be developed and evaluated in light of clearly specified outcomes. It is impossible to evaluate learning without measurable outcomes, even if the criteria are not clear-cut correct or incorrect responses. As with all learning objectives, you will need an action verb that matches the appropriate action or decision on the job. In addition, you need to consider your delivery media. If you plan on a self-study scenario-based e-learning course, you will need to specify an action that can be implemented through computer response interactions, such as clicking on or dragging on-screen objects, selecting options from a menu, and/or typing short statements.

## TABLE 3.1.    Typical Learning Objectives by Domain

| Domain | End-Task Deliverable | Objective |
|---|---|---|
| 1. Interpersonal | Communicate effectively to achieve operational goals | Given client specifications and query, the learner will select optimal responses to engage the client. Given common classroom disruption scenarios, the learner will identify the source of the problem and select an optimal response. |
| 2. Compliance: Policies and Procedures | Select options that best comply with legal and company policy guidelines | Given depictions of adherence or violation of corporate information security policy, the learner will identify violations and select appropriate remedies. |
| 3. Diagnosis and Repair | Access and interpret relevant data, diagnose problem, perform repair, or prescribe treatment | Given a virtual shop and equipment failure, the learner will select and interpret tests to determine the source of the failure. |
| 4. Research, Analysis, Rationale | Identify and assess data sources; make optimal decisions or recommendations based on rationale | Given a client loan application and multiple data sources, the learner will recommend approval or rejection of the request with supporting rationale. |
| 5. Tradeoffs | Apply knowledge to take actions or make decisions for which there may be multiple solution paths or solutions | Given situations requiring decisions with positive and negative consequences, the learner will research options, select an action, and reflect on consequences. |
| 6. Operational Decisions | Take actions in simulated production or operational environments to optimize performance | Given an operational failure requiring immediate response, the learner will categorize the problem and take a series of actions to optimize the system, monitoring and adjusting as appropriate. |

*(Continued)*

*Table 3.1 (continued)*

| Domain | End-Task Deliverable | Objective |
|--------|---------------------|-----------|
| 7. Design | Create an original product to meet scenario constraints—no single correct solution | Given product specifications and resource constraints, the learner will develop a prototype product that meets stated criteria. |
| 8. Team Coordination | Communicate and deploy resources to optimize team goal | Given a surgical situation and patient specifications, the learner will apply a communication model and assign tasks to co-workers to optimize resources. |

In some highly structured types of problems, your task deliverable may be relatively straightforward with a clear correct or incorrect response. Identifying a single failure source in malfunctioning equipment is one example. In other cases, you may want to focus not only on a correct or incorrect answer, but also on the process used to derive the answer. For example, in the auto troubleshooting lesson, the student's path through the test options is tracked. At the end of each case, the learner can compare his path with that of an expert as shown in Figure 1.2. Therefore, the task deliverable includes not only a correct answer but also the most efficient path to derive the answer. In still other situations, the outcome may not be a correct answer but rather one of several alternative responses, each of which has benefits and drawbacks. This is the basis for scenarios that I call "tradeoffs." In a tradeoff scenario, the goal is not so much the end point as the knowledge acquired on the journey. Finally, with ill-structured problems such as many design scenarios and some interpersonal situations, there are no correct solutions but numerous outcomes which may be appropriate.

Your job analysis should provide the basis for your task deliverables, which will serve as your starting point as you define the other major elements of your design. In many cases, you will find that your subject-matter experts are unable to readily articulate the critical thinking knowledge and skills listed in Table 2.1. The heuristics and knowledge that underpin skilled problem solving are frequently tacit knowledge in the minds of your expert performers. Therefore, you will need to supplement your traditional job analysis techniques with some form of cognitive task analysis. In cognitive task analysis, the expert typically voices aloud his or her thoughts as he or she performs or reflects back on a scenario that incorporates the skills you need to teach. In Chapter 11 you can review several cognitive task analysis techniques that you can adapt to your own context.

Once you have defined objectives, you may or may not want to explicitly state them in the scenario. Those opposed to stating objectives argue that objectives can make the learning experience artificial and impose a barrier to immersion in the

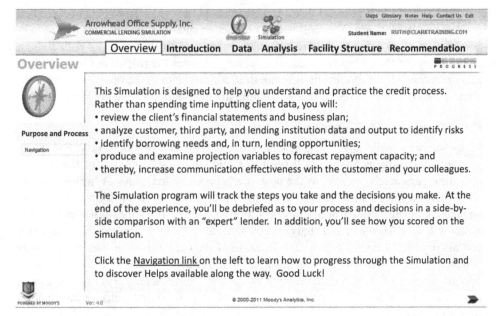

**FIGURE 3.2.** *An Introductory Screen in a Bank Analysis Scenario-Based e-Learning Lists Anticipated Outcomes.*
With permission from Moody's Analytics.

scenario. The bank loan simulation presents the list of anticipated analytic behaviors shown in Figure 3.2 as a substitute for traditionally stated objectives.

### Core Component 2: The Trigger Event

When the learner opens the program, what will she see? The trigger event is how the scenario kicks off. In many lessons it takes the form of an assignment from the manager. The assignment may be formatted in a brief video statement appearing in a pop-up screen or via an e-mail. In other situations the trigger event may be a contact from a customer—for example, a customer walks up to your desk or you see a client meeting scheduled on your smart phone calendar.

The goal of the trigger event is to set a realistic stage for the scenario and to provide the learner with any initial background knowledge or advice needed. As you consider your kick-off event, think about how a situation would be initiated in the workplace and how you can duplicate it in an online environment.

A unique approach to the trigger event is what I call "The Murphy's Law trigger." This basically takes the form of a "disaster" outcome to a scenario in which just about everything goes wrong. As the learner clicks on the start-up graphic, she sees a video, an animation, or even a few static visuals that depict a failed situation. At the end of the introductory scene, the learner is assigned the role of the decision-maker and has the opportunity to go back in time to make better decisions that avert the negative trigger scene.

For example, in Figure 2.1, I showed the introductory video from Gator 6 designed for new combat officers. The Hollywood production-quality video plays a five-minute combat scene that unfortunately results in too many preventable deaths—both civilian and military. At the end of the video, the learner assumes the role of the commanding officer. In this role he can revisit different time periods prior to the operational engagement to make better decisions that will culminate in a more positive outcome.

### Core Component 3: Scenario Data

Many scenarios will require data unique to each assigned problem or task. For example the automotive technician will need to know the model and year of the car and operating parameters, as well as the customer's problem statement. A hiring supervisor will need information about the position requirements, the working conditions, and the candidates' backgrounds to select useful interview questions. The bank underwriter will need to collect and analyze extensive data about the applicant such as financial history, illustrated in Figure 2.3. Because of the central role of data in diagnosis and analysis scenarios, the lessons must incorporate navigational devices to access the various sources of information relevant to the task deliverable. Typically, the data is represented in the form of documents, charts and graphs, observations, or information derived from interviews.

In some situations the goal is to learn which data sources are most relevant and credible, which data sources to access at a particular stage of problem solving, and/or how to interpret test data. In the automotive troubleshooting scenario, some tests are irrelevant to the failure symptoms. Running these tests wastes time. The instructional goal is not only to identify a correct answer but also to follow an efficient process. Therefore, the interface makes available the full range of data sources (shop testing tools) found in the normal work environment. For these types of goals, you will need to select an interface and program that offers moderate levels of learner control as well as tracking of options selected. The full-screen active object interface shown in Figure 1.1 incorporates all basic tools found in a repair bay. Similarly, a menu-driven interface such as the one in Figure 2.3 offers access to a variety of scenario data.

### Core Component 4: Guidance and Instruction

Since scenario-based e-learning is about learning, the what, when, and where of the learning opportunities demand careful thought. Guidance and instruction can include traditional tutorials available either online or in a classroom setting, online experts, online agent advice, and model answers. For example, in the Bridezilla lesson shown in Figure 1.3, the learner can select online advisors for knowledge and skills related to religious, design, financial, and negotiation aspects of wedding planning.

In some situations, your organization may already have relevant online guidance available. In these circumstances, you can leverage these online resources by integrating them into your interface. For example, in the auto shop, clicking on the computer links into the corporate troubleshooting references.

Evidence shows that pure discovery lessons are suboptimal for learning. Instead you will want to incorporate guidance and structure in your scenarios to replace discovery with guided discovery. Instructional psychologists refer to this type of guidance as *scaffolding*. As an example, in the automotive troubleshooting scenario, when the learner clicks on some test objects he receives a message stating: "This is not the appropriate test to use at this time." Effective guidance requires a balance between giving the learner enough freedom to make decisions and learn from mistakes and, at the same time, enough structure to circumvent unproductive and frustrating trial-and-error approaches.

### Core Component 5: Feedback

All learning requires feedback. By feedback I mean knowledge of what happens when actions are taken. As an experienced trainer, you are likely familiar with traditional instructional feedback often referred to as "corrective" feedback. I call this type of feedback *instructive* feedback. Instructive feedback tells the learner whether he or she is correct or incorrect and gives an explanation. One of the main roles of the coach in the Bridezilla course is to provide instructive feedback about choices made during the interview. You can see the coach's response in the bottom left panel of the screen in Figure 1.3.

Scenario-based learning offers a second unique form of feedback that I call *intrinsic* feedback. Intrinsic feedback is simply a visible illustration of how the scenario plays out or responds to the learner's actions. An everyday example of intrinsic

FIGURE 3.3. *Persistent Failure Symptoms Provide Intrinsic Feedback to Selection of an Incorrect Failure Cause.*
With permission from Raytheon Professional Services.

feedback is found in most sports. When putting the golf ball, the player immediately sees the path of the ball and can assess what she did effectively or ineffectively. In an interpersonal scenario-based e-learning, if a suboptimal response is made to a customer, the customer's body language and statements reflect a negative response. If an incorrect failure is selected in the automobile troubleshooting scenario, the failure symptoms persist, as shown in Figure 3.3.

Multimedia can display intrinsic feedback of environmental responses that would normally not be visible in the workplace. For example, in a scenario-based e-learning for restaurant workers, a germ meter showed the level of contamination as foods were handled incorrectly. In the Bridezilla lesson (Figure 1.3), an attitude meter illustrates how the clients are feeling as the interview progresses.

Feedback can be offered immediately after a learner's response, such as by the coaching comments and attitude meter shown in Figure 1.3. Alternatively, it can be withheld until after a number of actions or decisions are made. For example, feedback on the troubleshooting process shown in Figure 1.2 only appears *after* the learner has successfully identified the fault.

### Core Component 6: Reflection

Feedback has little value unless the learner reviews the feedback and considers how his or her actions or decisions led to the outcomes seen. Some learners are naturally inclined to be reflective, while others are more impulsive and may not carefully review feedback. Therefore, it's a good idea to incorporate an overt opportunity for reflection. As shown in Figure 3.4, at the close of an interview in Bridezilla, the learner is asked to review the interview questions while referencing a checklist of effective questioning techniques. The learner records observations in the form of follow-up questions and lessons learned in the right-hand boxes.

## MODES AND MEDIA IN SCENARIO-BASED e-LEARNING

So far we've reviewed examples of diverse communication modes, including the Bridezilla and bank loan lessons that rely primarily on text supplemented by a few simple still visuals, the automotive shop interface that uses computer-generated animations, and Gator 6 that makes heavy use of video. As you consider your design, you will also begin to think about your use of communication modes. In Chapter 10 I review some research that compares learning from text to various types of visuals, including video. The evidence points to the value of visuals rather than text alone in the interface. However, the research is limited, so until we obtain more definitive guidelines, I recommend the following:

1.  Use realistic images such as computer animation or video when visual or auditory cues are important to any of the design components I've discussed. For example, in a medical scenario, interpreting the visual appearance and sounds of the patient may be a major focus of your instruction.

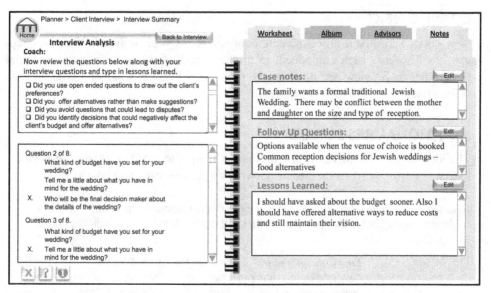

**FIGURE 3.4.** *Questions (Upper Left) Promoting Review and Reflection on Interview Techniques in Lessons Learned Box (Lower Right).*

2. Consider video if the emotional impact is an important element and will add appreciably to engagement in the scenario. For example, the video combat scene that initiates Gator 6 is more compelling than if the same scene were described in text.

3. Consider your production facilities and the volatility of your content. It is generally easier to update computer-generated graphics than to update video. Something as simple as a military uniform change could mark a well-executed video as dated but be easily updated if rendered in a computer-generated graphical interface.

4. Consider the amount of mental load that could affect learning. Video projects large amounts of visual and auditory information, which could overload a novice audience. One research team recommends computer animation over video because irrelevant visual noise inherent in the video can be eliminated in an animated version (Moreno & Ortegano-Layne, 2008).

5. Don't rule out text supplemented with a few visuals. In this book I include several excellent examples that rely heavily on on-screen text. Text is faster and less expensive to produce and update and may be adequate to communicate the core components of your design.

## COMING NEXT

Now you have a first draft of the core components of your design. In the next chapters I will discuss each component in greater detail. You can flesh out your initial design plan as I review and illustrate the specifics. I begin in Chapter 4 with the task deliverable.

## ADDITIONAL RESOURCES

The idea of scenario-driven instruction is not unique to me. For alternative perspectives and guidelines, I recommend reviewing any of the following books:

Jonassen, D.H. (2004). *Learning to solve problems.* San Francisco: Pfeiffer.
  An interesting book that provides some different perspectives on building critical thinking skills.

Merrill, M.D. (2012). *First principles of instruction.* San Francisco: Pfeiffer.
  A comprehensive new book with many examples that emphasizes task-centered instruction and provides a detailed design model called Pebble in a Pond.

Van Merrienboer, J.J.G., & Kirschner, P.A. (2007). *Ten steps to complex learning.* New York: Routledge.
  A less technical explanation of Van Merrienboer's Four Component Instructional Design model for task-centered instruction.

## SCENARIO-BASED e-LEARNING AND YOU:
## YOUR DRAFT DESIGN MODEL

Now that I have overviewed the main components of any scenario-based e-learning design, you may have some initial ideas about how you will apply one or more of these to your own scenario-based e-learning lessons. Take a minute to complete the table below with your initial ideas. Include your thoughts regarding the appropriate media (video, animation, text, still visuals) you might use to communicate these components. In the chapters to follow we will dig into each component in more detail to help you refine your initial plans.


Your Task(s)


Your Scenario-Learning Domain(s)

- ☐ Interpersonal skills

- ☐ Compliance

- ☐ Diagnosis and repair

- ☐ Research, analysis, and rationale

- ☐ Tradeoffs

- ☐ Operations

- ☐ Design

- ☐ Team coordination

- ☐ Other

**Your Design Model: First Draft**

| Design Element | Description | Your Ideas |
|---|---|---|
| Task Deliverable | The actions or decisions made in the scenario that will demonstrate intended knowledge or skill gains. May include correct-incorrect answers, prioritizations of evidence, product production, or the following of an optimal sequence of actions. | |
| Trigger Event | How the scenario will open. May be an assignment, a new customer, or a Murphy's Law scene. | |
| Scenario Data | What information will be needed to select actions or decisions linked to the task deliverable? Are the identification, interpretation, and sequence of data accessed important to your learning goals? Is scenario-data normally contained in organizational reference sources? | |
| Guidance and Instruction | Resources available to teach knowledge and skills linked to the task deliverable, such as: Classroom instructors Traditional tutorials Virtual experts Worksheets | |
| Feedback: Instructional Intrinsic | How will learner receive knowledge of results of choices? Instructional feedback provides traditional "right" or "wrong" comments. Intrinsic feedback shows how the learner's choices play out. | |
| Reflection | Explicit opportunities for learners to review a sequence of actions taken or decisions made and to identify lessons learned or alternative actions. | |

# CHAPTER

## 4

# DEFINING SCENARIO OUTCOMES

All effective training begins with the end(s) in mind. As we do a traditional job analysis, we specify tasks in terms of their demonstrable outcomes or worker actions and write learning objectives to match. In scenario-based e-learning, the outcomes are often strategic and may require critical thinking skills. Defining the desired actions and decisions to reflect critical thinking skills is more challenging than defining outcomes for procedural skills. Furthermore, depending on your problem-solving domain, your outcomes often include not only an "answer" but an optimal path of accessing case data, evaluating data credibility, and/or stating hypotheses or a rationale for decisions made. One of the challenges of scenario-based e-learning is translating your learning objective into specific online interactions—behaviors such as clicking on objects, selecting multiple-choice options, or manipulating slider bars. The behaviors must reflect your intended learning outcomes, your technologies, and your learners. In this chapter I discuss in greater detail the task deliverable component of your lesson design, including:

■ Defining outcomes for the different scenario-based e-learning domains

■ Determining the level of complexity of your outcome deliverable(s)

■ Translating learning objectives into learner actions supported by your multimedia environment

## OUTCOME DELIVERABLES FOR LEARNING DOMAINS

Recall from Chapter 3 that the outcome deliverable is defined as the actions or decisions the learner must make as they investigate, resolve, and complete the scenario. You will define these outcomes by interviewing and observing experienced performers and identifying the physical and mental work flow, that is—how they resolve situations calling for judgment and decision making. For example, an automotive technician must verify the problem, select a series of tests, analyze the results, and identify the failure source and associated repair actions. A veterinarian in an emergency situation must rapidly collect and interpret data, determine treatment priorities, and monitor changes. Sometimes you will need to go beyond traditional job analysis observations and interviews in order to identify tacit knowledge and skills underlying expert performance. The process of eliciting tacit knowledge and skills is called *cognitive task analysis*. I'll review some techniques you can use in Chapter 11.

After you write the learning objectives in your usual manner, for design and development purposes, you will need to translate those objectives into specific computer actions such as clicking on links or dragging and dropping objects. I've found that this translation can be a major hurdle for designers unfamiliar with e-learning design and development. The translation will depend on a number of factors that in turn will impact the complexity of your design. In the next section I will review some of the factors you need to consider as you convert higher-level learning objectives into specific online behaviors.

## ASSESS THE COMPLEXITY OF YOUR OUTCOME RESPONSES

The learning domain, your technology, and the prior knowledge of your learners are among the major factors that will influence your translation from a task-specific learning objective to a scenario-based e-learning objective. In Figure 4.1. I summarize four of the most important factors to consider.

| | MULTIMEDIA DESIGN COMPLEXITY | |
| | LOWER | HIGHER |
|---|---|---|
| 1. Number of outcomes | One at a time | Multiple<br>• Solutions<br>• Solution paths<br>• Rationale |
| 2. Outcome precision | High<br>• Right or wrong answers | Low<br>• Nuanced answers<br>• Multiple correct responses |
| 3. Interface response options | Limited<br>• Yes– No<br>• Multiple choice | Multiple<br>• Checklist<br>• Object select |
| 4. Social presence | High<br>• Instructor facilitated | Low<br>• Self-paced, self-study environment |

FIGURE 4.1. *Factors Influencing the Complexity of Multimedia Design.*

## 1. Number of Outcomes

If you have a learning objective with a single outcome verb, your lesson may focus on only one main result. For example, in a compliance scenario, the learner may simply indicate whether the action depicted does or does not violate policy or law. In more complex situations, you may have multiple objectives that require more than one outcome—not only a right or wrong answer but also an optimal process for collecting data and acting on it. For example, in the automotive troubleshooting lesson, it's important to identify the failure, but it's also important to do so in an efficient manner. The program tracks the learner's path and gives feedback allowing the learner to compare his path with that of an expert, as shown in Figure 1.2. Identifying the failure *and* using an efficient testing process to diagnose the failure represent two different outcomes. In the wedding counselor course Bridezilla, the learner selects from three multiple-choice response options during the interview, selects pull-down options to fill in worksheets, and can type in notes. In Figure 4.2 you can see the multiple-choice interview options in the left panel and the worksheet with pull-down menus and note-taking window in the right.

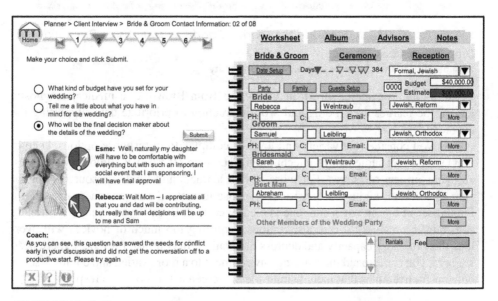

**FIGURE 4.2.** *Multiple-Choice Response Options on Left Panel and Pull-Down Type in Response Fields on the Right Worksheet.*

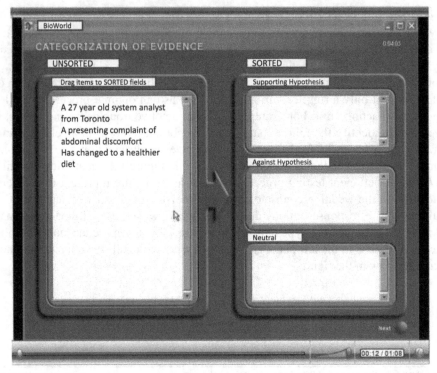

**FIGURE 4.3.** *In Bioworld the Learner Prioritizes Data Using Drag-and-Drop Interactions.*
With permission from Susanne LaJoie, McGill University.

In another example, shown in Figure 4.3 from Bioworld, a medical diagnostic lesson, the learner uses a drag-and-drop interaction to prioritize data supporting the diagnosis.

As you consider the variety and level of complexity in response options, keep in mind your target audience, your technological constraints, such as authoring resources, and your project resources. For more novice learners and limited resources, opt for simpler solutions and a few consistent response formats. Set up interfaces that offer a limited set of options of which one is clearly correct. Even if you need to artificially constrain the real-world response options, requiring too much of novices will overload their memory capacity and depress motivation. In contrast, for more experienced learners, you can expand the learning environment to a more varied and complex set of outcome deliverables that include multiple on-screen actions or open responses.

### 2. Outcome Precision

By outcome precision I mean the degree of ambiguity in potential responses. High precision outcomes imply response options that are correct or incorrect. The scenario has a fairly clear-cut right or wrong answer. For example, in a compliance course, the learner must decide whether a client offer of two $300 tickets to the local basketball game does or does not violate policy. A *yes* or *no* option that reflects a clear-cut correct or incorrect answer makes for a relatively simple interface design.

In many critical thinking domains black and white answers are scarce—the options are grayer or open-ended. For example, in an interpersonal branched scenario course, the learner may face four possible responses to an angry customer, of which three are both plausible and somewhat effective. The authoring system can give scoring weights to each learner response and then at each decision point or after several decision points lead to a different outcome. Alternatively, in a scenario requiring engineers to design a well-fracturing fluid system, there may be multiple solutions, several of which may be acceptable. Scenarios with multiple acceptable outcomes will often require human mediation for evaluation and feedback.

### 3. Interface Response Options

Interface response options are the different methods learners use to engage with the interface, such as clicking links or dragging on-screen objects. You will need to consider the affordances of your technology—in terms of authoring software, programming expertise, and delivery hardware. For a more constrained environment, you might limit response options to a single choice from two or more options, as in a branched scenario. Alternatively, you might incorporate a slider bar to indicate a response that falls along a continuum. For example in Figure 4.4 I show a screen from Bioworld—a scenario-based e-learning program focusing on medical problem solving. On this screen the learner has

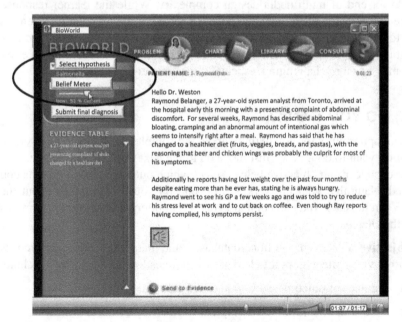

**FIGURE 4.4.** *Learners Indicate Confidence in Their Hypotheses with the Belief Meter Slider Bar (Upper Left Corner).*
With permission from Susanne Lajoie, McGill University.

selected an initial hypothesis of Salmonella from a pull-down menu and now slides the "Belief Meter" to indicate his or her level of confidence in the hypothesis.

Interface response options, including checklists, pull-down menus, links, slider bars, or selection of on-screen objects, allow the learner to respond in a variety of ways to the scenario. In general, a simpler program will use only one or two response formats such as multiple choice and clicking on links. A more complex program may require multiple forms of input, including clicking on links, dragging objects, and typing in responses.

### 4. Social Presence

Scenario-based e-learning can be designed to be used in an instructor-led environment— for either traditional in-person or virtual online classes. At the other extreme, it can be designed as a stand-alone self-study module. Intermediate solutions involve a stand-alone package supplemented by social media—resources such as wikis or shared media pages where learners can collaborate, exchange outcomes, or obtain expert advice.

In a high social-presence environment such as a physical classroom, it is generally easier to accommodate outcomes that are more open-ended, more nuanced, and that involve multiple deliverables. For example, role-play exercises that always have multiple correct responses can be facilitated and critiqued by classmates and instructors. Likewise, design domains that require development of an original product can be more readily produced and critiqued in an environment with higher social presence. Because of their higher level of social presence, I classify synchronous facilitated environments at the lower end of multimedia design complexity. While the learner response may be more complex for a role play compared to selecting predefined on-screen options, access to peers or an instructor takes some of the burden off your multimedia design. In contrast, in environments with lower social presence, the scenario-based e-learning design may be more challenging, especially for open-ended outcomes.

## WHAT DO YOU THINK?

Here is an opportunity for you to think about the complexity involved in several examples. Don't want to do it now? Just move on to the next topic in this chapter.

For each learning objective below, select which outcome design options could be indicated. Naturally, your answers will depend on your assumptions about the scenario. When finished, you can compare your assumptions and responses to mine at the end of the chapter.

**Objective 1**   Given multiple databases and data on reader preferences, the learner will write a news article that incorporates four of six interest techniques.

A. Number of outcomes:   ○ one or ○ multiple

B. Precision of solutions:   ○ high or ○ low

C. Number of interface response options:   ○ limited or ○ multiple

D. Optimal level of social presence:   ○ high ○ medium ○ low

**Objective 2**    Given patient signs and symptoms, the health provider will order appropriate lab tests and make optimal treatment decisions

    A. Number of outcomes:    ○ one or ○ multiple

    B. Precision of solutions:    ○ high or ○ low

    C. Number of interface response options:    ○ limited or ○ multiple

    D. Optimal level of social presence:    ○ high ○ medium ○ low

**Objective 3**    Given a scenario about use of email in the work environment, the learner will indicate whether the situation violates organizational information security policy

    A. Number of outcomes:    ○ one or ○ multiple

    B. Precision of solutions:    ○ high or ○ low

    C. Number of interface response options:    ○ limited or ○ multiple

    D. Optimal level of social presence:    ○ high ○ medium ○ low

## TRANSLATE YOUR LEARNING OBJECTIVES

As you plan the design of your scenario-based e-learning lessons, you will usually need to reframe your learning objective into specifications of online learner actions that your environment can support. On the simpler end the response may be a yes-or-no box to click or a selection among three or four options. On the more complex end, it may involve clicking on any of a number of on-screen objects, selecting options from a pull-down menu, or selecting one answer from a lengthy list. In a virtual world or instructor-led environment, a design task or a role play may offer almost unlimited response options. Keep in mind, however, that the more complex outcomes will also require more complex evaluation criteria and feedback. A design task of any complexity warrants a debriefing or evaluation in an environment of high social presence, such as from subject-matter experts, instructors, or peers. Review and feedback of open-ended outcomes will require a rubric (checklist) to guide evaluation. You can read more about scenario evaluation in Chapter 9.

Table 4.1 lists some examples of learning objectives accompanied by higher and lower complexity translations for each of the major learning domains. For example, under the interpersonal domain, a less complex response format uses a branched scenario in which the learner makes one choice from three or four options on each screen. In contrast, a more complex response requires a role play. In a blended solution, you may decide to use the multimedia scenarios as prework for a face-to-face session. Recent research has shown that blended solutions that leverage the strengths of synchronous and asynchronous learning environments support optimal learning (U.S. Department of Education, 2012).

TABLE 4.1.  **Some Typical Objectives and Associated Response Options for Learning Domains**

| Learning Domain | Objective | Response Options | Examples |
|---|---|---|---|
| Interpersonal | Given a respondent, learner will select or generate optimal statements to achieve task goals | Select a series of responses to optimize communication outcomes<br>Role play to exhibit behaviors most likely to achieve communication goals | 1. Customer service rep selects best option among four responses to resolve customer inquiry<br>2. Sales person role plays responding to client objections |
| Compliance: Policies and Procedures | Learners will respond to situations by taking actions congruent with organizational policies and procedures | Select options that comply with legal and company policy guidelines<br>Construct optimal products to comply with policy guidelines | 1. Worker responds to client offer of a gift by clicking on one of four options<br>2. Supervisor writes valid and legal questions for new hire interview |
| Diagnosis and Repair | Given symptoms and testing options, learner will apply efficient diagnostic process to select tests, interpret results, and make a repair | Click on appropriate testing tools<br>Select appropriate test interpretation from a pull-down menu<br>Select or state treatment or repair option | 1. Technician identifies cause of auto malfunction by clicking on one option from a list<br>2. Veterinarian selects treatments from a pull-down menu based on patient symptoms and diagnostic test results |
| Research Analysis and Rationale | Given an assignment and sources of case data, learner will apply efficient research process to select data, interpret results, and make a decision or produce a product | Click on productive data sources<br>Evaluate data credibility with a slider rating scale<br>Select or state optimal decision/action<br>Enter or select hypothesis or rationale | 1. Underwriter accesses applicant records, interviews applicant, makes recommendations, and states rationale<br>2. Journalist identifies relevant sources and synthesizes data into a report that reflects reader's profile |

| Learning Domain | Objective | Response Options | Examples |
|---|---|---|---|
| Tradeoffs | Given a business goal or dilemma, learner will identify and evaluate various perspectives to make and justify a decision | Click on sources of perspectives; access policies/procedures; select decision and enter/select rationale Identify and review alternatives; prepare a position giving evidence for your position | 1. Staff member reviews a situation that possibly warrants whistle blowing and prepares pro and con arguments 2. Wedding counselor identifies compromise options that reflect expectations and accommodate clients' constraints |
| Operational Decisions, Actions | Given equipment interfaces and relevant data, operator will adjust controls to optimize outcomes | Click or slide controls to adjust operational parameters Select rationale for adjustments | 1. Plant operator adjusts simulated control interfaces to optimize production at maximum cost-benefit 2. Pilot adjusts controls to respond to system alarm |
| Design | Given requirements and resource data, learner will construct a product that optimizes resources and meets requirements | Click on options to identify requirements and resources Drag and drop or select pull-down on-screen elements into a first draft design Construct a design | 1. IT student designs a website to meet client constraints 2. Engineer develops a design spec to meet production, time, and cost requirements |
| Team Work | Given a goal requiring collaborative synergy among team members of diverse expertise, learner will ensure effective team communication, make decisions, take action to optimize outcomes | Click to review situation and resources Drag and drop resources to optimize outcome; select best response or communication option | 1. Emergency response team lead coordinates activities to manage and contain crisis 2. Military commander makes combat personnel assignments that minimize causalities |

*Multimedia Response Options*

If you are familiar with e-learning, either as a designer, developer, or student, you are likely aware of the various options commonly available in a multimedia interface, summarized in Table 4.2. As you translate your learning objective into specific online behaviors, review this list—keeping in mind the options supported by your authoring environment, your desired learning outcomes, and learner prior knowledge. For example, in the Bridezilla lesson (see Figure 4.2) we used multiple-choice questions, links, pull-down lists and input fields. In Bioworld (see Figures 4.3 and 4.4), case research and solution activities use drag and drop, links, pull-down menus, and slider bars.

One of the pitfalls of scenario-based learning is open ended environments that fail to provide the structure and guidance your learners need. One feature of your design that influences structure and guidance is your interface, including the type and number of response options allowed in the interface. I will return to this issue in greater detail in Chapter 6 on guidance in scenario-based e-learning.

## SCENARIO OUTCOMES AND MULTIMEDIA INTERFACES

In Chapter 2 I introduced four navigational interfaces: branched scenario, menu, open object, and virtual world. As you define and translate outcomes and their associated response options, you may need to revisit your initial decisions. For example, a learning objective that focuses on the best work flow sequence to accomplish the goal must offer an interface and be supported by a program that allows multiple solution paths that can be tracked. An open design with on-screen objects to select is a common interface for that kind of task deliverable. In contrast, as I mentioned previously, an open-ended task deliverable such as a product design may require an instructor-facilitated

TABLE 4.2.  **Common Multimedia Response Options**

| Option | Description | Use for |
|---|---|---|
| Yes-No | Learner makes one choice from two options | Selecting decisions or actions |
| Multiple-Choice | Learner makes one choice from several options | Selecting decisions or actions |
| Checklist | Learner makes several choices from a list of options | Selecting multiple reasons for a decision<br>Selecting multiple interpretations of data |

| Option | Description | Use for |
|---|---|---|
| Links | Learner selects from several text links | Accessing scenario case data and resources<br>Making scenario decisions |
| Pull-Down Menu | Learner selects one choice from several options | Selecting hypotheses, decisions, actions, or rationale |
| Drag and Drop | Learner moves content from one screen area to another | Classifying objects or data |
| Click on Object | Learner selects an on-screen object | Identifying object as source of problem<br>Selecting data to be saved for review |
| Slider Bar | Learner slides bar to indicate a degree | Indicating confidence in a decision or hypothesis<br>Indicating likely validity of a data source |
| Type in | Learner types in short text entry | Summarizing rationale |
| Virtual World | Learner moves and takes action in 3D world | Role playing responses<br>Taking actions on equipment<br>Designing product |
| Social Media | Learner can search or contribute to social media available in your organization | Building a shared media page such as Facebook<br>Soliciting feedback from an online expert or team |
| Search Engines | Learner can use organizational or external search engines to identify facts or procedures relevant to scenario | Searching online technician manual to identify correct schematic<br>Searching database to find background information relevant to scenario product |

environment. If you are getting started in scenario-based e-learning, I recommend starting with smaller and less complex lessons, learning from your experience, and gradually evolving to more complex levels as needed.

## WHAT DO YOU THINK? REVISITED

Here are my answers. If you have different choices, don't worry—there are multiple interpretations of each objective which could lead to different answers.

For each learning objective below, select which task deliverable design options could be indicated.

**Objective 1**  Given multiple databases and data on reader preferences, the learner will write a news article that contains four of six interest factors.

A.  Number of outcomes:    ● one or ● multiple

B.  Precision of solutions:   ○ high or ● low

C.  Number of interface response options:   ○ limited or ● multiple

D.  Optimal level of social presence:   ● high ○ medium ○ low

In this scenario, the main focus is on the final product, a news article with a single open-ended outcome with multiple solutions. However, the focus may be not only on the product itself but also on the search and decision process involved in identifying and verifying source content. That's why I selected both one and multiple for number of outcomes. The outcome report will have low precision, that is, no single right or wrong answer. In addition, the learner will need a number of response format alternatives to select and search different databases. Because the news article is a very open product, this objective would likely benefit from high social presence in a virtual or physical setting.

As prework for an instructor-led session, the scenario-based e-learning lesson could focus on a subset of the final skills, such as identifying and searching relevant databases, assessing the credibility of the data, and assembling pre-constructed report "pieces" to build an online article. This type of lesson could support the basic knowledge and skills prior to instructor-led sessions that emphasize open-ended tasks, such as writing the article.

**Objective 2**  Given patient signs and symptoms, the health provider will order appropriate lab tests and make optimal treatment decisions.

A.  Number of outcomes:   ○ one or ● multiple

B.  Precision of solutions:   ● high or ○ low

C.  Number of interface response options:   ○ limited or ● multiple

D.  Optimal level of social presence:   ○ high ● medium ○ low

For this learning objective, I assume that learners will make multiple responses as they select tests, select interpretations, and ultimately select a treatment. The complexity of the scenario could vary, but for a straightforward case, I would incorporate treatment choices that are right or wrong and an outcome deliverable that would include not only the final selected treatment but the tests ordered and perhaps some indication of rationale. Depending on the complexity of the case, discussions among learners would promote learning. At the same time, for relatively straightforward situations, a lower level of social presence might suffice. I took a middle ground and selected medium.

**Objective 3**   Given a scenario about use of email in the work environment, the learner will indicate whether the situation violates organizational information security policy.

   A.  Number of outcomes:   ● one or ○ multiple

   B.  Precision of solutions:   ○ high or ● low

   C.  Number of interface response options:   ● limited or ○ multiple

   D.  Optimal level of social presence:   ○ high ● medium ○ low

Objective 3 is the least complex of the three scenarios. I assume a fairly straightforward scenario requiring a single decision that is correct or incorrect and can be indicated with a yes or no response. This type of scenario-based e-learning could easily be implemented in a self-study multimedia learning environment. High social presence is not needed, although it could add value if learners wanted to discuss "What if's?" or if scenarios were of sufficient complexity.

## COMING NEXT

Now that you have specified your outcome deliverables and associated responses, you are ready to plan the trigger event as well as specify what scenario case data will be needed by the learner and how best to represent it in your multimedia interface.

## ADDITIONAL RESOURCE

Horton, W. (2006). *e-Learning by design*. San Francisco: Pfeiffer.
   In this comprehensive guide to design of all types of e-learning, you can review a wide variety of activities, some of which could be used in your scenario-based e-learning design.

# SCENARIO-BASED e-LEARNING AND YOU: TRANSLATING YOUR OBJECTIVES

At this stage, you need to identify and translate your general learning objectives into a more specific format as a bridge between high level outcomes and specific online learner responses. Consider your learning domain and write out your learning objectives. Based on your objectives, define the main outcome elements involved in a successful scenario conclusion. For example, could the learning objective be translated into a yes or no response, a product, or a research and analysis process? Next consider which specific response interface formats your environment can support and rewrite your objective if needed to reflect those options.

## Scenario-Learning Domain
**Check all that apply.**

- ☐ Interpersonal skills
- ☐ Leadership and compliance
- ☐ Diagnosis and repair
- ☐ Research, analysis, and rationale
- ☐ Tradeoffs
- ☐ Operations
- ☐ Design
- ☐ Team coordination
- ☐ Other

## Your Learners

Novice          Some Experience          Apprentice          Mixed

## Your First Draft Learning Objective(s)

**Complexity of Outcome Responses**

A. Number of outcomes: ○ one or ○ multiple

B. Precision of solutions: ○ high or ○ low

C. Number of interface response options: ○ limited or ○ multiple

D. Social presence: ○ high ○ medium ○ low

**Your Revised Learning Objective(s) for Design Purposes**

**Your Interface Response Options**

As you consider your revised objectives and your authoring resources, which interface response formats can you use for your desired task deliverables:

- ☐ Yes or no
- ☐ Multiple choice
- ☐ Checklist
- ☐ Links
- ☐ Pull-down menu
- ☐ Drag and drop
- ☐ Object select
- ☐ Slider bar
- ☐ Type in
- ☐ Virtual world
- ☐ Classroom
- ☐ Virtual classroom
- ☐ Social media: _____
- ☐ Search engines:_____
- ☐ Other: _____

# CHAPTER

## 5

# DESIGNING THE TRIGGER EVENT AND CASE DATA

Think about the first slides you see in a typical training session. A text title sometimes augmented with a photograph comes first. Next are slides with learning objectives and an agenda. Imagine as an alternative that the first image you see is a video scenario similar to the example shown in Figure 2.1 in which a number of civilians and soldiers die in a failed combat operation. Following the video, you assume the role of the commanding officer. In a series of scenarios you have the opportunity to turn back time and make decisions that will lead to a better outcome.

In this chapter, I'll describe two key components of a scenario-based e-learning design—the lead-off or trigger event and the case data. Both of these can be derived from the "given" statement of the learning objective, which typically specifies the conditions, tools, and resources learners will have when performing a task. For example, the automotive technician lesson objective is "Given a work order and typical shop testing equipment, the learner will conduct appropriate tests to identify and resolve the failure." Therefore the trigger event is a work order and the case data will be derived from multiple on-screen testing tools.

## WHAT DO YOU THINK?

Before we delve into the specifics of trigger events and case data, which of the following statements do you think is true? You can compare your answers with mine at the end of the chapter.

❑   All scenarios should include a trigger event.

❑   Some learning domains will require greater emphasis on case data than others.

❑   Access to case data should be flexible, allowing learners to choose what they want when they want it.

❑   Trigger events should use video to deliver an engaging lesson start.

## PLANNING THE TRIGGER EVENT

When learners log into the lesson, what is the first thing they will see? The trigger event is the kick-off or launch of your scenario. It is typically displayed on the first or second screen. The trigger event incorporates the setting as well as the specific event that initiates the scenario. You will want to craft a trigger event that pulls your learners into the scenario right away. Therefore, the trigger event should be job-realistic, compelling, and provide the learner with a clear idea of outcome expectations. To define the setting and trigger event, ask your subject-matter experts one or more of the following:

▪   How would an assignment or situation requiring actions that will lead to the desired outcome be presented or appear in the normal work environment?

▪   What is the physical setting in which the initiating event would occur?

▪   When a worker needs to [*fill in verb*], what initiates her actions? Where is she?

▪   How might a mishandled situation look [if you are considering a Murphy's Law trigger]?

In Table 5.1, I summarize some typical trigger events for the learning domains introduced in Chapter 2.

In many cases the trigger event is simple—a workplace setting in which a situation is initiated by a phone call, an e-mail, or a co-worker. A more elaborate approach is what I call the Murphy's Law trigger. In the Murphy's Law trigger, the lesson starts with a situation in which incorrect decisions and actions were made and just about everything went wrong. The failed combat scene in Figure 2.1 is one example. A Murphy's Law trigger may be elaborate, such as the failed combat mission. Alternatively, it may be simple, for example, the Bridezilla course could start with a screen shot showing a disorganized wedding reception and negative comments from the bride, parents, and guests.

**TABLE 5.1.** **Some Settings and Trigger Events for Scenario-Based e-Learning Domains**

| Domain | Setting | Triggers | Examples |
|---|---|---|---|
| Interpersonal | Office, meeting room, telephone | Sales call, client phone call, meeting with staff member | 1. Account rep sees sales call on calendar<br>2. Staff member enters manager's office |
| Compliance | Office, restaurant, operational area | Scene relevant to policy or procedure: office, factory floor, client meeting, etc. | 1. In office learner sees an unsecured computer<br>2. In marketing department colleague proposes discriminatory ad campaign |
| Diagnosis | Shop, clinic, hospital, laboratory | Work order, sick patient, customer request | 1. Work order in auto shop<br>2. New patient in examination room |
| Research and Analysis | Office, computer | Boss assignment, e-mail, client request | 1. Loan application assignment<br>2. E-mail with report assignment |
| Tradeoffs | Combat scene, office, shop, laboratory, field site | Situation initiator: customer request, customer interview, Murphy's Law lead-in | 1. Failed combat engagement (see Figure 2.1)<br>2. Customer interview |
| Operational | Equipment panels | Alarms, work order | 1. Alarms—auditory and visual<br>2. Failed emergency response—post-event investigation |
| Design | Computer, laboratory, workbench, drafting table | Boss or client assignment Specifications for product | 1. Phone request from design team<br>2. Text message from boss |
| Team Collaboration | Disaster scene, operating room, oil field, meeting room | Situations requiring team coordination, Gantt chart | 1. Cockpit situation requiring crew resource utilization<br>2. ER team responding to patient |

## DEFINING CASE DATA

Case data refers to specific information about the scenario needed to complete the assignment. For some learning objectives, finding and interpreting case data is one of the outcome deliverables and assumes a major focus of the scenario. This is usually true in diagnosis and research and analysis domains and often true in other domains such as design, team coordination, and operational.

When the access and interpretation of case data is an intended outcome, your interface must offer multiple sources of case data, such as the testing equipment in the automotive shop. While the auto shop uses a very graphical interface, you may decide instead to use a menu design to provide access to case data. For example, in Figure 5.1 the bank loan scenario (research and analysis domain) includes a tab along the top row labeled "data." When selected, left submenus appear with main categories of "financial data," "third-party data," and "client-supplied data." In this example the learner has selected market research data and has access to various documents relevant to the applicant's industry.

Both the whole screen and menu interfaces support high levels of navigational control so that learners can select the data sources they feel are most relevant at any given time. When your goal is to teach an efficient or logical process for access and interpretation of data, the learners will need a higher level of control to exercise their decision-making skills.

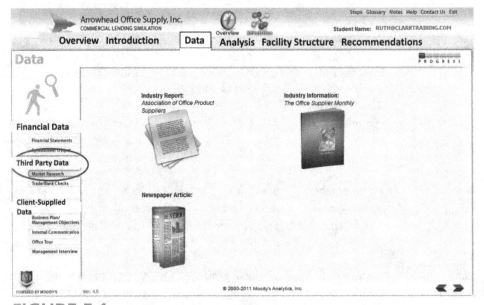

**FIGURE 5.1.** *The Upper Tabs and Left Menu Links Link to Scenario Data.*
With permission from Moody's Analytics.

### Formats for Case Data

Case data usually can be represented in the form of documents, charts and graphs, interviews, or objects for observation and assessment. For example, in the bank scenario shown in Figure 2.3, the financial data is displayed in a spreadsheet. In the cat anesthesia lesson, case data is displayed through the chart summary of physical signs. In the bank scenario, the learner has the opportunity to gather data through client interviews. As you can see in Figure 5.2, the learner can select from a list those questions she deems most relevant. Because the amount of time allocated to the interview is limited to about 15 minutes, the learner will need to be selective in picking the most relevant questions to ask.

Case data that might be hidden in the normal work setting can be displayed in a multimedia lesson. For example, in the Bridezilla interview shown in Figure 1.3 we used an attitude meter as a graphic source of "invisible" client data. If interpretation of sensory data is a focus of your learning objective, it will be important to display objects of sufficient fidelity to support the needed discrimination. For example, when assessing a patient, the color of the skin, the breathing pattern, the lung sounds, the voice quality—all might be relevant and would need realistic rendering. If those discrimination skills are *not* the focus of learning, the same case data could be provided in descriptive text, such as "patient lips are cyanotic," "breathing is irregular," etc.

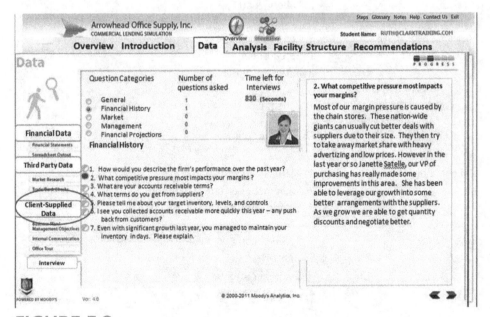

**FIGURE 5.2.** *To Interview Client Managers, the Learner Must Select Relevant Questions in a Limited Time Frame.*
With permission from Moody's Analytics.

Compared to the automotive troubleshooting and bank loan lessons, some scenarios may require very little case data. For example, in a compliance scenario, a couple of screens showing a co-worker's actions or decisions may be all that is needed.

In Table 5.2 I list some examples of case data associated with the scenario domains listed in Chapter 2.

**TABLE 5.2.  Examples of Case Data for Scenario-Based e-Learning Domains**

| Learning Domain | Examples |
|---|---|
| Interpersonal | 1. Sales rep queries client needs<br>2. Manager reviews employee file |
| Compliance | 1. Records of current or previous incidents<br>2. Previous records of case<br>3. Legal judgments |
| Diagnosis | 1. Test data from shop tools<br>2. Interview of accident witness<br>3. Patient chart |
| Research and Analysis | 1. Loan application<br>2. Spreadsheet<br>3. Interview of manager |
| Tradeoffs | 1. Patient chart<br>2. Customer interview<br>3. Gantt chart |
| Operational | 1. Alarms—auditory and visual<br>2. Equipment performance graphs<br>3. Equipment specifications and schematics |
| Design | 1. Specification document<br>2. Gantt chart<br>3. Customer interview<br>4. User testing data |
| Team Collaboration | 1. Team members' skill documents<br>2. Situation updates via radio or telephone |

## Saving and Tracking Case Data

In scenarios requiring learners to access and to interpret multiple sources of case data such as the automotive troubleshooting lesson, consider an on-screen element that allows the learner to save data for later review. For example, in the Bridezilla lesson, much of the case data is derived from the client interview. As the data is gathered, it is annotated in the worksheets under categories of bride and groom, ceremony, or reception. For example, in Figure 5.3 we see a screen from the end of the initial interview with the bride and her mother. Much of the worksheet has been completed and a note about the budget has been made in the lower left field of the worksheet.

In scenarios that involve identification, accumulation, and interpretation of data, ask yourself how workers save this data on the job and build similar mechanisms into your interface.

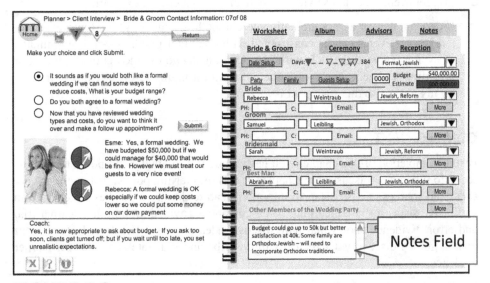

**FIGURE 5.3.** *Client Data Is Saved in the Worksheet on the Right, Including the Lower-Left Notes Field.*

## WHAT DO YOU THINK? REVISITED

Here are my thoughts about which statements are true or false:

❑   All scenarios should include a trigger event.

*True.* Initiating your scenario with a real-world event—something as simple as an e-mail assignment or as complex as a video of a failed situation—will set the stage and engage the learner right away.

❑   Some learning domains will require greater emphasis on case data than others.

*True*. Domains that involve research and analysis, by definition, will require case data. Your scenario lessons may emphasize the selection and interpretation of case data as a major outcome. In contrast, other domains may not rely significantly on case data for resolution.

❑   Access to case data should be flexible, allowing learners to choose what they want when they want it.

This is true when your goal is to teach the best resources and/or an efficient process for accessing and interpreting resources. If this is not a goal, you may display relevant case data as a part of your introductory scenes. Remember that novice workers may be overwhelmed by too much learner control and require higher levels of structure.

❑   Trigger events should use video to deliver an engaging lesson start.

Video can deliver a very dramatic and compelling trigger event. However, effective trigger events can be constructed with computer graphics—still or animated or even a few static visuals with text. One challenge to video is the high cost of updating. A benefit, however, is the potential for higher levels of emotive impact. So my answer to this statement is *false*.

## COMING NEXT

By the completion of this chapter, you have thought through the end-point, that is, the scenario outcomes (discussed in Chapter 4) and the starting points, that is, the trigger event and sources of case data. An important feature that distinguishes effective from ineffective scenario-based learning is the guidance provided to minimize learner trial and error. Evidence shows that pure discovery learning is ineffective. Instead, your goal is guided discovery. Chapter 6 will describe and illustrate strategies for learner guidance.

## SCENARIO-BASED e-LEARNING AND YOU:
## DEFINING YOUR TRIGGER EVENT AND CASE DATA

In Chapters 3 and 4 you identified your learning domain and specified your desired outcomes from your lesson. At this stage you can plan your setting, trigger event, and sources of case data.

**My Scenario Setting(s)**

☐ Office, meeting room

☐ Computer

☐ Technical shop, laboratory

☐ Clinic, hospital, surgical suite

☐ Equipment and instrument panels

☐ Factory

☐ Field site, such as oil well, combat zone:

☐ Other:

**My Trigger Event**

**Trigger**                          **Description**

☐ Phone call

☐ E-mail, text message

☐ Interview

☐ Failure or crisis

☐ Murphy's Law scenario

☐ Other

Does your scenario outcome require identification and analysis of data? If yes:

A. How will the learner navigate to the data sources?

- ☐ Graphic representations
- ☐ Tabs
- ☐ Other:

B. How will the learner save accumulated data for later reference?

- ☐ Clipboard
- ☐ Electronic files
- ☐ Note pad
- ☐ Spreadsheet
- ☐ Worksheet
- ☐ Other:

C. How will you represent your case data?

| Format | Description |
| --- | --- |
| ☐ Documents | |
| ☐ Charts, graphs | |
| ☐ Interviews | |
| ☐ Objects | |
| ☐ Other: | |

# CHAPTER

# BUILDING GUIDANCE IN SCENARIO-BASED e-LEARNING

Perhaps your most important design decisions involve the amount and type of guidance you provide in your scenario-based e-learning environment. Research tells us that pure discovery learning does not work. "Instructional programs evaluated over the past fifty years consistently point to the ineffectiveness of pure discovery" (Mayer, 2004, p. 17). Learning environments that lack guidance fail to manage what I call the *flounder factor*. Learners engage in unproductive trial-by-error explorations. The results at best inefficient learning and, at worst, no learning and/or learner dropout. In this chapter I review some common techniques you can use to build a guided discovery (versus a discovery) learning environment through use of guidance techniques, also known as scaffolding.

## WHAT DO YOU THINK?

Compare Figures 6.1 and 6.2. Based on what you can see in these screen shots, answer the questions that follow. You can see my answers at the end of the chapter.

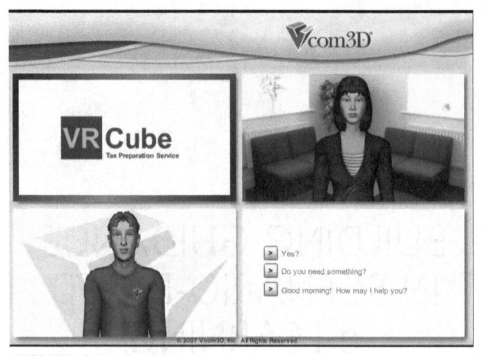

**FIGURE 6.1.** *A Customer Service Scenario-Based e-Lesson.*
With permission from VCOM 3D.

**FIGURE 6.2.** *An Automotive Troubleshooting Scenario-Based e-Lesson.*
With permission from Raytheon Professional Services.

1. Which example is more guided or close-ended?

   ❏ A. The customer service sample

   ❏ B. The automotive troubleshooting sample

2. In the more guided or close-ended example, what sources of guidance (or structure) do you see?

   ❏ A. Limited on-screen response options

   ❏ B. On-screen coach

   ❏ C. Complexity of the scenario

3. Which example is better?

   ❏ A. Depends on the learners' prior knowledge

   ❏ B. Depends on intended outcomes of the instruction

   ❏ C. Depends on the immersive quality of the interface

## WHAT IS GUIDANCE?

Typically, we classify overt sources of help such as online coaches or feedback as guidance. However, I use the term *guidance*—also called scaffolding—to designate any element in a scenario-based e-learning design that minimizes the flounder factor. In other words, any design element that converts discovery learning into guided discovery is a form of guidance. For example, an interface that offers a choice of only one response option at a time (such as Figure 6.1) is more "guided" or constrained than an open-ended environment that allows higher levels of learner control.

In this chapter I will summarize nine different design techniques you can use for guidance. These techniques don't span all possible options. However, they will give you a rich menu of the most common support techniques that you can adapt to your own context. Which techniques you select will depend on your target audience—primarily their topic-relevant prior knowledge and your outcome goals. For Question 3 under What Do You Think?, I would select options A and B as the most important factors. Regarding target audience, novice learners will need much higher levels of guidance compared to apprentice workers. Some learning domains, such as diagnosis and repair, focus on process goals for which the desired outcome is a solution and also the process the learner uses to derive the solution. For example, in Figure 6.2 the learner has a choice of various tests, and only if the learner is given an environment in which she can select among multiple testing options and testing sequences, can that process be practiced and refined. However, offering a higher level of learner control also imposes a less structured environment. In other situations such as many compliance goals, the outcome may be more limited, for example, a yes or no decision calling for only two or three response options. In Table 6.1 I summarize nine guidance options to be described in this chapter. Feel free to peruse these techniques and dive into those most relevant to your context.

## TABLE 6.1.   Techniques for Guidance in Scenario-Based e-Learning

| Technique | Description | Example |
| --- | --- | --- |
| Faded Support | Initial scenarios offer more guidance than later scenarios. | The first scenario solution is a demonstration followed by a scenario that is partially worked out for the learner. |
| Simple to Complex Scenarios | Each module includes a progression of simple to more complex scenarios. Complexity can come from the number of variables in the scenario, the amount of conflict in case data, or from unanticipated events. | Straightforward failure scenario resolvable with five tests in initial troubleshooting followed by more complex scenario requiring eight tests. |
| Open vs. Closed Response Options | On-screen response options range from limited-choice responses to open-ended responses. | A multiple-choice response option in a branched scenario is more closed than a multiple-select response option, which in turn is more closed than a role play. |
| Interface/ Navigation Options | Branched scenario designs offer fewer options at one time compared to full-screen displays. Menu titles can reflect the recommended work flow. | Figure 6.1 compared to Figure 6.2. In bank loan scenario (see Figures 5.1, 5.2), the tabs are labeled: introduction, data, analysis, facility structure price, and recommendations. |
| Training Wheels | Constrain the interface to allow only partial functionality. For example, some on-screen elements (visuals or menu items) remain inactive for a given problem or until a given state in problem solution. | The automotive shop allows only limited functionality in the beginning. Some tool options respond with "do not use for this problem" when selected. |
| Coaching and Advisors | A virtual helper that often takes the form of an on-screen agent that offers hints or feedback. As lessons progress, agent help is reduced. | In Bridezilla the coach comments on each choice made during the interview process. In later lessons, the agent comments only when selected. |

| Technique | Description | Example |
|---|---|---|
| Worksheets | For complex decisions that rely on collection and analysis of multiple data sources, a worksheet stores data and guides the analysis. | In an underwriting scenario, a series of worksheets is used to help learners assemble and analyze client data. |
| Feedback | Knowledge of results given either as the learners progress or at the end of the scenario is an essential source of guidance. | In Bridezilla the coach comments on each choice made during the interview process. In addition, the attitude meter shows client feelings based on questions asked. |
| Collaboration | Opportunities to collaborate during scenario solution with experts or other learners via synchronous or asynchronous methods supports learning. | In Bridezilla the learner can e-mail some of the expert advisors with questions not addressed in the lesson. |

## OPTION 1: FADE SUPPORT FROM HIGH TO LOW

Let's begin with a general principle for the imposition and fading of learner guidance. In Figure 6.3 I illustrate the concept of faded support. In this model, the support consists of a three-part progression starting with a solution demonstration followed by two partial assignments and ending with a full problem assignment.

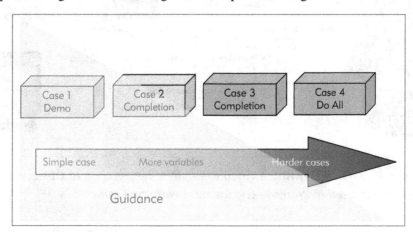

**FIGURE 6.3.** *Fade Support and Increase Complexity as Scenarios Progress.*

So in a simple situation, imagine that for one class of scenarios—for example, overcoming objections—your first case would be relatively simple and would be viewed by the learner as a demonstration in which the on-screen expert describes how an objection was handled. Figure 6.4 from a pharmaceutical sales course, uses a video to demonstrate an expert performance. To encourage engagement in the demonstration, we added questions next to the example. The next scenario would be a bit more complex—perhaps involving more variables or a prescriber who is already happy with a competitor's product. This scenario would be partially demonstrated and the learner would finish it. The final scenario would involve a complex situation requiring the learner to resolve the entire case. Initial cases might use a more structured branched scenario response format, whereas later cases might require a role-played response in a virtual classroom or face-to-face setting.

For this illustration I used a fading technique of evolving from demonstration to full problem assignment. However, the basic principle—to offer higher levels of support on initial cases and gradually remove it in later scenarios—can apply to any of the guidance techniques to follow.

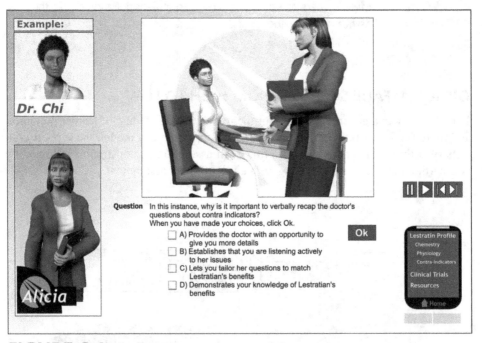

**FIGURE 6.4.** *Following a Video Example of Responding to Objections, Questions Are Used to Promote Engagement with the Example.*

## OPTION 2: MOVE FROM SIMPLE TO COMPLEX

This technique is also illustrated in Figure 6.3. As an experienced instructional professional, you are familiar with developing practice exercises or case studies that range
from simple to complex. Similar strategies apply here. Scenario complexity may be
determined by several factors, depending on your learning domain. For example,
a simple case may have fewer variables and more clear-cut correct and incorrect
responses. Alternatively, a simple case may have as many variables as a more complex
case, but the more complex case offers conflicting variables or unanticipated obstacles
that surface mid-stream. Typically, each course module will incorporate several scenarios that focus on a cross-section of the tasks. For example, in a pharmaceutical
selling course you might find the following modules: (A.) Selling to a family practice;
(B.) Selling to a specialty practice; and (C.) Selling to an HMO. Within each module
you will include three or four scenarios, each incorporating the major selling stages,
such as "assess client needs," "present relevant product features," "answer questions,"
"respond to objections," and "set the stage for the next visit." Within each module the
scenarios will range from simple to complex.

### Use SMES to Identify Complexity Factors

To derive factors that contribute to case complexity, ask your subject-matter expert
team members to individually write three situations they have faced in a particular
class of scenarios, ranging from simple to more complex. For each situation, they
should write enough detail so that the setting, obstacles, and their solution actions and
rationale are clear. Next assemble your team of experts to share their simple, moderate, and complex scenarios and agree on the classifications. Guide the experts to use
their examples as a basis to derive the key factors that make a scenario simple or
complex. You can then reverse engineer your process, using the complexity factors and
samples to build cases at an appropriate level.

For example, if you were developing scenario-based e-learning on presenting a
new drug to a specialty group practice, you might ask your top sales performers to
independently write out simple, moderate, and complex situations in which they effectively worked with such a practice. Consider giving your experts a template as well as a
model example to ensure that you receive sufficient detail. For example, provide a completed table with headers for relevant information such as the drugs involved, a brief
profile of the practice and prescribers, the main presentation points, the objection(s)
raised, the objection response techniques, and a summary of the outcomes.

## OPTION 3: CONSIDER OPEN VS. CLOSED RESPONSE OPTIONS

In Chapter 4, I reviewed the different types of outcome deliverables your learning goals may dictate, as well as how to translate those deliverables into on-screen
responses, including multiple choice, multiple select, fill-in, drag and drop, and click
on-screen objects. In addition, I discussed options for outcome deliverables that

require open-ended responses such as shared media pages, breakout rooms, spread-sheets, PowerPoint slides, Word documents, role plays, etc. For novice learners, you may design scenarios with frequent limited response choices and clear-cut right versus wrong answers. For example, in the branched scenario course shown in Figure 6.1, each screen offers three response options, which in turn trigger immediate audio feed-back from the on-screen agent. Alternatively, for more experienced learners, you may offer a multiple-choice screen with many options, such as that shown in Figure 6.5, requiring the learner to select one correct answer from a list of ten or more alterna-tives. As a general guideline, offer fewer response options such as multiple choice for more novice learners and more complex response options, including multiple select, fill in, drag and drop, shared media pages or role plays, for more experienced learners.

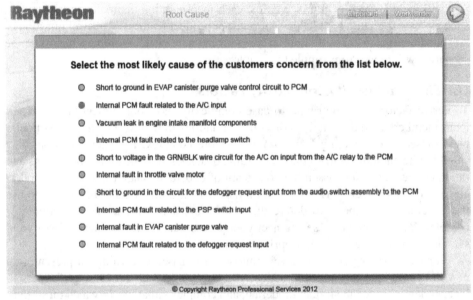

**FIGURE 6.5.**  *A Multiple-Choice Response Screen in Automotive Troubleshooting Lessons with Many Solution Options.*
With permission from Raytheon Professional Services.

## OPTION 4: CONSIDER INTERFACE/NAVIGATION DESIGN

The branched scenario design as shown in Figure 6.1 is a more straightforward response template in the form of multiple-choice options with immediate feedback on each screen. In contrast, for more advanced learners and when your goal is not only an "answer" but also the data-gathering and analysis process, a menu or whole-screen design offers the potential for less constrained responses. Menu or whole-screen navi-gational layouts provide multiple paths for progressing through the lesson and may be

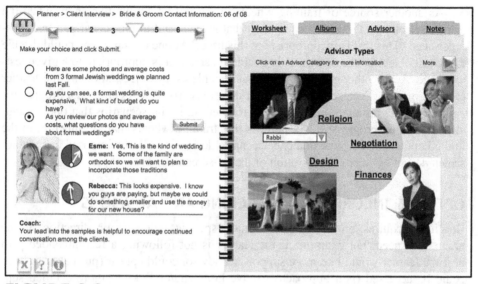

FIGURE 6.6.  *The Album and Advisor Tabs (Upper Right) Link to Guidance in the Bridezilla Lesson.*

essential if your goal is to teach a problem-solving flow as well as analysis decisions. As a general guideline, the more response alternatives available in the interface, the more unguided the learning environment. A classroom role play or project assignment offers the most unguided environment in which the learner can construct free-form responses.

A menu design such as that used in the bridal consultant course offers an intermediate level of structure. You can use menu links to lead to guidance resources, as shown in Figure 6.6. Alternatively, you can use menu links to reflect the workflow, as shown in the bank underwriting training in Figures 5.1 and 5.2. The learner can choose to access any of the menu options, but the options themselves provide a structure to the environment. In a blended learning environment, you may start with a multimedia introductory lesson using a branched scenario design and later evolve to more open-ended responses in an instructor-led setting.

## OPTION 5: ADD TRAINING WHEELS

Before my grandsons could really ride their bikes, they spent several months riding with training wheels. The training wheels gave them enough freedom to learn balance maneuvers but also prevented ugly spills. In more open interfaces such as the automotive shop, you can add training wheels by constraining the response options. For example, at the start of the automotive troubleshooting scenario, when the learner mouses over the various testing objects, the car is the only active object, as indicated by a halo effect and a callout. Verifying the fault is the first step in the troubleshooting process and is the only response allowed in the beginning of the scenario.

As another source of training wheels in the virtual automotive shop, when the learner selects certain testing equipment that is irrelevant to the scenario, a text message sates: "This test is inappropriate at this time." At one extreme, you could disable every test object on the screen, only enabling each as it is appropriate to a given testing stage. At the other extreme, you could enable every object, allowing the learner to make multiple incorrect or inefficient decisions. You may decide on a progressive approach using a more constrained environment in initial scenarios that open gradually as learning progresses. My point is that training wheels that are inherent in the limited options of a typical branched scenario design can also be imposed in a whole-screen design by selective activation of the on-screen objects.

## OPTION 6: INCORPORATE COACHING AND ADVISORS

Coaching requires providing brief context-specific guidance or direction at the moment of need. For example, if the learner is not following a recommended path or if the learner would like more support, an advisor could appear (push approach) or could be accessed (pull approach) to give hints and/or links to more detailed support. Coaching guidance may come from an avatar represented as a persistent on-screen guide, as shown in lower left section of Figure 6.1, or from a pop-up text box. Whatever the form, the coaching message should be short and specific to an on-screen action recently taken by the learner. Branched scenario designs could provide a coaching message with each response taken. Open designs may offer less frequent guidance, only appearing when learners deviate significantly from recommended paths.

Does it matter whether the coach takes the form of a person, a cartoon, or some other representation? Research comparing different representations, including cartoon figures, video of a person, or no figure at all, found that the actual representation did not make a great deal of difference to learning (Clark & Mayer, 2011). There is some evidence that whatever figure you decide to use (animated or still—nonhuman or human), incorporating some human embodiment features in the form of eye movement and hand gestures promotes learning.

The voice quality is important. For example, learning was better from an avatar using a native-speaker-friendly voice than one with a machine-generated or foreign-accented voice. We need more research on avatar representations, but you are probably okay with whatever you select as long as the avatar serves a relevant instructional role such as coaching or giving feedback, the voice is natural and friendly, the language is personal, and there is some human embodiment such as eye glances and gestures. You may want to test your graphic approach with your target audience. For example, among different job roles you may find different reactions to a cartoon avatar.

Advisors can be used to offer perspectives on one or more facets of a scenario. In Table 6.2 I list some alternative advisors you might consider for the eight scenario domains. As shown in Figure 6.6, when the learner clicks on the advisors tab in the Bridezilla case, a screen appears with four visuals representing clergy, design, negotiation, and finances. Each of these in turn leads to specialist advisors such as a rabbi, priest, minister, or imam. As illustrated in Figure 6.7, upon selecting a specific

## TABLE 6.2. Potential Advisors for Each Learning Domain

| Domain | Potential Advisors |
| --- | --- |
| Interpersonal | Manager, top performer, expert negotiator, virtual clients, product expert |
| Compliance | Manager, colleague, human resources representative, legal representative, government agency official |
| Diagnosis and Repair | Tech support, journeyman performer, product engineer, quality assurance, diagnostic expert |
| Research, Analysis, Rationale | Critical thinking expert, senior performer, resource expert, manager |
| Tradeoffs | Various perspectives relevant to decisions to be made, such as client feedback, financial, legal, ethical, religious |
| Operational Decisions | Equipment engineer, quality assurance, lead technician, senior operator |
| Design | Expert designer, previous clients, quality assurance, project manager, accountant |
| Team Collaboration | Project manager, senior performer, senior leadership, accountant, communication expert, team members |

resource such as Rabbi Feinberg, questions on the left side of the screen serve as menus to access unique expertise of that advisor.

In an online course for nurses on fetal alcohol syndrome, links led to emails of real advisors, including a public health nurse and a guardian for a child with fetal alcohol syndrome. These advisors had volunteered for the duration of the course to offer their experience. If your organization has established social networks of experts, perhaps their expertise could be leveraged as an instructional resource. Note in Figure 6.7 a link to the Rabbi's email for additional questions.

## OPTION 7: EMBED WORKSHEETS

A worksheet is a template in which learners can select or input intermediate products as they progress through a scenario. Worksheets offer structure by focusing the learner on specific intermediate data or decisions. They can also offer memory support as

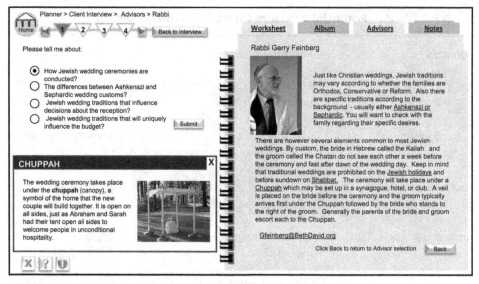

**FIGURE 6.7.** *Selecting a Specific Advisor (See Figure 6.6) Leads to Topic-Specific Information.*

repositories for data as it is accessed. For complex decision-making processes, your organization may already provide various tools to guide the workflow, as well as for memory support and decision making. Use the same tools in your learning environment. Alternatively, you may have to design some tools that may then later extend into the actual workplace as performance support. In Figure 5.3 you can review the worksheet used by the wedding consultant during the client interview.

## OPTION 8: ADJUST FEEDBACK

One of the most powerful instructional strategies for any kind of training is feedback. In fact I devote a full chapter to feedback in scenario-based learning in Chapter 8. Here I mention feedback specifically as a guidance resource. Feedback offered with each decision, as in the customer service branched scenario shown in Figure 6.1, provides more immediate guidance than feedback that is withheld until the learner has progressed through a number of intermediate stages to reach a solution, such as in the automotive troubleshooting scenario.

In Chapter 3 I distinguished between traditional instructional feedback and consequential feedback that I call *intrinsic* feedback. For more guidance, consider using both instructional feedback and intrinsic feedback. Intrinsic feedback will show consequences of actions and decisions but may not provide sufficient rationale to guide learners. See Chapter 8 for more details on the what, when, and how of feedback in scenario-based e-learning designs.

## OPTION 9: MAKE LEARNING COLLABORATIVE

Collaboration during problem solving offers a popular and potentially helpful source of guidance. Research has shown that, when producing a novel product or solving a problem, a collaborative effort yields better results than solo work (Clark & Mayer, 2011). Kirschner, Pass, Kirschner, and Janssen (2011) report that collaboration is most effective when scenarios are challenging. In contrast, learning from easier scenarios was best when tackled by individual learners. Collaboration imposes additional mental load, and if a scenario is already relatively easy, the extra load will not add much instructional value.

Consider using structured argumentation as a proven collaborative technique. In structured argumentation, teams of two are given a position or facet of a problem to research. After a research period, each team presents their position or product to another team working on a different position or facet of the problem. Teams reverse roles, and when all presentations are completed, teams merge and create a combined product that synthesizes all perspectives. Structured argumentation is well applied to tradeoff scenarios in which the goal is not so much a solution per se but rather an understanding of diverse perspectives on the scenario.

Social media offer multiple opportunities for virtual collaboration through breakout rooms, shared media pages, and wikis, among others. A combination of synchronous and asynchronous collaboration might offer the best option. Synchronous team activities such as virtual or face-to-face breakout sessions have proven effective for brainstorming multiple solutions. Asynchronous team activities work well to give everyone time for reflection. Whatever forms of collaboration you decide on, in general you should keep team sizes small enough to promote optimal engagement and consider techniques to motivate equal participation. For more details on collaboration, see Chapter 13 in Clark and Mayer (2011).

## WHAT DO YOU THINK? REVISITED

In my introduction to this chapter, I suggested that you compare Figures 6.1 and 6.2 and respond to the questions below:

1.  Which example is more guided or close-ended?

    ❑   A. The customer service sample

    ❑   B. The automotive troubleshooting sample

2.  In the more guided or close-ended example, what sources of guidance do you see?

    ❑   A. Limited on-screen response options

    ❑   B. On-screen coach

    ❑   C. Complexity of the scenario

3.  Which example is better?

☐ A. Depends on the learners' prior knowledge

☐ B. Depends on intended outcomes of the instruction

☐ C. Depends on the immersive quality of the interface

Here are my thoughts. The branched scenario customer service lesson shown in Figure 6.1 offers more guidance because response options are limited to a single choice among three options and the on-screen coach provides immediate feedback. In contrast, the whole screen virtual shop offers more choices and feedback is not available until after a number of decisions are made. However, even in the automotive shop, some guidance is provided by inactivating some of the objects and by responding with *"don't go there"* advice when some tools are selected. Therefore, while the branched scenario design does impose more guidance, a whole-screen design can also manage the flounder factor by limiting response options.

I selected all of the options for Question 2. The customer service lesson is much less complex due to limited choices on each screen, immediate feedback from the coach, as well as response options that lack nuance. For Question 3, I would select Options A and B. Learners with more prior knowledge and outcomes that focus not only on correct answers but also on problem-solving processes may be better served by interfaces with more choices such as a menu or whole-screen layout.

## COMING NEXT

Now that you have considered the guidance you plan to provide, a closely related design issue relates to instructional resources. The goal of scenario-based e-learning environments is learning. Therefore, instructional resources are usually an essential element of your design. In the next chapter I will review some common options, including tutorials, examples, and reference resources.

## ADDITIONAL RESOURCES

Kirschner, F., Paas, F., Kirschner, P.A., & Janssen, J. (2011). Differential effects of problem-solving demands on individual and collaborative learning outcomes. *Learning and Instruction, 21*, 587–599.
A helpful research-based review of situations in which collaboration is and is not effective.

Mayer, R.E. (2004). Should there be a three-strikes rule against pure discovery learning: The case for guided methods of instruction. *American Psychologist, 59*, 14–19.
A classic review and discussion of the shortfalls of discovery learning.

## SCENARIO-BASED e-LEARNING AND YOU:
## DEFINING GUIDANCE

At this stage, you should have defined the core elements of your scenario and have some ideas about the knowledge and skills needed to resolve it. Answer the questions below to plan your guidance:

1. Your Task(s):

2. Your Learners:

   ☐   Novice

   ☐   Journeymen

   ☐   Experienced

   ☐   Mixed

   ☐   Other:

3. Scenario-Learning Domain: Check all that apply.

- ☐ Interpersonal skills
- ☐ Leadership or compliance
- ☐ Diagnosis and repair
- ☐ Research, analysis, and rationale
- ☐ Tradeoffs
- ☐ Operational
- ☐ Design
- ☐ Team collaboration
- ☐ Other:

4. What approaches to guidance might be the best fit for your audience, learning goals, and technology features:

- ☐ Response options—open versus closed
- ☐ Interface/navigation design
- ☐ Training wheels
- ☐ Scenario complexity from low to high
- ☐ Amount of guidance from high to low
- ☐ Coaches and advisors
- ☐ Worksheets
- ☐ Feedback
- ☐ Collaboration

# CHAPTER

7

# PUTTING THE "L" IN SCENARIO-BASED e-LEARNING

In Chapter 6 I reviewed some design techniques to build in guidance (often referred to as scaffolding) for guided discovery learning environments. The main goal of guidance is to keep the learners on the right track as they work the scenario. One form of guidance I describe separately in this chapter involves instructional resources. There is a fine line between techniques for guidance and instruction. Regarding instructional resources, I emphasize techniques that are explicitly designed to teach knowledge and skills at the right time to help the learner make a decision or take an action. Since the ultimate goal of each scenario is to promote learning of specified knowledge and skills in the context of solving a problem, you need to consider the type of and format for instructional resources. Instructional resources can precede or be embedded in the scenario—or both. Some of the more common instructional strategies include tutorials, instructors, references, examples, and social media knowledge resources.

## WHAT DO YOU THINK?

Which of the following statements do you find true regarding instructional resources in scenario-based e-learning? I'll offer my opinion on each at the end of the chapter.

❑ Tutorials should be sequenced separately from a scenario (before or after) to avoid disrupting engagement in the scenario.

❑ Instructional resources should be available, but only when the learner selects them.

❑ Examples are one of your most powerful instructional strategies.

❑ Instructors will play a different role in scenario-based e-learning than they do in traditional in-person instruction.

## INTEGRATING KNOWLEDGE AND SKILL RESOURCES

As an experienced instructional professional, you are most likely familiar with how to design job-related knowledge and skill training based on your learning objectives and the background of the learners. When you defined your scenario outcomes in Chapter 4, you specified your terminal learning objective. As you consider your scenario outcomes and their associated knowledge and skills listed in Table 2.1, you can also write the enabling or supporting objectives to serve as milestones to the final goal. In Table 7.1, I list some typical enabling knowledge and skills based on the terminal objectives presented in Chapter 4. These objectives need not be displayed to the learner, but will be useful to guide the design and development of the lessons. Having defined your learning goals—both major and supporting—you can consider the when, what, and how of instructional resources to include in your instruction.

Regarding the *when*, you may determine that a standard tutorial (either in an instructor-led or multimedia environment) should be offered *prior to* the scenario-based learning lessons or embedded as a resource to be accessed within the scenario interface—or both. Recent evidence I review in Chapter 10 suggests situations that benefit from tutorials provided before problems as well as tutorials provided after problem solving. Regarding the *what,* you may opt for several instructional resources drawing from the suggestions in this chapter. Regarding the *how*, you may need to decide whether to:

1.  Make instructional resources available on demand, such as in an on-screen book or on a virtual computer screen with embedded menus (pull).

2.  Insert instruction in predetermined junctions in the scenario, for example, in the form of a coaching mini-session (push).

3.  Align instructional resources to individual on-screen objects such as elements of a worksheet or stages in a process, or

4.  Use an adaptive approach that offers tutorials based on tracking of learner actions against an expert path.

In the next paragraphs I will review the most common instructional resources, including tutorials, reference, examples, and instructors.

**TABLE 7.1.** **Some Sample Terminal and Enabling Learning Objectives by Domain**

| Learning Domain | Sample Terminal Objective from Table 4.1 | Sample Enabling Objectives |
|---|---|---|
| Interpersonal<br>  Sales<br>  Customer Service<br>  Management | Given a respondent, learner will select or generate optimal statements to achieve task goals. | Review respondent history and identify features relevant to outcome goal.<br>Explain relevant information tailored to respondent needs or situation (product specs, policies, processes).<br>Anticipate and respond to questions or objections.<br>Offer a solution or follow-up plan. |
| Compliance | Learners will respond to situations by taking actions congruent with organizational policies and procedures. | Identify actions or statements as congruent or in conflict with organizational or legal policy.<br>Locate/identify specific applicable policies or laws.<br>Select action or decision aligned to policy or legal requirements. |
| Diagnosis and Repair | Given symptoms and testing options, learner will apply efficient diagnostic process to select tests, interpret results, and make a repair. | Identify failure symptoms.<br>Define potential hypotheses.<br>Identify which tests are most appropriate for hypotheses.<br>Interpret results from tests.<br>Narrow potential causes.<br>Justify diagnosis with rationale.<br>Perform repair/treatment and monitor results. |
| Research, Analysis, Rationale | Given an assignment and sources of case data, learner will apply efficient research process to select data, interpret results, and make a decision and/or produce a product. | Based on assignment, identify relevant resources.<br>Search, access, and interpret data.<br>Rate data based on relevance to or impact on research goal.<br>Make decision congruent with data.<br>Justify decision with appropriate rationale. |

*(Continued)*

*Table 7.1 (continued)*

| Learning Domain | Sample Terminal Objective from Table 4 .1 | Sample Enabling Objectives |
|---|---|---|
| Tradeoffs | Given a business goal or dilemma, learner will identify and evaluate various perspectives to make and justify a decision. | Identify alternative responses to dilemma. Review perspectives on the issue. Identify pros and cons on decision or action alternatives. Justify decision made or action taken. |
| Operational Decisions | Given equipment interfaces and relevant data, operator will adjust controls to optimize outcomes. | Interpret signals from interface. Gather and interpret additional relevant data. Identify equipment process likely underlying signal. Form hypothesis as to cause of abnormal signals. Prioritize operational goals. Respond to remedy situation. Monitor and repeat process as needed. |
| Design | Given requirements and resource data, learner will construct a product that optimizes resources and meets requirements. | Gather and interpret project constraints. Gather and interpret design criteria. Review previous product solutions. Select or create prototype. Test prototype. Interpret test results. Revise prototype based on test results. |
| Team Collaboration | Given a goal requiring a collaborative synergy among team members of diverse expertise, learner will ensure effective team communication, make decisions, and take action to optimize outcomes. | Assess desired outcomes or team goal. Assess team resources and constraints. Apply communication model to optimize team resources. Prioritize team alternatives. Coordinate team activities based on team input. Monitor and adjust as needed. |

## TUTORIALS

As instructional professionals, I assume you are experienced creating basic tutorials to teach procedures or concepts linked to work-relevant tasks. In fact, you may even have access to some relevant tutorials related to your scenario-based e-learning goals in your organization's training repository. Your main challenge in scenario-based e-learning will be to first locate, create, and segment tutorials that support required knowledge and skills needed to resolve the scenario and then decide how you want to link them to your interface. One approach is to review the different elements in your design plan in terms of their visual representations. For example, you may want to construct tutorials linked to the on-screen objects representing sources of case data to help learners know whether a specific object is relevant to a specific case and how to interpret data from it. If you have designed a worksheet as a support tool, you could provide links to tutorials on each major element of the worksheet. For example, the Bridezilla lesson includes three worksheets. A short procedural tutorial on each worksheet can be accessed by clicking the lower-right tutorial button, as shown in Figure 7.1.

Alternatively, if you have used a menu to represent the major elements of your design or stages in the workflow, you could add specific links for tutorials associated with menu items. Another option is to add on-screen objects to serve specifically as repositories for tutorials, such as books, computer screens, or even a virtual office wall poster with some type of process graphic on it.

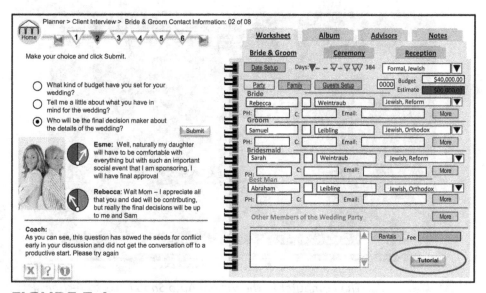

**FIGURE 7.1.** *Clicking on the Tutorial Button (Lower Right) Leads to a Short Demonstration on Completing the Form.*

In a simple implementation, learners can access tutorials on demand. In a more sophisticated approach, tutorials can be assigned or advised based on a tracking of the actions of the learner in the scenario. For example, in the automotive troubleshooting scenario, if one or more inappropriate tests are selected, a brief tutorial on diagnosing the specific type of fault in the scenario could be offered by the tech support telephone line or by an on-screen coach.

## REFERENCE

Consider embedding references into your scenario interface. If you are lucky, there are existing references available. For example, the automotive troubleshooting scenario was able to take advantage of pre-existing online technical manuals on the various systems unique to each automotive make and year. By clicking on the on-screen computer in the auto shop, the corporate intranet reference menu appears, as shown in Figure 7.2. Clicking on the service manual opens it to a list of parts or systems, which in turn lead to specific schematics or descriptions of each element.

If you don't have pre-existing reference resources, it's common practice to develop them as part of any instructional effort. For example, in a compliance scenario, an online book can open to relevant policy statements. In a sales scenario, online references can summarize product features and benefits. If your scenario will focus on

**FIGURE 7.2.**  *The Computer in the Virtual Auto Shop Links to Technical References.*
With permission from Raytheon Professional Services.

a process, consider a poster displayed prominently on the workstation wall illustrating a high-level graphic summary of the stages. Clicking on any stage on the poster zooms into more detailed explanations.

As with any instructional effort, as you review your learning objectives, ask yourself: "What memory support would be useful here?" "What facts or steps would be needed to achieve the goal?" "Are there pre-existing references we could repurpose?" If not, what kinds of references would you want to include and what would be the best way to represent them?

Keep in mind the need for visual contiguity. If the learner has the opportunity to open a reference resource, avoid covering up your interface with the resource or find a way to make that resource information easily accessible when it is closed. For example, a relevant procedure could be printed out or a procedure window minimized. Alternatively, a relevant resource could be copied and pasted into a persistent on-screen area such as a clipboard or file that could drop down as a small window that does not obscure the action field. In the laboratory simulation shown in Figure 7.3, the learner refers to a wall chart that summarizes the correct reagent dilution proportions to achieve a desired concentration. When clicking on the wall chart, a zoom effect magnifies its contents.

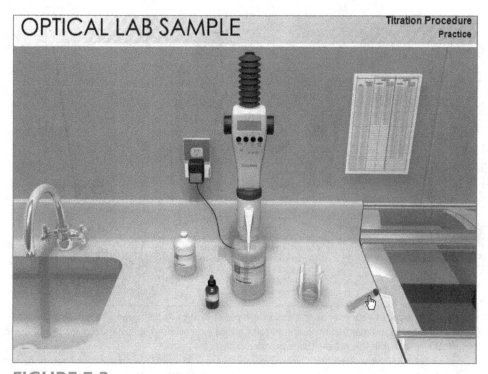

**FIGURE 7.3.** *A Wall Chart Provides a Reference for a Laboratory Procedure.*
With permission from Raytheon Professional Services.

## EXAMPLES

I have found examples to be underutilized in the scenario-based e-lessons I have reviewed. A lack of examples is a missed opportunity for support, as they are a well-proven, powerful learning aid. An example might take the form of a behavioral model in which a video or animated "expert" demonstrates how best to respond to a similar problem, as shown in Figure 6.4. Alternatively, examples may take the form of stories. Experts are famous for swapping war stories of challenging and memorable situations they have faced (Green, Strange, & Brock, 2002). In fact, much expertise is based on a repository of examples indexed in memory in a way that facilitates retrieval when facing a problem with similar features. It's not uncommon to hear experts talking over breaks or at lunch with phrases like: *"Yeah–I remember a case I had like that once. At first I thought. . . ."*

As you plan examples, consider the format, the type, the focus, and how examples might be accessed. Do you need to provide an example illustrating an entire solution process to a problem similar to the one the learner is assigned? This could be accessed by a "show me" button that activates a step-by-step demonstration of how a similar scenario was resolved. Alternatively, you could plan mini-examples linked to

Alicia: Are many of your overweight and obese patients already taking weight-reducing drugs?
Dr. Chi: No, you see many of my patients can't afford expensive weight management drugs so I'm not sure how viable this drug is to my practice.

FIGURE 7.4. *A Cognitive Modeling Example Illustrates Not Only the How But Also the Why.*

specific elements of your scenario. For example, if your lesson incorporates a number of objects, such as various testing equipment that could be used to diagnose a failure, you could link an example to each test individually. Each example would consist of a brief commentary from an expert describing when and why he or she has used that test in the past.

To help build critical thinking skills, consider a specific type of example called a *cognitive modeling* example. In a cognitive modeling example, the expert illustrates what he or she did, but also describes the rationale or mental heuristics. In Figure 7.4 the expert sales representative demonstrates not only her actions but also her thoughts. Multimedia is an excellent tool for making tacit knowledge explicit during a demonstration of expert performance.

You might consider building a repository that offers examples indexed to the actions, decisions, or rationale of your scenarios. If your organization has a repository of examples as part of its knowledge base, exploit it by cross-indexing related examples into your course. For example, the Bridezilla course uses a virtual album as a repository of examples. Each wedding example in the album includes photographs, client reviews, and a budget summary.

Research on examples has shown that, for building critical thinking skills in a domain, offering several examples in which the specifics vary somewhat but the underlying principles remain the same is a more effective approach than providing only a single example or two examples with the same surface features. As you collect multiple examples, consider a repository that indexes examples to the scenario categories or elements.

### Make Examples Engaging

One drawback to examples is that learners fail to process the example deeply or may even bypass it completely. Overcome this potential stumbling block by adding questions to your examples—questions that force the learner to carefully review and process the example. For example, in Figure 6.4, the learner views an expert modeling the optimal response to a client's objection. The multiple-choice question prompts the learner to carefully study the example. Research has shown that adding questions to examples yields better learning than when the same examples are included without questions.

## INSTRUCTORS

Will your scenario-based e-learning be facilitated by an instructor—either online or in a face-to-face learning environment? If so, consider what roles that instructor might serve. In some cases, the instructor might actually play a role in the scenario. For example, he could play the role of the client, the project manager, or even inanimate objects such as equipment. In a troubleshooting class, teams review the symptoms and suggest what test they would try first. The instructor, assuming the role of the equipment, displays the results of a given test and asks the learners to interpret the results and decide whether that test was appropriate and what they learned from it. Next moving into a more traditional role, the instructor could suggest alternative actions he would take commenting on the team's choices.

Alternatively, the instructor may focus more on the problem-solving process than on the outcomes. In this role, the instructor models and monitors the critical thinking process stages. For example, if individuals or teams are problem solving, the instructor could ask questions such as "What are you doing now?" "What other alternatives did you consider?" "How will you know whether your current activity is moving you forward in solving the problem?"

### Give Your Learners an Instructional Role

In my e-learning design course, participants tackle an assignment in several rounds. They initially work in teams for about an hour to produce a prototype product—a storyboard. Next, the instructor provides background knowledge for all participants, who are then individually assigned to a specialized content area to research. For example, some research best practices relevant to use of visuals, to use of audio and text to describe visuals, or to navigational facilities. Each participant then gives a mini-tutorial to others on his or her area of expertise. After the teach-back sessions, teams revisit their projects to evaluate what they created initially and to revise it based on new knowledge.

In sum, as you consider your desired outcomes, define the role of the instructor. Should she serve as an expert practitioner providing domain-specific instruction to correct misconceptions or advance thinking? Should she play the role of a critical thinker ensuring a logical train of thought and domain-specific problem-solving approaches? Should she assume the role of the object of the scenario, such as the equipment or patient, or test response to a selected action? Should she emphasize thinking process behaviors guiding students to identify, discuss, and refine their own learning with minimal instructional input? Many of these roles are quite different from traditional didactic activities and instructors habituated to such a traditional role will likely need support in transitioning to new activities.

## WHAT DO YOU THINK? REVISITED

Which of the following statements do you find true regarding instructional resources in scenario-based e-learning? Here are my thoughts:

❑   Tutorials should be sequenced separately from a scenario (before or after) to avoid disrupting engagement in the scenario.

We have research showing benefits of both options with different instructional interfaces and learners. My guess is that tutorials prior to the scenario might be most useful for a more novice audience or an unfamiliar learning environment such as a simulation. In contrast, tutorials either embedded or following problem-solution attempts might best serve a mixed or advanced audience. In Chapter 10 I will summarize research supporting both alternatives.

❑   Instructional resources should be available but only when the learner selects them.

Again, I have not seen research on this specific issue. We do know that resources that are optional, such as links, are often bypassed. Additionally, many learners do not make accurate self-assessments of their instructional needs. Making resources optional risks their underutilization. On the other hand, many learners prefer to make their own choices—especially in a scenario-based e-learning environment. At this point in time, I'm neutral on this question.

❑   Examples are one of your most powerful instructional strategies.

In my experience, examples are one of the most under-utilized instructional methods in the trainer's toolkit. We have a wealth of research on the kinds of examples that are most effective and on how to make those examples engaging. The main exception to the use of examples is for experienced learners. Research has shown that more advanced learners can experience a deterioration of learning because examples provided may conflict with their own established mental models (Kalyuga, Rikers, & Paas, 2012).

❑   Instructors will play a different role in scenario-based e-learning than they do in traditional in-person instruction.

I believe this is generally a true statement. In a traditional role, the instructor often serves the role of a content expert by giving explanations, demonstrating tasks, assigning exercises, and giving feedback. In a scenario-based e-learning setting, the instructor may play one of several different roles discussed in this chapter.

## COMING NEXT

Now that you have addressed techniques to minimize the flounder factor and to support learning, it's time to consider two final essential elements: feedback and reflection. As the learner responds to the scenario, she needs at some point to know whether she has made appropriate selections. Further, she needs to step back, review her thoughts and actions, and consider what worked well and what needs improvement. No scenario-based e-learning lesson can fully achieve its goals without these two critical elements.

## ADDITIONAL RESOURCES

Renkl, A. (2011). Instruction based on examples. In R.E. Mayer & P.A. Alexander (Eds.), *Handbook of research on learning and instruction.* New York: Routledge.
A very comprehensive and somewhat technical review of research on examples in learning environments.

Schank, R.C., & German, T.R. (2002). The pervasive role of stories in knowledge and action. In M.C. Green, J.J. Strange, & T.C. Brock (Eds.), *Narrative impact: Social and cognitive foundations.* Mahwah, NJ: Lawrence Erlbaum Associates.
This book reviews the key roles that stories play in shaping our memories, knowledge, and beliefs.

## SCENARIO-BASED e-LEARNING AND YOU:
## DEFINING INSTRUCTIONAL RESOURCES

At this stage, you should have defined the core elements of your scenario, including different forms of guidance you will provide. Keeping in mind your outcome goals and supporting learning objectives along with their associated knowledge and skills, take some time now to consider what instructional resources you will include and how they will be represented in your learning environment.

1. Your Scenario-Learning Domain (Check all that apply.)

   ☐   Interpersonal skills

   ☐   Compliance

   ☐   Diagnosis and repair

   ☐   Research, analysis, and rationale

   ☐   Tradeoffs

   ☐   Operational decisions

   ☐   Design

   ☐   Team collaboration

   ☐   Other:

2. What are the main knowledge and skill topics (supporting learning objectives) needed to accomplish the final task? What would be the best instructional resource for each of these topics? As you check off an alternative, describe how you might incorporate it into your program.

**Terminal Learning Objective (copy or refine from Chapter 4)**

| Enabling Objective | Instructional Alternatives | How to Implement/Represent |
|---|---|---|
| EO 1 | Tutorials | Reference |
| | | Pre-existing |
| | | To be developed |
| | | Examples |
| | Expert solution demonstrations | Questions in demonstrations to promote engagement |
| | | Cognitive modeling examples to illustrate tacit knowledge |
| | | Example repositories linked to organizational knowledge base |
| | Instructors | Traditional role |
| | | Socratic role |
| | | Scenario role |
| EO 2 | Tutorials | Reference |
| | | Pre-existing |
| | | To be developed |
| | Examples | Expert solution demonstrations |
| | | Questions in demonstrations to promote engagement |
| | | Cognitive modeling examples to illustrate tacit knowledge |
| | | Example repositories linked to organizational knowledge base |
| | Instructors | Traditional role |
| | | Socratic role |
| | | Scenario role |

# CHAPTER

8

# DESIGNING FEEDBACK AND REFLECTION

Imagine you are taking a lesson on diagnosing and treating a sick cat. You have access to the owner's description of symptoms, your own examination results, as well as data from various tests you ordered. You begin by reviewing the data, then ordering and interpreting test data, and, finally, selecting a treatment plan. However, you receive no response to your selections. You don't know whether the cat died or improved. You don't know whether you ordered the right tests or whether you interpreted them correctly. In fact, you don't know much more at the end of the episode than you did at the start. Imagine, in contrast, that after you make a treatment decision, the clock fast forwards, and you see a healthy cat and happy owner twenty-four hours later. You can be satisfied that your decisions were appropriate, but you still might wonder why. You see the consequences of your actions, but perhaps have not learned the reasons for your success—or a more efficient, less expensive way to solve the problem. Detailed feedback on your solution, your problem-solving process, and your rationale makes all the difference between an effective and an ineffective learning experience.

## THE POWER OF FEEDBACK

Among experimental research studies comparing the efficacy of various instructional methods, feedback gets a high score. Based on a review of twelve meta-analyses, Hattie and Gan (2011) found the average effect size for feedback was .79, which is twice the average effect size of other instructional methods. An effect size of .79 means that, given feedback, learners will average about eight-tenths of a standard deviation higher scores on an assessment than learners not given feedback.

The bad news is the high variation of effects noted among all of the experiments. In some experiments feedback diminished learning. According to Kluger and DeNisi (1996), one-third of all feedback in the studies they reviewed actually *depressed* learning! From the research we have learned that feedback has huge potential to improve learning, but not all feedback is effective. In this chapter I will look at the unique forms of feedback you can design into scenario-based e-learning and offer guidelines you can adapt to your instructional context.

## LEARNING FROM MISTAKES

Are mistakes good or bad for learning? Following a disastrous collapse in the final round of the 2011 Master's golf tournament, Rory Mcillroy commented: "It was a very disappointing day, obviously, but hopefully I'll learn from it and come back a little stronger. I don't think I can put it down to anything else than part of the learning curve" (downloaded from *The Telegraph*, June 22, 2011). Anyone who watched his record-breaking win just two months later at the U.S. Open witnessed first-hand the potential of mistakes to shape and improve performance.

Directive courses, reflecting their behaviorist roots, are designed to minimize errors. If a mistake is made, the learner receives immediate corrective feedback. For example, if an incorrect formula is entered in an Excel lesson, instructional feedback immediately displays a message such as: "Remember to use the '*' operator when you need to multiply." Behaviorist psychology applies the premise that incorrect responses, if not immediately corrected, can embed the wrong knowledge and skills in memory. Mistakes are to be avoided and, when they occur, are to be immediately remedied. In contrast, scenario-based learning makes different assumptions—mainly that mistakes can provide a useful learning experience. In fact, sometimes the most memorable lessons learned are those born from errors.

You can probably identify some lessons learned from your own mistakes—big or small. Recently, during my Italian lesson I wanted to say that I was disgusted with a particular situation. Instead, I said that I was disgusting. Fortunately, the instructor stopped me immediately and explained the differences—*disgustoso* meaning disgusting and *disgustata* meaning disgusted. This was such a memorable mistake that I am unlikely to ever make it again—thanks to immediate feedback from the instructor.

## INSTRUCTIONAL VS. INTRINSIC FEEDBACK

In scenario-based e-learning training design you have multiple feedback opportunities. You can include both *instructional* and *intrinsic* (consequential) feedback. With intrinsic feedback, the learning environment responds to decisions and action choices in ways that mirror the real world. For example, if a learner responds rudely to a customer, he will see and hear an unhappy customer response. Intrinsic feedback gives the learner an opportunity to try, fail, and experience the results of errors in a safe environment.

In this chapter I will provide guidelines for feedback targeted at three major levels: scenario solutions, problem-solving processes, and learning needs. Additionally, to ensure that learners process the feedback provided, you can require learners to reflect on the feedback and draw conclusions from it. In this chapter I will discuss several important feedback parameters for you to consider in your design, including:

- *Specificity:* general to focused

- *Type:* instructional and intrinsic

- *Frequency:* immediate or delayed and,

- *Focus:* solution, process, or learning needs

## WHAT DO YOU THINK?

Read the feedback provided in each scenario and indicate whether it is (a) specific or general, (b) instructional, intrinsic, or both, (c) immediate or delayed, and (d) focused on solutions, process, or learning needs. My answers appear at the end of this chapter. If you would rather do the exercise after reading the chapter, move on to the next section.

1. In a safety scenario, when the wrong ladder is selected, the worker is injured. The on-screen safety-specialist coach explains the features of the correct ladder for the job and asks the learner to input the location of safety ladders in the warehouse.

| Specificity | Type | Frequency | Level |
|---|---|---|---|
| ❏ Specific | ❏ Instructional | ❏ Immediate | ❏ Solution |
| ❏ General | ❏ Intrinsic | ❏ Delayed | ❏ Process |
| ❏ Can't tell | ❏ Can't tell | ❏ Can't tell | ❏ Learning |
| | | | ❏ Can't tell |

2. In an underwriter scenario, when a recommendation to fund a loan is lacking sufficient rationale, the loan committee refuses to review the deal. The learner is directed to gather more data on applicant credit and sales projections.

| Specificity | Type | Frequency | Level |
|---|---|---|---|
| ❏ Specific | ❏ Instructional | ❏ Immediate | ❏ Solution |
| ❏ General | ❏ Intrinsic | ❏ Delayed | ❏ Process |
| ❏ Can't tell | ❏ Can't tell | ❏ Can't tell | ❏ Learning |
| | | | ❏ Can't tell |

3.  In a branched scenario on selling skills, after several responses to the customer, an expert sales representative models how she would have responded. The learner is asked to compare his responses to the model and to select a specific tutorial to address gaps in his skills.

| Specificity | Type | Frequency | Level |
|---|---|---|---|
| ❏ Specific | ❏ Instructional | ❏ Immediate | ❏ Solution |
| ❏ General | ❏ Intrinsic | ❏ Delayed | ❏ Process |
| ❏ Can't tell | ❏ Can't tell | ❏ Can't tell | ❏ Learning |
| | | | ❏ Can't tell |

## FEEDBACK IN A NUTSHELL

Based on evidence and the design opportunities inherent in scenario-based e-learning, I will describe some guidelines for feedback which are summarized in Table 8.1.

## TABLE 8.1.  A Summary of Feedback Features

| Feedback Feature | Alternatives | Comments |
|---|---|---|
| Specificity | Specific or General<br>A. Conduct the sss test (specific)<br>B. You are not using the best test for this situation (general) | Specific feedback is more helpful and also more expensive to produce. |
| Type | Intrinsic and Instructional<br>A. Customer frowns (intrinsic)<br>B. You should have asked an open-ended question (instructional) | Intrinsic feedback requires a realistic environmental response to learner actions. Instructional feedback can explain the reasons for the outcomes and suggest alternative actions to consider. |
| Frequency | Frequent or Delayed<br>Feedback could be given with each learner response, at the end of a segment, or at the end of the lesson. | Frequent feedback imposes more guidance; delayed feedback might be better for process-focused scenarios. Consider your learning goals and background knowledge of your learners |
| Focus | Level 1—correctness of solution<br>Level 2—solution process<br>Level 3—learning or problem-solving gaps; recommendations for additional learning resources | Level 1: Useful, especially for highly structured problems with right or wrong answers<br>Level 2: Useful when the learning goal focuses on the problem-solving process<br>Level 3: Useful if the program can make valid inferences about knowledge gaps as the basis for additional training |

### 1. Be Specific

In general, evidence shows that more specific feedback leads to better learning than generalized feedback. For example: "You need to rule out electrical malfunctions in the drive shaft" is more helpful than "It looks as if you are not following the correct solution path." Feedback that not only tells learners whether they are right or wrong but also gives a brief explanation has proven to lead to more learning than feedback that simply states "right" or "wrong." Of course, more specific feedback takes more time to construct, so you will need to consider the cost-benefit tradeoffs. In particular, you may decide to offer specific feedback linked to some actions and more generalized feedback in other places where specific feedback would not be cost-beneficial.

### 2. Provide Intrinsic and Instructional Feedback

As an experienced instructor, you are familiar with instructional feedback. In instructional feedback, commonly known as corrective feedback, you give information about the accuracy of a solution, along with an explanation. One of the unique opportunities of scenario-based learning lies in intrinsic or consequential feedback. In intrinsic feedback, the learner takes an action or makes a decision and experiences the results of that action. For example, in the customer-service branched scenario example in Figure 6.1, with each response the learner makes to the customer, she can hear and see the customer's reply. In addition, she will hear instructional feedback from the virtual coach in the bottom left portion of the screen.

Multimedia can be designed to incorporate "invisible" forms of intrinsic feedback. For example, we used an attitude meter to show how the mother and bride-to-be are responding to each statement made by the wedding planner. Other examples I've seen include a money bar chart or scale illustrating income and outflow over time as decisions are made, a germ meter reflecting levels of contamination based on actions taken, and a virtual clock used to accelerate the passage of time.

In general, I recommend that you incorporate both intrinsic and instructional feedback into your lessons.

### 3. Adjust Feedback Frequency Based on Guidance Needs and Learning Goals

In a branched scenario, similar to the lesson shown in Figure 6.1, feedback—both instructional and intrinsic—appears with every learner selection. Immediate feedback on each action provides a high level of guidance and is most appropriate for novice learners. In contrast, if the goal of your scenario is to teach a troubleshooting or problem-solving process, immediate feedback on each action might not give the learner sufficient latitude to learn from inefficient or ineffective paths. For example, in the automotive troubleshooting course, feedback is delayed until the learner selects a failure. As a general guideline, I recommend you provide more frequent feedback in initial scenarios intended for novice learners and delay feedback in more advanced lessons.

## 4. Focus the Feedback Based on Your Goals

Kluger and DeNisi (1996) reported that a large proportion of instructional feedback did not improve learning—and in some cases even depressed learning. Evidence shows that feedback that focuses the learners' attention to themselves hinders learning. For example, feedback that incorporates praise ("Great work!") or gives comparative scores ("You're in the top 10 percent!") tends to draw attention to the ego and away from the learning task. Instead, you should focus feedback onto the task in general and the gap between the outcome criteria and the learner's achievement in particular.

Based on an analysis by Hattie and Gan (2011), I recommend three levels of feedback: (1) solution focused, (2) task-process focused, and (3) learning focused. Which combination of these you provide will depend on your instructional goals. If the goal is relatively bounded, for example, a correct application of corporate compliance policies, instructional feedback may simply state whether the learner's response is correct or incorrect and give a reason based on the policies. If the learning goal involves a problem solving process that requires research, analysis, and decisions, both solution and task-process focused feedback will be helpful. For example, in Figure 8.1 the service technician can compare her solution process with an ideal solution shown on the left. Finally, you may also want to provide learning feedback that directs the learner's attention to his or her personal instructional needs. For example, if the learner

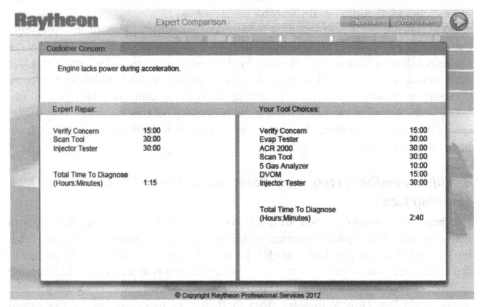

FIGURE 8.1. *A Summary of the Learner's Actions (on the Right) Is Displayed Next to an Expert Solution Process (on Left).*
With permission from Raytheon Professional Services.

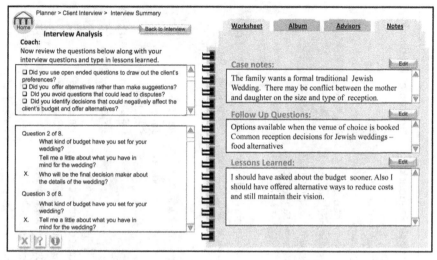

**FIGURE 8.2.** *Response Windows (on the Right Side of the Screen) Encourage Learners to Reflect on Feedback.*

is floundering in selecting a logical progression of research or testing options, the program could offer a tutorial addressing specific knowledge gaps.

### Embed Reflection Opportunities for Learners

As you design your program, keep in mind not only the feedback you offer, but whether or how that feedback is received by the learner. Often learners give feedback only a cursory review. They might look at the overall outcomes of their solution responses but not really consider what they have learned and how they might respond more effectively next time. I recommend that you find ways to encourage reflection on feedback. In a self-study environment, you might provide an end-of-lesson window that asks learners to input how they would approach a similar situation differently. For example, in Figure 8.2 at the end of the wedding planning interview, learners can review their questions and use the checklist on the left side of the screen to evaluate themselves. Input boxes on the right offer a place for the learners to document follow-up questions and lessons learned. Alternatively, learners can review their outcomes and construct an action plan focusing on future developmental efforts.

## FEEDBACK AND REFLECTION IN LEARNING DOMAINS

I've given some brief and general guidelines on feedback, and those may be enough for your needs. In the next section, I'll consider how these guidelines might be applied to several of the learning domains we've discussed throughout the book. I summarize some ideas in Table 8.2 and will elaborate on each, along with some examples.

**TABLE 8.2.** Some Feedback Options by Scenario Domain

| Learning Domain | Focus on Learning | Instructional Feedback | Intrinsic Feedback | "Invisible" Feedback |
|---|---|---|---|---|
| Interpersonal | Questions asked<br>Responses made | Comments on productive questions, interpretation of responses, application of prior knowledge | Respondent body language<br>Respondent questions<br>Respondent statements<br>Scenario outcome (sale, customer satisfaction, response of target) | Attitude meter for respondent<br>Fast-forward clock or calendar to see long-term results |
| Compliance | Responses made to accurately apply policies and procedures | Comments on how choices reflect policies, legal directives | Consequences of policy violation or compliance | Hidden or delayed costs of violations, such as fines, financial impact |
| Diagnosis and Repair | Tests ordered<br>Test interpretation<br>Treatment or repair decisions | Comments on appropriateness and sequence of tests, interpretation of tests and treatments<br>Effectiveness of treatments | How the equipment or patient responds to repair actions | Test costs<br>Time costs<br>Client satisfaction<br>Impact of treatment on system function |
| Research and Analysis | Identification of requirements<br>Identification of appropriate data sources<br>Access of appropriate data<br>Interpretation of data<br>Final product | Comments on identifying and searching appropriate data sources, evaluating data credibility, and interpreting it in light of requirements | Consequences of failing to identify and abstract appropriate resources<br>Client reactions | Time costs<br>Dollar costs<br>Credibility meter<br>Fast forward to future states |

| Learning Domain | Focus on Learning | Instructional Feedback | Intrinsic Feedback | "Invisible" Feedback |
|---|---|---|---|---|
| Tradeoffs | Mixed consequences of choices made; facts, concepts, processes associated with the domain | Comments on alternatives | Outcomes of decisions made | Fast-forward calendar or clock to see future consequences |
| Operational Decisions, Actions | Interpretation of equipment indicators<br>Understanding of equipment dynamics<br>Process followed<br>Actions taken | Comments on interpretation of indicators;<br>Comments on decision path<br>Guidelines for actions | Consequences to operational status based on analysis path and decisions made | Time<br>Equipment status<br>Cost meter<br>Safety meter |
| Design | Specifications met<br>Constraints optimized | Comments based on rubric | Consequences of the design in terms of production, client satisfaction, sales, etc. | Time costs<br>Materials costs<br>Originality meter<br>Client satisfaction |
| Team Collaboration | Actions in accordance with roles and goals<br>Activity coordination<br>Planning<br>Prioritization of decisions and actions | Comments based on replay or review of scenario with rubric | Time<br>Efficiency<br>Consequences on team goal | Team satisfaction scale<br>Team utilization scale |

At this point you may want to use the following section of the chapter as a reference by reviewing specifically the learning domains most relevant to your context.

### Interpersonal Skills

As we saw in Figure 6.1, you can make interpersonal skill training highly guided by offering a combination of intrinsic and instructional feedback with each response. In contrast, you may opt for a less guided experience in which the learner will make several statements or responses before receiving feedback. Intrinsic feedback can be represented with respondents' body language, replies, or an attitude meter. If instructional feedback is delayed for several learner responses, the attitude meter can offer intermediate intrinsic feedback, giving the learner clues about the general effectiveness of her choices. In the most open interpersonal skills design, learners respond in a role play—often with another class participant or the instructor playing the role of the client. In this situation, the interactions can be recorded and replayed, with feedback given by peers, the instructor, and/or actual clients (compensated for their participation). Feedback to very open responses should be focused with a checklist to provide structure. In Figure 8.3 you can review a checklist for a needs assessment interview. When constructing checklists, write observable behaviors based on an analysis of top performers. Reviewing samples and giving feedback promotes not only learning of the individual performer but also of those giving the critiques.

### Compliance

In designing scenario-based e-learning for compliance purposes, you can decide how much guidance is appropriate for the policies to be reviewed as well as for the learners. You may decide to stick with relatively clear-cut applications of organization policies

---

**Needs Assessment Interview Behaviors**

- ❑ Greets client and conveys interest in the situation
- ❑ Asks an open-ended question about the situation
- ❑ Asks probing questions to elicit elaboration on the situation
- ❑ Summarizes client initial statements
- ❑ Asks client about desired outcomes and their indicators
- ❑ Identifies client's perceptions of potential causes and solutions
- ❑ Identifies constraints
- ❑ Suggests multiple performance factors that may be involved
- ❑ Provides a brief specific example of non-training solutions
- ❑ Identifies data sources
- ❑ Identifies client preference for report

FIGURE 8.3.  *A Feedback Checklist for a Needs Assessment Interview Role Play.*

and procedures. A branched scenario design includes a situation (described in text or illustrated with still or animated graphics), three or four response options, and instructional feedback for each. In a more complex version, you may provide sources of case background information, such as an employee file, an employee interview, or a worksheet. Instructional feedback may suffice. However, you may also want to add intrinsic feedback such as a fast-forward clock and an animation illustrating the adverse consequences of policy violations.

### Diagnosis and Repair—Research and Analysis

I'm combining these domains since the critical thinking skills in both typically involve reviewing and assessing the initial state or request, identifying supporting data needed, interpreting that data, and making a decision based on the interpretation. We discussed guidance options in Chapter 6 and, based on those decisions, you can adjust your feedback accordingly. At some point in the learning progression, you will need to give learners freedom to identify and interpret different sources of case data. In these situations you may want to provide feedback only after the learner makes a repair or treatment decision. It will be important to give solution feedback (instructive and intrinsic), as shown in Figure 8.4, as well as process feedback, as shown in Figure 8.1. To ensure maximum value from that feedback, add a structured reflection interaction as well. In general, for these domains I recommend feedback that is specific, intrinsic, and instructional, and somewhat delayed with a focus on solution, process, and learning needs.

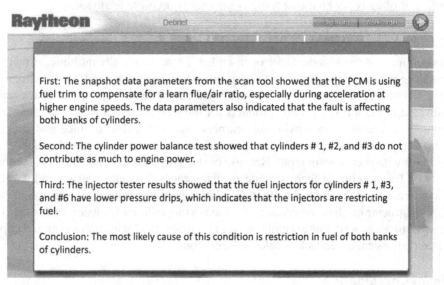

**FIGURE 8.4.** *Instructional Feedback for the Automotive Repair Scenario.*
With permission from Raytheon Professional Services.

## Tradeoffs

In tradeoff scenarios, there is often no single correct answer. Intrinsic feedback is used to show a realistic potential outcome from any decision made. Each choice will have an outcome with a combination of desirable and undesirable features. For example, you may have improved sales, but the cost of your solution outweighs financial gains. Or you may have made the bride happy but upset the bride's mother, who is paying for the wedding. Additional learning can be promoted by instructional feedback that comments on the decisions made. For example, next to the spreadsheet showing improved sales but increased costs, the coach may comment on ROI, discussing factors to consider when taking actions to improve sales. In tradeoff scenarios, the goal is to review different perspectives on a problem and the advantages and disadvantages of each. The feedback is typically not corrective and may not be overly concerned with process. After the learner completes a segment of the scenario, you may ask some reflection questions such as those shown in Figure 8.2, followed by an option to reconsider the decision or rerun the scenario.

## Operational Decisions

In most operational scenarios, intrinsic feedback plays a major role. As the learner takes an action, the environment responds as it would in the actual equipment. Based on the new environmental state, the learner makes further adjustments. Consider the opportunity to augment visible intrinsic feedback with some invisible indicators as well. For example, in a power plant, changing the control settings will be reflected on equipment gauges, but you could also add an internal view of the equipment or an indicator of costs per hour as a source of normally invisible feedback.

## Design

By definition, design products are open-ended. There are usually multiple correct outcomes in the form of products or solutions that meet requestor needs and environmental constraints. In a self-study environment without instructor support, feedback can be provided in the form of sample products for the learners to compare with their solutions. The feedback can provide the learners with a checklist to guide and structure their comparison. Naturally, this type of review can also make a useful collaborative exercise with peer or team input. Because of the open nature of the outcome, feedback may be less specific. If there are intermediate stages in product design and development, feedback can be attached to each, allowing adjustments along the design path. If an instructor or client representative is available, tailored feedback can come from these sources as well. For example, at one pharmaceutical sales training site, compensated doctors gave feedback to sales presentations.

## Team Coordination

If your focus in a team coordination lesson is on communication and coordination actions an individual might make in a team setting, you can provide feedback on those individual decisions similar to previous domains we have discussed. However, if your environment allows for multiple simultaneous decisions among team members, you may want to keep a record of the various decisions made and replay or review them as a extended debriefing with a discussion of lessons learned. For example, in a military simulation, the exercise is video recorded and replayed with a discussion debrief. As mentioned previously, for more open-ended environments use a checklist of optimal behaviors to focus feedback.

## WHAT DO YOU THINK? REVISITED

Take a minute to review the answers you entered at the start of the chapter. Keep in mind that your assumptions might be different from mine and we can both be correct in our analysis.

1.  In a safety scenario, when the wrong ladder is selected, the worker is injured. The on-screen safety-specialist coach explains the features of the correct ladder for the job and asks the learner to input the location of safety ladders in the warehouse.

| Specificity | Type | Frequency | Level |
|---|---|---|---|
| ✓ Specific | ✓ Instructional | ✓ Immediate | ✓ Solution |
| ❑ General | ✓ Intrinsic | ❑ Delayed | ❑ Process |
| | | | ✓ Learning |

In this compliance scenario focusing on safe working practices, the feedback to an incorrect answer is specific, indicating the correct ladder, and immediate. The injury is an example of intrinsic feedback coupled with instructional feedback from the coach. The feedback focuses primarily on the solution and also prompts learning needs by asking the learner to identify the correct equipment in his setting.

2.  In an underwriter scenario, when a recommendation to fund a loan is made without sufficient rationale, the loan committee refuses to review the deal. The learner is directed to gather more data on applicant credit and sales projections.

| Specificity | Type | Frequency | Level |
|---|---|---|---|
| ✓ Specific | ✓ Instructional | ❑ Immediate | ✓ Solution |
| ❑ General | ✓ Intrinsic | ✓ Delayed | ✓ Process |
| | | | ❑ Learning |

The intrinsic feedback arises from the loan committee's refusal to review the deal but is supplemented by specific instructional feedback regarding the types of data the learner should review. Because feedback is only given after the learner has submitted a recommendation, it is delayed. The feedback comments on the solution, but even more on the process by which the solution was derived.

3.  In a branched scenario on selling skills, after several responses to the customer, an expert sales representative models how she would have responded. The learner is asked to compare his responses to the model and to select a specific tutorial to address gaps in his skills.

| Specificity | Type | Frequency | Level |
|---|---|---|---|
| ☐ Specific | ✓ Instructional | ☐ Immediate | ☐ Solution |
| ✓ General | ☐ Intrinsic | ✓ Delayed | ✓ Process |
| | | | ✓ Learning |

The feedback does not appear to be directed at the learner's specific behaviors but rather provides a model of effective behaviors. Therefore, I classify this feedback as general. It does not seem to include the customer's response as a source of intrinsic feedback but rather focuses on instructional feedback that is delayed until the end of the exchange. The feedback focuses on the communication process and the instructional needs of the learner.

The feedback descriptions I provided in the previous exercise were brief, so if you made different decisions regarding the features of the feedback, don't worry. In your own domain you will have a clearer and more comprehensive idea of the scenario outcomes and the types of feedback to provide.

## COMING NEXT

This chapter completes my discussion of the core elements of a design model for scenario-based learning lessons. As you have seen, quite a few resources can go into creation of lessons using a guided discovery approach. Before making such a commitment, you may wonder whether your efforts will pay off. The next two chapters will address evaluation techniques and outcomes from guided scenario learning designs. In Chapter 9, I review strategies you can use for your own evaluation—with an emphasis on evaluating learning. In Chapter 10 I summarize experimental research that has focused on guided discovery instructional environments.

## ADDITIONAL RESOURCES

Hattie, J. (2009). *Visible learning*. New York: Routledge. See Chapter 9: The contributions from teaching approaches, part 1.
    An interesting book that synthesizes volumes of research on instructional issues and provides guidance for instructional professionals. If you like data, this book is for you.

Hattie, J., & Gan, M. (2011). Instruction based on feedback. In R.E. Mayer & P.A. Alexander (Eds.), *Handbook of research on learning and instruction*. New York: Routledge.
    A recent evidence-based review of feedback effects. I found the second half of the chapter most relevant from a practitioner perspective.

Shute, V.J. (2008). Focus on formative feedback. *Review of Educational Research, 78*(1), 153–189.
    A comprehensive and well-written review of research and application of feedback in instruction.

# SCENARIO-BASED e-LEARNING AND YOU:
## DEFINING FEEDBACK

As you near the end of your scenario-based learning design process, you can consider how and when you will provide feedback and opportunities for reflection.

**Your Terminal and Enabling Objectives**

**Your Scenario-Learning Domain**
Check all that apply.

- ☐ Interpersonal skills
- ☐ Compliance
- ☐ Diagnosis and repair
- ☐ Research, analysis, and rationale
- ☐ Tradeoffs
- ☐ Design
- ☐ Team Coordination
- ☐ Other:

**Feedback Features Planner**

| Specificity | Type | Frequency | Level |
|---|---|---|---|
| ❑ Specific<br>❑ General | ❑ Instructional<br>❑ Intrinsic | ❑ Immediate<br>❑ Delayed | ❑ Solution<br>❑ Process<br>❑ Learning |

Describe "invisible" sources of feedback you might incorporate:

Will you need a checklist (rubric) to focus feedback?

How will you encourage reflection:

☐ Ask learners to submit an action plan to their manager.

☐ Insert boxes for learners to enter lessons learned.

☐ Ask learners to compare how their solution differs from an expert solution.

☐ Ask learners to replay the scenario applying lessons learned.

☐ Other:

General comments on your feedback and reflection design:

# CHAPTER

## 9

# EVALUATION OF SCENARIO-BASED e-LEARNING

Outcomes from scenario-based e-learning can be dramatic. For example, Will Interactive designed and developed a suicide prevention scenario-based e-learning course for the U.S. Army called *Beyond the Front*. The learner can assume the role of a soldier facing personal problems while deployed and/or the role of an officer overseeing soldiers exhibiting symptoms of depression. For example, in Figure 9.1, we see the negative emotional effects of a soldier discovering that his girlfriend is pregnant (not his baby!). *Beyond the Front* was required training for all active duty Army personnel. The following year Army suicide rates dropped 58 percent! While your training may not have life-or-death consequences, the outcomes can be just as profound. But without evaluation you will never know what effects your program has.

When launching a new approach to learning—especially one that might be more expensive than previous courseware—the stakeholders usually want to know whether it's working. That seemingly simple question can easily balloon into multiple evaluation questions. In fact, there may be more questions than you have the resources to answer. Some of the questions may be impractical or even impossible to answer in your context. There may be other questions that, once answered, won't lead to any actions or decisions. Many evaluation questions will require some data gathering *before the new training is deployed*. For all these reasons, it's a good idea to define and focus the evaluation questions sooner rather than later.

**FIGURE 9.1.** *A Screen from* Beyond the Front, *Suicide Prevention Scenario-Based e-Learning.*
With permission from Will Interactive.

As evaluation questions are raised, ask yourself and your clients: "What will we do with this information?" For example, if we find that scenario-based e-learning is a more expensive approach, but is popular with learners, will we scrap the program for less-costly approaches or invest in a more popular approach? Where you receive an actionable response to that question, and the context and resources lend themselves to an evaluation project, put together an evaluation plan. When there is no real answer and/or the evaluation would consume too many resources or is unrealistic in your context, reframe or drop the question.

Early on, also consider whether you or your stakeholders want to compare the effects of scenario-based e-learning with a different (traditional or older) approach or whether you want to focus only on the effects of scenario-based e-learning. For example, if you have developed a new-product course in a traditional format, you might want to know whether using a scenario-based e-learning approach for similar learning objectives and content will cost more to design and develop, take learners longer to complete, and lead to higher student ratings, better learning, or better sales. Alternatively, your focus may not be a comparison with other training designs, but rather an evaluation of scenario-based e-learning on its own. Typical evaluation questions fall into any of five major categories: motivation, learning effectiveness, learning efficiency, transfer of learning, and return on investment. In Table 9.1 I summarize these categories, along with example indicators of each. Feel free to add to my list or adapt the indicators to your own context. In the first part of this chapter I will summarize strategies for evaluation within these major categories. Then I will devote the second half of the chapter to a discussion of how to use tests to evaluate learning from scenario-based e-learning courses.

## TABLE 9.1.  Some Typical Evaluation Questions for Scenario-Based e-Learning Courses

| Evaluation Category | Description | Typical Indicators |
| --- | --- | --- |
| Motivation | Learner satisfaction with, engagement, and persistence in the training. | Student survey ratings<br>Course completion rates<br>Course enrollments when optional<br>Social network ratings |
| Learning Effectiveness | Achievement of the learning objectives of the course. Usually measured with some form of test. | Tests measuring:<br>    Factual and conceptual knowledge<br>    Strategic or principle knowledge<br>    Near or far transfer procedural skills<br>    Near or far transfer open-ended skills |
| Learning Efficiency | The average time students take to complete the training.<br>Time to achieve competency. | Average time required to complete training<br>Time to acquire expertise needed for competent job performance |
| Transfer to the Workplace | The extent to which new knowledge and skills are applied in the workplace.<br>The extent to which scenario knowledge and skills are adapted to different contexts. | Job performance metrics, such as sales, customer satisfaction<br>Supervisor ratings<br>Tests measuring use of skills in related but different context |
| Return on Investment | The ratio between performance gains in the workplace and costs to produce and take training. | Performance gains in workplace translated into monetary values divided by costs to design, produce, and deliver training multiplied by 100 |

## WHAT DO YOU THINK?

Before we jump into the details, check off the statements below that you think are true about evaluation:

❏ 1. Student end-of-course satisfaction ratings are pretty accurate indicators of the instructional effectiveness of that course.

❏ 2. In most situations you should calculate a return on investment (ROI) for your scenario-based e-learning program.

❏ 3. You can use multiple-choice tests to measure learning in a scenario-based e-learning program.

❏ 4. It's not practical to measure learning from scenario-based e-learning courses.

❏ 5. Eighty percent is a good general cutoff score for passing scenario-based e-learning tests.

## FOCUSING YOUR EVALUATION

Which questions will be of greatest interest to your stakeholders? Which questions could be readily answered using data already collected by the organization? How would you adapt evaluation questions to your context? What additional questions have not been raised by your stakeholders? Evaluations require a balance between value judgments and resources. Different organizations and even different contexts within an organization will have different values and diverse resources. Below are the most common questions you or your clients might ask about the outcomes of scenario-based e-learning courses.

### Do the Learners Like It?

In some cases, motivation—that is, the satisfaction of your learners—is sufficient to support instructional product decisions. Some managers may feel that, if the learners see value in the training, that's sufficient justification. Motivation is typically measured with student rating sheets completed during and after the training. Other sources of motivational data include comments and ratings on social networks, enrollment in similar courses, and course completion statistics. Indicators of student satisfaction may be all that your stakeholders need to sell them on the scenario-based e-learning approach. Design your motivation questions carefully. Research comparing test scores to responses on course evaluations found best correlation with questions asking the learners to assess their level of confidence (Sitzmann, Brown, Casper, Ely, & Zimmerman, 2008). An example question from the pharmaceutical sales course is: *Rate your level of confidence in handling objections to Lestatin.*

### Is Instruction Effective?

Often, however, you will also need direct measures of instructional effectiveness— if for no other reason than to improve the instructional quality of your product. Comparisons of student course ratings with student test scores have shown almost no relationship (Sitzmann, Brown, Casper, Ely, & Zimmerman, 2008). Some learners whose test scores reflect minimal learning give the course high ratings, while others who achieved more give the course low marks. In other words, you can't rely on participant ratings as accurate indicators of participant learning.

To assess learning objectively, you need some form of test. Since most scenario-based e-learning programs are targeted toward problem-solving skills, appropriate tests may be more challenging to construct and validate than tests you have developed in the past that measure conceptual or procedural knowledge. Tests that are not valid and not reliable are a waste of time at best, and misleading and/or illegal at worst. Therefore, you need to carefully plan your learning measurement goals, development, and validation processes. I will devote most of this chapter to guidelines on assessing learning from scenario-based e-learning courses.

### Is the Learning Environment Efficient?

Instructional efficiency is another important metric, especially in organizational settings where staff is paid to attend training. Given two instructional programs with comparable learning outcomes, one of which requires twice as long for students to complete, the more efficient program may be the better choice—even if it is not the coolest or most popular option. Instructional efficiency can best be measured during the pilot stages of the training. By measuring and recording the time a small group of pilot students requires to complete the lessons, you can gain a reasonable estimate of efficiency. You may want to compare this efficiency estimate with time to reach similar instructional goals in a face-to-face classroom setting or online via a traditional training design. Be careful, however, to balance learning and efficiency metrics. For example, a face-to-face class may have required less time to complete but at the same time yielded either lower or inconsistent learning outcomes.

### Does Learning Transfer?

Training transfer is an important outcome in organizations, where the goal is to improve bottom-line outcomes such as productivity, sales, efficiency, safety, regulatory compliance, etc. As you will see in the next chapter, in some experiments scenario-based e-learning resulted in better transfer of learning compared to a traditional part-task design. However, bottom-line productivity metrics reflect many factors, and it's often challenging to claim a solid cause-and-effect relationship between training and job transfer.

In some situations, job metrics reflecting operational goals are routinely captured and, without too much effort, you could look at how these metrics might be affected by your training program. For example, in the suicide prevention course, suicide rate records are maintained by the Army, and it was easy to compare those rates before and after the training. Sales and customer service are two domains that routinely collect operational data. If you were going to use scenario-based e-learning to build optimal behaviors in customer service, you might be able to roll out the training in stages and compare job metrics, such as call monitoring data or customer complaints, between those trained first and others scheduled for later training. Alternatively, you might create two versions of the training—a traditional version that incorporates the core content of the scenario-based e-learning lessons as well as the scenario version— and compare metrics between the two groups. However, it's often not practical to set up a true scientific comparison in an operational setting, so I recommend caution in making too many judgments (positive or negative) based on bottom-line metrics.

### Is There a Good Return on Investment?

Basically, good return on investment (ROI) means that the tangible benefits accrued to the organization outweigh the costs to design, develop, and deliver the training. In terms of dollars, benefits are measured by cost savings, increased sales, increased customer satisfaction, fewer accidents, fewer audits, less employee turnover, more efficient work, and better compliance with regulatory requirements, among others. Time to reach competency is another potential benefit of scenario-based e-learning with ROI implications. For example, if automotive troubleshooting competencies that would require several weeks in a hands-on environment can be accomplished in several hours in a scenario-based e-learning environment, these time differences can be quantified. Along the same lines, scenario-based e-learning may reduce the amount of time spent in a face-to-face class, thus lowering travel expenses and other costs associated with in-person training.

To determine ROI, calculate the costs of the training and the monetary returns of the benefits. How you determine training costs is not always a straightforward process. It's usually pretty easy to determine the resources in terms of time or dollars devoted to analysis, design, and development of a training program. However, you may also want to include the delivery costs—the instructor's time and travel, the participant's time and travel, facilities, administration, etc. To calculate the ROI, divide the net program benefits by the program costs and multiply by 100.

In many situations it is difficult to obtain bottom-line operational data that will reflect the benefits of training. I recommend considering a ROI evaluation when (1) training is targeted toward skills closely linked to bottom-line quantitative metrics, (2) relevant metrics are already being captured and reported by the business unit, and (3) your client is interested in ROI and is willing to devote the resources needed. Sales can offer a good opportunity. One organization developed a two-day instructor-led course for account representatives selling high-end computer products. The course focused on a process for sales staff to define customer needs and match products accordingly. Twenty-five account representatives were randomly selected to participate in the training, and for two months the following metrics were collected: number of proposals submitted, average pricing of proposals, average close rate, and average value of won orders. The data from the twenty-five trained staff were compared to twenty-five different randomly selected sales staff who did not attend training, and the outcomes were divided by the training costs to calculate a return on investment. They found the average close rate of trained sales staff was 76.2 percent, compared to 54.9 percent for untrained. By multiplying the close rate by the average value of won orders, dividing that figure by the training costs, and multiplying the result by 100 the research team determined an ROI of 348 percent (Basarab, 1991).

A recent report on the ROI from a coaching intervention asked hotel managers to set business goals and measure their achievement with the aid of an external business coach (Phillips, 2007). For example, several managers set goals of reduced turnover. As managers calculated the return on goals achieved, they multiplied that return by their own estimate of how much the coaching intervention led to that result. For example, if reduced turnover resulted in a savings of $50,000 and a manager estimated that 70 percent of that reduction was due to coaching, the program benefit was calculated at $35,000. The estimated returns were divided by coaching costs to calculate a return on investment.

### Plan Evaluation in Stages

Evaluations can be resource-intensive. Therefore, set evaluation goals that are realistic in light of your resources. If you are just getting started with scenario-based e-learning, you will learn from your early efforts and improve your product. I suggest that initially you gather data most helpful to revising and evolving your early drafts and postpone evaluations that measure longer term effects. Specifically, before rolling out a new scenario-based e-learning lesson, start with a couple of pilot tests that include a small group of experts and representative learners to cull out glaring technical, content, or instructional errors or omissions not previously spotted. Use a second pilot with a larger group of representative learners to assess average times to complete the program, student satisfaction ratings, and learning outcomes.

Note that, by the time of the second pilot, to evaluate learning, you will need to have a valid test in hand. Therefore, you will need a test development process completed by the time the training is ready for pilot testing. Based on lessons learned from these pilots, revise your scenario-based e-learning. For example, if the testing data shows gaps in specific knowledge or skills, add or revise scenarios or scenario elements to shore up the training. After piloting, as you scale up the program, collect the type of data you used for the pilots and, if your client is interested, add indicators of transfer and return on investment such as bottom-line operational metrics.

Unfortunately, evaluations beyond student satisfaction are relatively scarce in workforce learning settings. As I will discuss below, test design and development is a labor-intensive process in itself, and many organizations either lack the resources or have concerns about potential legal consequences of employee testing. Therefore, the learning value of the bulk of training products more often than not is unknown. Still, I believe that it is better not to test at all than to attempt to measure learning with poor quality tests.

In the remainder of this chapter I will primarily focus on measures of learning effectiveness and use as examples tests from research studies that have either compared learning from various forms of scenario-based e-learning or have compared scenario-based e-learning with other instructional designs.

## BACK TO THE BASICS: TEST RELIABILITY AND VALIDITY

To measure learning you will use some form of test. Even if you do not plan to evaluate individual learner achievement, a test is the best objective tool to assess the instructional effectiveness of your program. Because scenario-based e-learning often focuses on building problem-solving skills, you will need to construct tests that evaluate those skills. Nevertheless, the fundamentals of test reliability and validity still apply, and I would be remiss not to mention them. If a test is not valid, it does not tell you anything useful—in fact, depending on how the results are used, it might be very misleading. Additionally, a test is not valid if it is not reliable. In Appendix C, I review the basics of reliability and validity. I want to stress *review*! If you plan to construct tests, it's always a good idea to consult with your legal department as well as engage the services of a testing expert—a professional called a psychometrician. For detailed information, I recommend *Criterion-Referenced Test Development* by Shrock and Coscarelli (2007).

## TEST ITEMS FOR SCENARIO-BASED e-LEARNING

Many organizations either do not test at all or, if they do test, they may not have validated their test items. Therefore, I decided to draw upon published experimental research studies to identify the types of tests research teams used to assess learning effectiveness of scenario-based e-learning. In Chapter 10, I summarize a number of research studies that compared the instructional effectiveness of various forms of guided discovery learning (including scenario-based e-learning)—often to traditional training programs. To measure learning effectiveness in these experiments, the research team must develop and validate their tests. In reviewing the research studies, I noticed that most experiments used two or three different types of test items to assess both knowledge and problem-solving skills. In Table 9.2, I list six types of test items representative of the tests used in various experiments and include an example of each type.

TABLE 9.2.  **Sample Test Items to Measure Scenario-Based e-Learning Outcomes**

| Outcome | Item Type Description | Test Item Example |
|---|---|---|
| Factual and Conceptual Knowledge | Items to assess understanding of concepts and application of facts associated with lesson tasks. Typically presented in multiple-choice format. | From a lesson for medical practitioners: Which of the following substances are typically excreted at an increased rate due to pheochromycytoma? Hydroxyl indolic acid and hydroxyproline  Hydroxyl indolic acid and catecholamines  Catecholamines and metanephrine |

| | | |
|---|---|---|
| Strategic or Principle Knowledge | Items to assess deeper understanding of principles relevant to the learning objectives. Typically presented in multiple-choice or open-ended format. | From a lesson on electronics: You wire a subwoofer speaker with a resistance $R = 16\,\Omega$ and a regular speaker with a resistance of $R = 8\,\Omega$ in parallel and operate this circuit with a $V = 6\,V$ battery. What is the total resistance of this circuit? Draw a diagram for the electrical circuit described in this problem. |
| Near Transfer Procedural Tasks | Items to assess the ability to solve well-structured problems with correct or incorrect answers that are *similar to the problems* used in the training. Sometimes can be assessed by multiple choice, but may require a performance test. | From a class on setting up a grade book spreadsheet: Use the student names and scores entered in the attached spreadsheet to set up a grade book that will calculate a semester score in which unit tests are weighted four times more than weekly quiz scores. Review your calculation results to answer:<br>1. Anna's semester score is:<br>    68%<br>    73%<br>    75%<br>    78% |
| Far Transfer Procedural Tasks | Items to assess the ability to solve well-structured problems with correct or incorrect answers that are *different from the problems* used in the training. Sometimes can be assessed by multiple choice, but may require a performance test. | From a class on setting up a grade book spreadsheet: Use sales agents' names and weekly sales data entered into the spreadsheet to determine monthly commissions and total salary. Review your calculations to answer:<br>1. Mark's take home pay for May, including commission, is:<br>    $2,357<br>    $2,590<br>    $3,029<br>    $3,126 |
| Near Transfer Open Tasks | Items to assess the ability to solve a problem or demonstrate a skill for which there are multiple acceptable solutions. The test problem *is similar* to those practiced in training. | From pharmaceutical sales training: Review the account notes on Dr. Mendez and respond to her questions about Lestatin in a role play. |

*(Continued)*

*Table 9.2 (continued)*

| Outcome | Item Type Description | Test Item Example |
| --- | --- | --- |
| Far Transfer Open Tasks | Items to assess the ability to solve a problem or demonstrate a skill for which there are multiple acceptable solutions. The test problem *is different* from those practiced in training. | From pharmaceutical sales training: Drs. Oman and Smith want a consistent approach in their family practice that includes three nurse practitioners. Review their practice patient profile summary and role play a staff meeting in which you discuss a general treatment plan for obesity that includes Lestatin. |

As I mentioned previously, open-ended responses require human evaluation. To keep the evaluation consistent, provide raters with a checklist and/or suggested answers that assign points to various response elements. (See the Inter-Rater Reliability discussion in Appendix C.) For example, in Figure 9.2, I show a sample test question from lessons on heat transfer taken from an experiment that compared learning from physical hands-on labs to learning from virtual labs. Note that the test includes a multiple-choice question but also asks learners to explain their reasoning. The explanations were reviewed by rater teams. To boost rater consistency, the answer key includes statements to look for in the explanations, along with points to assign to those statements. By the way, the research team found conceptual learning was equivalent in a virtual lab to conceptual learning in a hands-on lab.

## DID I PASS THE TEST?

In experimental research, the goal is to compare the effectiveness or efficiency of one lesson version with a second version. For example, two scenario-based e-learning lessons are identical except one presents the scenario in text and the other presents the scenario with video. Upon completion, all learners take a validated test with items similar to those I described previously. The research team then compares the scores and runs statistical tests to determine whether one set of outcomes is significantly different from the other and whether the difference is of practical relevance.

However, in an educational or training setting, tests are used to determine (1) the effectiveness of the instructional material and (2) whether a given learner is competent to perform on the job. Therefore, unlike experimental studies, you will often need to determine a criterion for "passing" the test. Basically, a criterion is a

**Test Question:**

Suppose that 500 g of hot water at 60 C is mixed with 500 g cold water at 40 C.

      A. The temperature of the hot water increases, decreases, or remains the same? Explain your reasoning.

      B. The temperature of the cold water increases, decreases, or remains the same? Explain your reasoning.

**Scoring Guidance:**

Correct answer for Question A: The temperature of the hot water decreases (1 pt). Expected explanation:

- The two samples of water are in contact (0.5pt)
- The two samples of water interact thermally (0.5pt)
- The two samples of water have different temperatures (0.5pt)
- Given that the mass of the hot water times the temperature change of the hot water equals the  mass of the cold water times the temperature change of the cold water, the temperature of the hot water decreases (0.5pt)

**FIGURE 9.2.**   *A Sample Test Item with Rater Guidance.*
Adapted from Zacharia and Olympiou (2011).

"cutoff" score that distinguishes competent performers from individuals who lack the minimal knowledge and skills to perform effectively on the job. I often see an automatic 80 percent cutoff score assigned to tests. However, what does 80 percent mean? Is it acceptable to perform 80 percent of the key maneuvers while landing an airplane or performing surgery?

Cutoff scores can be important in situations in which learners are not allowed to do the job, blocked from promotion, not certified, etc., on the basis of a test score. Likewise, if you use the test as one metric of the effectiveness of your instruction, again the cutoff score will be important. Setting cutoff scores is a topic that exceeds the scope of this chapter. I will give some general guidelines and recommend that you consult your legal and psychometric resources.

First, all aspects of testing, including setting a passing criterion, involve judgment and you need to include input from stakeholders as you make this decision. Use a team to include job experts and management for guidance on cutoff scores.

Second, not all test items need be equal. Some items may be critical and must be performed at 100 percent proficiency. Others may be less critical and a lower cutoff score can be acceptable. For example, on a driver's performance test, I would hope that certain safety-critical maneuvers must be performed at 100 percent accuracy. Others, such as parallel parking, may carry less weight. I know when I took my driver's test, my parking score had to be quite low, but I passed based on such critical skills as forward and backward steering, stopping at stop signs, signaling turns, and so forth.

Third, you need to collect data to set a cutoff score and then review that data with your advisory team. Once you have built a test that is reliable and valid, per our previous discussion, you can give it to two different groups of individuals: fifteen workers who are known to be competent performers and fifteen workers who are non-masters. Don't use just anyone for your non-master group. Instead, select individuals who have relevant baseline skills—the type of individuals who would be taking the training. Plot the scores of each group and set the cutoff score in the vicinity of the intersection between the groups. Take a look at Figure 9.3. In this example, the intersection of scores was 65 percent. Note that a few known competent performers scored below that number and a few non-masters scored above. Should you set the cutoff score at 70 percent and thereby fail a few who are actually competent? Or should you set the cutoff score at 60 percent and thereby pass a few who are not competent? Here is where your advisory team can help. If the skills are critical, a higher cutoff score is appropriate. For less critical skills and perhaps a need for more workers assigned to a given task, a lower cutoff score might be chosen.

Fourth, remember that you need legal and psychometric consultation on any high-stakes test—tests that if not reliable, not valid, or defined with arbitrary cutoff scores could affect safety or other critical outcomes. Likewise, tests that are used for high-stakes personnel decisions such as hiring, promotions, and so forth should be carefully designed and developed. As you can see even from my brief summary, testing is a resource-intensive process in itself. Yet there really is no other valid path to objectively evaluating the instructional value of your scenario-based e-learning.

As I mentioned at the start of this chapter, for some organizations and contexts, tests may not be wanted or needed. In some cases, the learner's satisfaction, as indicated by rating sheets, focus groups, social media reviews as well as enrollment and completion statistics, may be sufficient. In other situations such as the soldier suicide prevention program, bottom-line data may be enough to sell your approach. No two

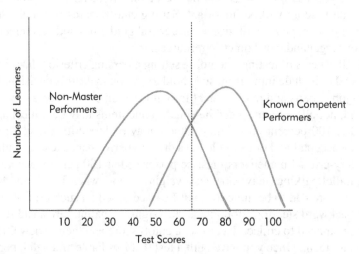

**FIGURE 9.3.** *A Distribution of Competent and Non-Master Performer Scores on a Test.*

evaluation situations are the same, but by now you should have the basics to adapt an evaluation strategy to your situation and to identify qualified experts to guide your project.

## TESTING WITH ONLINE SCENARIOS

In the previous sections I discussed traditional testing formats such as multiple choice and performance tests to assess the knowledge and skills learned from your scenario-based e-learning course. You could also use your scenario lesson interface as a testing tool. You would use a design similar to that described in this book, with the omission of guidance and learning resources other than the type of support that would be available in the normal work environment such as a reference resource. You would present scenarios not used in the instructional phases. Your scenarios could be structurally similar to those presented in the training to measure near-transfer learning as well as structurally different if you want to assess to what extent learners can adapt what they learned to different situations. For example, in a class on preparing a grade book with Excel, a near-transfer question would provide a different set of student data and ask learners to set up a grade book. A far-transfer question would provide data and ask learners to use Excel to set up a budget.

One of the challenges of testing with scenarios is scoring. If your scenarios are highly structured with correct and incorrect answers, you can set up a relatively traditional automated scoring and passing scheme applying standard testing methodologies for reliability and validity. For the automotive troubleshooting example used in this book (see Figures 1.1, 1.2, and 6.5), the client assigned a score for identifying a correct failure on the first attempt and also assigned points for the actual elapsed time to complete the scenario as well as the virtual time needed to complete the repair. The time data serves as a useful proxy measure for application of an optimal troubleshooting sequence. In contrast, if your scenarios are ill-structured, with multiple acceptable answers such as a role play, you may need human graders using a rubric to evaluate them.

In a blended testing approach, you could use traditional multiple-choice items to evaluate knowledge of facts and concepts, followed by scenario-based items to assess application of mental models, heuristics, or principles to job-relevant situations. If you need to evaluate hands-on procedures with shop equipment, for example, you will need a hands-on performance test. By defining the different knowledge and skills needed for a given level of competency, you may be able to automate part of the test and use human graders to assess just the important elements with high response variability.

If your professional domain has developed a validated certification test using traditional testing formats, you might be able to automate parts of it as a scenario-based test. For example, if an automotive technician is traditionally tested and scored in a hands-on shop environment, you could adapt the scoring and passing standards to a scenario-based test. The online scenario-based test could measure the troubleshooting problem-solving process but not procedural skills of manipulating equipment. If you need to evaluate both problem-solving and procedural skills, a blended testing approach might be best. If your domain does not have a validated certification test, you may need to validate and set passing scores yourself using the methodologies summarized previously in this chapter.

Because using a scenario-based environment for assessment of ill-structured problems is a relatively new approach, I recommend you consult with a measurement specialist for guidance.

## WHAT DO YOU THINK? REVISITED

Now that you have read the chapter, you may want to revisit the questions below to consider whether they are true or false.

- ❑  1. Student end-of-course satisfaction ratings are pretty accurate indicators of the instructional effectiveness of that course.

- ❑  2. In most situations you should calculate a return on investment (ROI) for your scenario-based e-learning program.

- ❑  3. You can use multiple-choice tests to measure learning in a scenario-based e-learning program.

- ❑  4. It's not practical to measure learning from scenario-based e-learning courses.

- ❑  5. Eighty percent is a good general cutoff score for passing scenario-based e-learning tests.

In my opinion, all of the statements are false, except Number 3. In some cases you can use a multiple-choice test to measure the knowledge topics targeted by your objectives as well as some skills that, when applied, result in clear-cut right-or-wrong answers. For example, you can provide a scenario and ask a series of multiple-choice questions about it. However, in many cases, scenario-based e-learning focuses on more ill-defined outcomes that require an open-ended response.

Regarding Number 1, there is good evidence that there is little relationship between how participants rate their class and their actual achievement as measured by a test (Sitzmann, Brown, Casper, Ely, & Zimmerman, 2008). You will need a reliable and valid test to assess the learning effectiveness of your scenario-based e-learning. Therefore, I consider this statement false.

For Number 2, in many cases it is difficult to show a bottom-line dollar gain from any training program. Therefore, I rate Number 2 as false. You may have the opportunity when outcome goals such as sales or suicide prevention are closely linked to bottom-line metrics that are routinely reported and you can show a difference in those metrics either before and after training or between a group that receives training and a group that does not. However, many factors will affect bottom-line measures, so it's often not practical to draw firm conclusions from these types of comparisons.

Regarding Number 4, I believe that there is nothing so unique about scenario-based e-learning that exempts it from being evaluated for its learning effectiveness.

Just as with any training program, your design should include learning objectives that are measurable. I mark this statement as false.

Number 5 is another false statement. Too often "passing" scores are set arbitrarily, rather than based on data—both objective and subjective. Previously in the chapter, I introduced a couple of techniques for you to consider if you need to set passing scores for certification purposes.

## COMING NEXT

In addition to (or in lieu of) conducting your own evaluation, I recommend that you review the research evidence on scenario-based e-learning. Because the approach is relatively new, the research base is somewhat limited—but growing. Some research compares learning outcomes from guided-discovery designs to outcomes from other designs. Other experiments aim to define which features of guided discovery optimize learning by comparing different versions of a guided-discovery lesson. In Chapter 10 I will summarize recent research on these questions.

## ADDITIONAL RESOURCES

Phillips, J.J. (2007). Measuring the ROI of a coaching intervention, part 2. *Performance Improvement,* 46, 10–23.
  A great practical article on measurement of ROI of management skills—often considered very hard to measure.

Schraw, G., & Robinson, D.R. (Eds.). (2011). *Assessment of higher order thinking skills.* Charlotte, NC: Information Age Publishing.
  A rather technical book with chapters from various scholars. Recommended for anyone interested in a more advanced/detailed set of perspectives on this important topic.

Shrock, S.A., & Coscarelli, W.C. (2007). *Criterion-referenced test development* (3rd ed.). San Francisco: Pfeiffer.
  The Shrock and Coscarelli book has always been my guide when it comes to any form of test development, and they have kept their classic book updated. Should be on every trainer's shelf.

## SCENARIO-BASED e-LEARNING AND YOU:
## PLANNING YOUR EVALUATION

Early in your project, you should consider what kind, if any, evaluation you and your stakeholders might use to demonstrate the value offered by scenario-based e-learning or to compare outcomes from scenario-based e-learning with outcomes from traditional approaches. Complete the survey below as a guide.

1. Your Task(s):

2. Your Learners (check all that apply)

- ☐ Novice
- ☐ Journeymen
- ☐ Experienced
- ☐ Mixed
- ☐ Management
- ☐ Senior management
- ☐ Other:

3. What evaluation questions and measures are of interest to you and/or your stakeholders?

- Do learners like scenario-based e-learning?
  - ☐ Rating sheets during and after instruction
  - ☐ Focus groups during and after instruction
  - ☐ Comments on social media
  - ☐ Enrollments in optional courses
  - ☐ Course completions
  - ☐ Other:

- Does your scenario-based e-learning lead to effective learning?
  - ☐ Test scores matched to learning objectives
  - ☐ Ratings from supervisors
  - ☐ Other:

- Is your scenario-based e-learning efficient?
  - ☐ Time to complete lessons
  - ☐ Time to achieve job competency
- Does your scenario-based e-learning lead to improved work performance?
  - ☐ Ratings from supervisors
  - ☐ Work performance metrics

- Does your scenario-based e-learning give a return on investment?
  - ☐ Costs to produce course
  - ☐ Costs to deliver course
  - ☐ Quantifiable outcomes such as sales, customer satisfaction, work efficiency
  - ☐ Other:

- Other evaluation questions you or your stakeholders might have:

# CHAPTER

## 10

# DOES SCENARIO-BASED e-LEARNING WORK?

Like most professional fields, workforce learning is no stranger to fads and fables. Take learning styles, for example. Millions of dollars have been spent on various learning style inventories, classes, books, and other resources. Yet there is no evidence for the validity of audio, visual, or kinesthetic learning styles (Clark, 2010). Before you make a significant investment in any new training method, product, or design, there are several questions worth asking. In this chapter I'll summarize the evidence on several key questions regarding scenario-based e-learning.

## DOES IT WORK?

The first question is *Does it work*? This question can be parsed into several related questions. First, *Does it work better than a different method or approach?* To answer this question, researchers will randomly assign one group of students to a lesson version using scenario-based e-learning and a second group to an alternative lesson teaching the same content using a different design, such as a traditional lecture or a directive approach. A second related question is *Does it yield some unique outcomes not readily achieved by other approaches?* For example, can scenario-based e-learning accelerate learning or does scenario-based e-learning result in better transfer of learning than alternative designs do? Finally, we could ask: *For what kinds of outcomes and for what kinds of learners is scenario-based e-learning most effective?* For example, *Is it effective for learning procedures or for learning strategic skills?* Alternatively, *Is it most effective for novice learners or for learners with some background experience?*

To answer this question, researchers may compare learning from scenario-based e-learning among learners of different backgrounds or assess learning from scenario-based e-learning with tests measuring different knowledge and skills.

## IS IT EFFICIENT?

Even if an instructional method works, we must also consider the cost. Does scenario-based e-learning take more time and resources to design and develop, compared with traditional multimedia training? And more importantly, will it require a longer learning period? The biggest cost involved in training in commercial organizations is the time that staff invests in the learning environment. Since most research comparisons allocate the same amount of time to the different experimental lesson versions to maintain equivalence, we don't have as much evidence about efficiency as about some of the other questions. However, in a recent experiment that measured learning and learning efficiency in a game compared to a slide presentation that presented the same technical content as the game, the game version resulted in equivalent or poorer learning than the slide version and required over twice as long to complete (Adams, Mayer, MacNamara, Koenig, & Wainess, 2012). I'm hoping to see more of this type of data in the future.

## DOES IT MOTIVATE?

If a given instructional method or program is equally effective for learning outcomes, but overall learners like it better, it might be a worthwhile investment. To answer questions about motivation, researchers ask learners to rate a scenario-based e-learning version and a traditional version of the same content and compare results. In addition, researchers can compare course enrollments and completion rates in instructional settings where learners have alternative courses to select and completion rates are tracked.

## WHAT FEATURES MAKE A DIFFERENCE?

For an instructional approach with as many variations as scenario-based e-learning, we might ask which components enhance learning and which either have no effect or even could be harmful. For example, is learning better when a scenario is presented with video compared to text? Are some elements of the design, such as guidance, feedback with reflection, or visuals, more important than others? To answer these questions, researchers design different versions of a scenario-based e-learning lesson and compare their effects. For example, an unguided version of a simulation might rely on the learner to discover the underlying principles, while an alternative version of the same simulation would provide structured assignments to guide its use. This approach to research is what Mayer calls "value added" (Mayer, 2011). In other words, what features of scenario-based learning designs add learning value and what features either have no effects or even hurt learning?

## WHAT DO YOU THINK?

Put a check by the statements that you think are true:

❑  A. Scenario-based e-learning can lead to better job transfer than traditional course designs.

❑  B. Learning is better when scenarios are presented in video or animation rather than in text.

❑  C. Overall, discovery learning has proven ineffective.

❑  D. Scenario-based e-learning has been demonstrated to accelerate expertise.

❑  E. Learners are more motivated by a scenario-based e-learning lesson than by a traditional lesson.

I'll review these questions and more as I summarize the research on the following pages. If you want to see the answers now, turn to the end of the chapter.

## LIMITS OF RESEARCH

Practitioners need much more research evidence than is often available. Hence, we need realistic expectations regarding how much wisdom we can mine from research—especially research on newer instructional methods or technology. Two major limitations regarding various forms of scenario-based e-learning include a rather low number of experiments conducted to date and inconsistency in terminology and implementation of scenario-based e-learning.

### The Evolution from Single Experiments to Meta-Analysis

Evidence on any new technology or instructional strategy will lag behind its implementation by practitioners. Only after a new approach has been around for a while and has been sufficiently salient to stimulate research might we see an accumulation of evidence. At first there will be a few reports of individual experiments. Eventually, after a significant number of studies accumulate, a synthesis called a meta-analysis is published. The conclusions of a meta-analysis give us more confidence than individual studies because they summarize the results from many experiments. The meta-analysis will report an effect size of the many studies combined, which gives us some idea about the degree of practical significance of the results. Effect sizes greater than .5 indicate sufficient practical potential to consider implementing a given method.

By coding different features in different studies, the meta-analysis can also suggest insights regarding which learning domains or audiences benefit most or, alternatively, which techniques used in a an instructional implementation might be more effective. In this chapter I summarize results of a meta-analysis that synthesized results from more than five hundred comparisons of learning from discovery lessons with either guided discovery or traditional lecture-based versions of the same content.

### What's in a Name?

Instructional practitioners and researchers are challenged to define what is meant by a specific instructional method or design. It's common to label quite different implementations of a given method with the same name. Likewise, we often see similar programs given different names. In professional practice as well as in the research literature, we see a range of terms for various guided discovery approaches, including problem-based learning, scenario-based learning, whole-task learning, project-based learning, case-based learning, immersive learning, inquiry learning, and so on.

It follows then that a given approach such as problem-based learning (PBL) may show conflicting results among different research reports because it is implemented differently in various settings. Hung (2011) has summarized a number of ways that the reality of PBL in practice often differs from the ideal definition and vision of what PBL should be. For example, PBL implementations may actually consist of traditional lecture-based instruction supplemented with problems. Alternatively, the PBL instructors may play quite different roles during the group sessions. For example, some facilitators may impose more structure and guidance regarding content, whereas others may primarily model problem-solving processes. In short, the label of PBL may in fact represent quite different instructional approaches. The result is research results about apples and oranges and, not surprisingly, inconsistent outcomes and conclusions. In a review of problem-based learning, Albanese (2010) concludes: "Research on the effectiveness of PBL has been somewhat disappointing to those who expected PBL to be a radical improvement in medical education. Several reviews of PBL over the past twenty years have not shown the gains in performance that many had hoped for" (p. 42).

In spite of these limits, I will review research on the following lessons learned from research on guided-discovery environments:

1. Discovery learning does not work.

2. Guided discovery can have learning advantages over "traditional" instruction.

3. Learner scaffolding is essential for success.

4. Domain information may be effective *before or after* problem solving.

5. Guided discovery can be more motivating than "traditional" instruction.

6. Feedback and reflection promote learning.

7. Visual representations should be congruent with your learning goals.

## DISCOVERY LEARNING DOES NOT WORK

Perhaps one of the most important lessons from years of instructional research is that pure discovery learning is not effective. In a review of discovery learning experiments conducted over the past forty years, Mayer (2004) concludes that "Guidance, structure, and focused goals should not be ignored. This is the consistent and clear lesson of decade after decade of research on the effects of discovery methods" (p. 17). Mayer's conclusion is empirically supported by a recent meta-analysis that compared discovery approaches with other forms of instruction (Alfieri, Brooks, Aldrich, & Tenenbaum, 2011). The research team synthesized 580 research comparisons of discovery learning to other forms of instruction, including direct instruction and guided-discovery approaches. Discovery learning *was the loser,* with more guided forms of instruction showing a positive effect size of .67.

Lessons that included guidance in the form of worked examples and feedback showed greatest advantage over discovery learning. A critical feature of any successful scenario-based e-learning will be sufficient structure and guidance to minimize what I call the "flounder factor." Instructional psychologists use the term "scaffolding" to refer to the structure and guidance that distinguish discovery learning from guided discovery. In Chapter 6 I described nine common strategies you can adapt to build structure and guidance into your scenario-based e-learning lessons.

## GUIDED DISCOVERY CAN HAVE LEARNING ADVANTAGES OVER "TRADITIONAL" INSTRUCTION

In part 2 of the meta-analysis summarized in the previous paragraph, the research team evaluated 360 research studies that compared guided discovery to other forms of instruction, including direct teaching methods. Overall, the guided-discovery methods excelled, with an average effect size of .35 which is positive but not large (Alfieri, Brooks, Aldrich, & Tanenbaum, 2011).

The *Handbook of Research on Learning and Instruction* (Mayer & Alexander, 2011) includes several chapters that summarize research on various forms of guided discovery compared to alternative teaching methods. For example, de Jong (2011) reviews results from instruction based on computer simulations. He summarizes the advantages of simulations as (1) opportunities to learn and practice in situations that cannot readily or safely learned on the job and (2) the opportunity to work with multiple representations such as graphs, tables, and animations, which stimulate deeper understanding. He concludes that "large-scale evaluations of carefully designed simulation-based learning environments show advantages of simulations over traditional forms of expository learning and over laboratory classes" (p. 458). One main theme of his chapter is that "Guided simulations lead to better performance than open simulations" (p. 451).

### Learning Excel in Scenario-Based Versus Directive Lessons

One of the defining features of scenario-based e-learning is learning in the context of solving problems or completing tasks. Lim, Reiser and Olina (2009) compared two sixty-minute classroom lessons that taught student teachers how to prepare a grade book using Microsoft Excel. One version used a traditional step-by-step directive approach in which twenty-two basic skills such as entering data, merging cells, and inserting a chart were demonstrated. At the end of the second session of the directive version, learners practiced completing a grade book.

In contrast, in the scenario-based version, learners completed two grade books during Session 1 and two during Session 2. In these classes, the instructor demonstrated how to create the grade book and students then created the same grade book just demonstrated. Next, students created a second similar grade book with a different set of data. The two grade books in Session 1 were simple and those completed in Session 2 were more complex. In summary, the directive class taught a number of small skills and concluded with one grade book practice, while the scenario-based version taught all of the skills in the context of setting up four grade books. All lessons were conducted in an instructor-led environment.

At the end of the two classes, all learners completed three tests. One test required learners to perform sixteen separate small skills such as entering data, merging cells, etc. The second task-based test asked learners to prepare a grade book using different data than that used in class. A third test measured transfer by providing a set of data and asking students to use Excel to prepare a budget. None of the lessons had demonstrated or practiced preparing a budget, so this third test measured the learners' ability to adapt what they had learned to a different task. In other words, this test measured ability to transfer skills to a different context. Take a look at the test results in Figure 10.1. Which of the following interpretations do you think best fits the data (select all that apply):

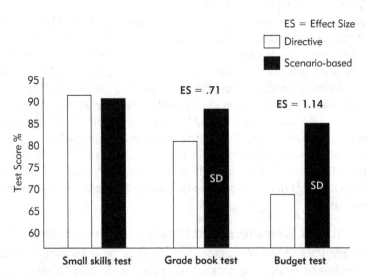

**FIGURE 10.1.** *Learning from Directive Versus Scenario-Based Versions of an Excel Class.*
Based on data from Lim, Reiser, and Olina (2009).

Scenario-based training was better for:

A.  Learning small skills such as entering data, etc.

B.  Learning to prepare a grade book

C.  Transfer of learning to a different spreadsheet task

As you can see, there were no major learning differences on the small-skills test. The scenario group did better on the grade-book test, but because they had four opportunities to practice grade books compared to one opportunity in the directive group, this is not surprising. Perhaps the budget transfer test offers the most interesting results. Here we see that the scenario-based group was much better able to transfer what they had learned to a new task. The correct answers to the question above are Options B and C. A take-away from this research is that transfer of learning may be enhanced when learners practice new skills in several real-world contexts rather than as separate smaller component skills.

Similar results are reported by Merrill (2012), who compared learning from a multimedia scenario-based version of Excel training based on five progressively more complex spreadsheet tasks with an off-the shelf multimedia version that used a topic-based approach. The test consisted of three spreadsheet problems not used during the training. The scenario-based group scored an average of 89 percent, while the topic-centered group scored 68 percent. The time to complete the test averaged twenty-nine minutes for the scenario-based group and forty-nine minutes for the topic-centered group.

We need more research comparisons of scenario-based with directive lesson designs in different problem domains and with different learners to make more precise recommendations regarding when and for whom scenario-based e-learning is the more effective approach.

## LEARNER SCAFFOLDING IS ESSENTIAL FOR SUCCESS

As I mentioned, one of the critical success factors for guided-discovery learning, including scenario-based e-learning, is guidance and structure. In Chapters 6 and 7, I outlined a number of techniques you can adapt to your projects. Scaffolding is an active area of research, so we don't yet have sufficient studies to make comprehensive recommendations. However, in the following paragraphs I summarize a few recent research studies that compared learning from two or more versions of guided discovery that incorporated different types of structure and support.

### Should Domain Information Come Before or After Problem Solving?

Whether relevant domain information in the form of explanations or examples should be provided before or after problem-solving attempts is a current debate among researchers. I'll review evidence on both sides of the question, ending with some guidelines that reflect both perspectives.

### *Assign Problems First—Then Provide Explanations*

If the instructional goal is to learn to solve problems, is it better to start by telling and showing a solution procedure (direct instruction) or by letting learners try to solve problems even if they don't derive a correct solution? Kapur (2012) compared the benefits of direct instruction followed by problem-solving practice versus problem-solving sessions followed by direct instruction. He refers to sequencing problem solving first, followed by directive instruction, as *productive failure.*

He taught the concept of and procedure for calculating standard deviation in one of two ways. The productive failure group worked in teams of three to solve a problem related to standard deviation, such as how to identify the most consistent soccer player among three candidates based on the number of goals each scored over a twenty-year period. No instructional help was provided during the problem-solving sessions. After the problem-solving sessions, the instructor compared and contrasted the student solutions and then demonstrated the formula for standard deviation and assigned additional practice problems.

In contrast, the direct instruction group received a traditional lesson, including an explanation of the formula to calculate standard deviation, some sample demonstration problems, and practice problems. All students then took a test that included questions to assess (1) application of the formula to a set of numbers (procedural items), (2) conceptual understanding questions, and (3) transfer problems requiring development of a formula to calculate a normalized score (not taught in class). In Figure 10.2 you can compare the test scores between the two groups for the three types of items.

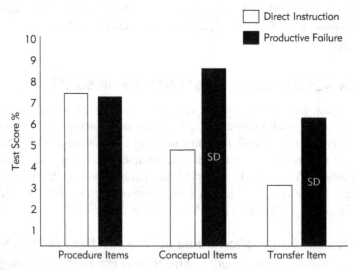

**FIGURE 10.2.** *Learning from Direct Instruction First Versus Productive Failure First.*
Based on data from Kapur (2012).

Which of the following interpretations do you think best fits the data? (Select all that apply.)

Compared to direct instruction, a design that starts with unguided problem solving (productive failure) leads to better:

A.   Procedural learning

B.   Conceptual understanding

C.   Transfer of learning

Kapur (2012) concludes that "Performance failure students significantly outperformed their direct instruction counterparts on conceptual understanding and transfer without compromising procedural fluency" (p. 663). Based on his data, options B and C are correct. This research suggests that designing problem activities—even activities that learners can't resolve—in the initial learning phase will benefit longer-term learning, as long as learners are provided with appropriate knowledge and skills afterward. The argument is not whether unguided solution activity is better or worse than direct instruction, but rather how they can complement one another.

This research focused on mathematical problems with a defined solution. We will need more evidence to see how productive failure may or may not apply to more ill-defined problems as well as the conditions under which it is best used. Applied to scenario-based learning, the results suggest the benefits of allowing learners to tackle a relevant problem (even if they don't fully or correctly resolve it), followed by direct instruction in the form of examples, explanations, and guided practice.

### Provide Explanations Before and During Learning

In contrast to the experiment described in the preceding paragraphs, two recent studies revealed better learning when domain information was presented prior to and/or during learning. Lazonder, Hagemans, and de Jong (2010) measured learning from three versions of a business simulation in which learners had to maximize sales in a shoe store by selecting the best combination of five variables, such as type of background music, location of the stockroom, and so forth. The simulation allowed learners to manipulate the value of each variable and then run an experiment to see the effect on sales. A guide included the key information about the variables and was available (1) only before working with the simulation, (2) before and during the simulation, or (3) not at all. Better learning occurred when domain information was available, with best results from learners having access both before and during the simulation.

Similar results were reported in a comparison of learning from a game with or without a written summary of the principles to be applied during the game (Fiorella & Mayer, 2012). Learners having access to a written summary of game principles before and during game play learned more and reported less mental effort. From these experiments, we learn that providing key information before and during a simulation or game leads to better learning.

Perhaps the type of instructional environment and the background knowledge of the learners are variables that guide the optimal sequence of problem solving and direct instruction. Both studies that showed benefits of receiving information first involved a simulation or game—relatively unstructured environments that required learners to try different actions and draw conclusions from responses. In contrast, the research showing better conceptual and transfer learning from unguided problem solving followed by direct instruction involved a more structured topic (deriving and applying the formula for standard deviation). In addition, problem solving first requires a sufficient knowledge base for learners to draw upon prior knowledge as they attempt to resolve new problems. Solution attempts among the productive failure groups, although not successful, did reflect an attempt to apply prior mathematical knowledge, such as mean, median, graphic methods, and frequency-counting methods.

Until we have more data, unguided problem solving as an initial activity is perhaps best for learners with background knowledge relevant to the problem domain and for high structure problems that have defined solutions. Alternatively, for more novice learners and a more open instructional interface such as a simulation, a directive initial approach might be best. We need more research on the sequencing of problem solving and direct instruction.

### Use Collaboration for More Challenging Scenarios

One potential source of support during problem solving is some form of collaboration—either face-to-face in a classroom environment or online via social media. Do we have evidence that learning from scenario-based e-learning is better when learners work in teams? Kirschner, Pass, Kirschner, and Janssen (2011) created four lesson versions teaching genetics inheritance problems. Easier lesson versions demonstrated how to solve problems with worked examples, while harder versions assigned problems instead. A large body of research has shown the learning benefits of providing worked-out examples in place of some problem solving (Clark & Mayer, 2011). Each of the two versions (easy and hard) was taken by either individual learners or teams of three. You can see the results in Figure 10.3.

The authors suggest that collaborative learning can help manage mental load because the workload is distributed across brains. At the same time, collaborative learning requires a mental investment in communicating and coordinating with others in the team. The experiment showed that collaborative work led to better learning, but only in the more demanding lessons. When assignments are more challenging, the benefits of teamwork offset the mental costs of coordination among team members. However, for easier lessons, individual problem solving was better. The authors suggest that: "It is better for practitioners NOT to make an exclusive choice for individual or collaborative learning, but rather vary their approach depending on the complexity of the learning tasks to be carried out" (p. 597).

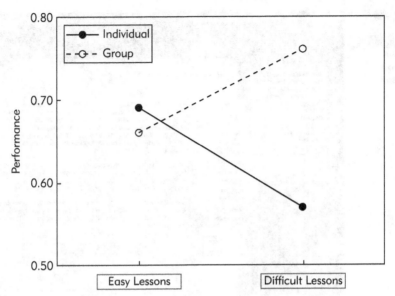

**FIGURE 10.3.**  *Collaboration Improves Learning from More Difficult Problems.*
Based on data from Kirschner, Pass, Kirschner, and Janssen (2011).

A second experiment on productive failure that focused on standard deviation, as described in the Kapur (2012) study summarized previously in this chapter, found that learning in productive failure designs was best with collaborative groups of three that included a mix of higher and lower ability students rather than all high or all low ability (Wiedmann, Leach, Rummel, & Wiley, 2012).

Taken together, the studies to date indicate that collaboration is beneficial for more challenging learning goals such as problem solving prior to instruction—especially when the teams include a mix of background experience among the learners.

### Make the Instructional Interface Easy to Use

In some scenario-based e-learning lessons, learners are required to type in responses such as hypotheses or explanations of examples. Alternatively, in other versions the interface is configured to allow a pull-down menu to select specific hypotheses. Selecting preformatted responses imposes less mental load than constructing a response from scratch and has been found to lead to better learning. For example, Mayer and Johnson (2010) found that a game designed to teach how circuits work benefitted from self-explanation questions when the learner could select

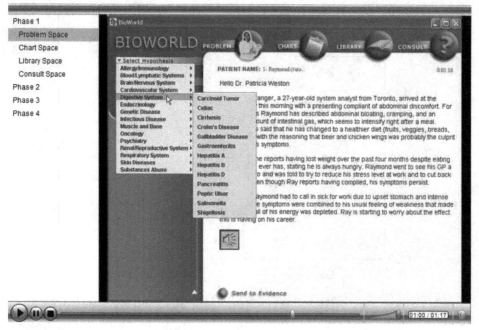

**FIGURE 10.4.** *The Bioworld Interface Uses a Pull-Down Menu to Offer Hypotheses Options.*
With permission of Susanne Lajoie, McGill University.

a self-explanation from a menu rather than construct one. In Bioworld, shown in Figure 10.4, the learner can select a hypothesis from a pull-down menu rather than type in a hypothesis.

In addition to developing an easy-to-use interface, also consider providing instruction on how to use the interface. Holzinger, Kickmeier-Rust, Wassentheurer, and Hessinger (2009) compared learning of arterial blood flow principles from a simulation with a traditional text description of the concepts. Group 1 studied the text description. Group 2 used the simulation unaided, while Group 3 used the simulation preceded by a thirty-second video explaining its use and the main parameters involved. Learning was much better from the simulation, but only when preceded by the explanatory video. The research team concluded that "It is essential to provide additional help and guidance on the proper use of a simulation before beginning to learn with the simulation" (p. 300). A colleague reported that orientation to a scenario-based e-lesson is critical to its success. For example, Figure 10.5 shows a screen taken from the orientation for the Bridezilla lesson. Here the coach introduces herself, summarizes the goal of the lesson, and leads into a demonstration of support resources accessible in the interface.

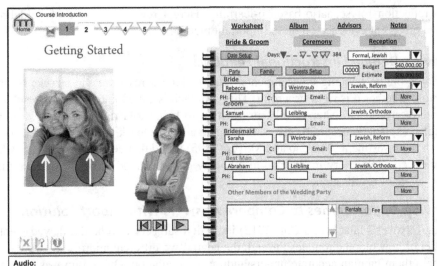

**FIGURE 10.5.**  *The Coach Orients the Learner to the Bridezilla Scenario.*

## GUIDED DISCOVERY CAN BE MORE MOTIVATING THAN "TRADITIONAL" INSTRUCTION

With only a few exceptions, evaluation reviews of problem-based learning (PBL) have found that medical students in the PBL curriculum are more satisfied with their learning experience compared to students in a traditional science-based program. Loyens and Rikers (2011) reported higher graduation and retention rates among students studying in a PBL program than in a traditional curriculum. My guess is that most medical students find learning in the context of a patient case more relevant than learning science knowledge such as anatomy and physiology out of context. Because of relevance and multiple opportunities for overt engagement, it is possible that scenario-based e-learning will prove more motivational to your workforce learners as well. If your scenario-based lessons result in higher student ratings and greater course completions, the investment might pay off. We need more research comparing not only learning but completions and satisfaction ratings from scenario-based e-learning environments.

## FEEDBACK AND REFLECTION PROMOTE LEARNING

For any kind of instruction, feedback has been shown to be one of the most powerful instructional methods you can use to improve learning (Hattie, 2009; Hattie & Gan, 2011). In Chapter 8 I discussed some alternatives to consider in the design of feedback and reflection for scenario-based e-learning. Here I review a couple of guidelines based on recent evidence on these important methods.

### Provide Detailed Instructional Feedback

In some online learning environments, after making a response the learner is simply told whether it is right or wrong. This approach is called knowledge of results or corrective feedback. Alternatively, in addition to being told right or wrong, a more detailed explanation could be given. Writing detailed feedback takes more time, so is it worth the investment? Moreno and Mayer (2005) found that detailed feedback—what they called explanatory feedback—in a botany game resulted in better learning than knowledge of results alone.

### Provide Opportunities to Compare Answers with Expert Solutions

Gadgil, Nokes-Malach, and Chi (2012) identified subjects who held a flawed mental model of how blood circulates through the heart. Two different approaches were used to help them gain an accurate understanding of circulation. One group was shown a diagram of the correct blood flow and asked to explain the diagram. A second group was shown an incorrect diagram that reflected the student's flawed mental model along with the correct diagram. Students in this group were asked to contrast and compare the two diagrams and in so doing explicitly confront their misconceptions. Both groups then studied a text explanation of correct blood flow and were tested. One of the test items asked learners to sketch the correct flow of blood through the heart. Ninety percent of those asked to compare the incorrect and correct diagrams drew a correct model, compared with 64 percent of those who only explained the correct diagram. The research team concluded that instruction that included compare and contrast of an incorrect and correct model was more effective than an approach that asked learners to explain correct information. Asking learners to compare their own misconceptions with a correct representation proved to be a powerful technique.

From this study, we can infer that a useful feedback technique involves requiring learners to contrast and compare their solutions, especially solutions with misconceptions to an expert solution. Therefore, include two elements in your design. First, save and present the learner's solution with an expert solution on the same screen to allow easy comparison. Second, to encourage active comparison, add reflection questions that require the learner to carefully compare the solutions and draw conclusions about the differences. In Figure 8.2 you can review how I adapted this technique to the Bridezilla lesson.

## VISUAL REPRESENTATIONS SHOULD BE CONGRUENT WITH YOUR LEARNING GOALS

A wealth of research shows the benefits of adding relevant visuals to instructional text (Clark & Lyons, 2011). How can we best leverage visuals in scenario-based e-learning? Does the type of visual, for example, animation or still graphics, make a difference? We are just starting to accumulate evidence on how best to use different types of visuals for different learning goals. Here I will summarize research that can be applied to the visual design of scenario-based e-learning.

### *Use Visual Representations Rather Than Text Alone When Visual Discrimination Is Important*

In a comparison of learning from examples of classroom teaching techniques presented in text narrative descriptions, in video, and in computer animation, both visual versions (video and animations) were more effective than text (Moreno & Ortegano-Layne, 2008). The research team suggested that computer animations might be more effective than video because extraneous visual information can be "grayed-out" as a cueing technique that helps the learner focus on the important visual elements. From a practical perspective, it is generally faster to update an animated version than to update a video. In this research, the goal was to teach student teachers classroom management—a skill set that relies on complex visual discrimination and implementation of verbal and physical actions. Since the visual representations offered more relevant detail related to the skill, it is not surprising that learning from visual examples was better than learning from a text narrative example.

We need much more evidence regarding the optimal modes, that is, text, video, animation, or stills to represent scenario-based e-learning cases. For skills that are based on discrimination of auditory and visual cues, such as teaching or medical diagnostics, visual representations via computer animation or video have proven more effective than text. In some situations animations may be more effective for updating scenarios and for drawing attention to the most relevant features of the visual display. In other cases, the higher emotional impact of video, seen, for example, in Gator 6 and Beyond the Front, may be more engaging to learners.

## CAN SCENARIO-BASED e-LEARNING ACCELERATE EXPERTISE?

It seems logical that opportunities to practice tasks—especially tasks that would not be safe or convenient to practice on the job—would accelerate expertise. After all, expertise grows from experience. From chess playing to typing to musical and athletic performance, research on top performers finds that they have invested many hours and often years in focused practice (Erickson, 2006, 2009). Chess masters, for example, have typically devoted more than ten years to sustained practice, resulting in over 50,000 chess play patterns stored in their memories. Many businesses, however, don't have ten years to build expertise. Perhaps scenario-based e-learning can provide at least a partial substitute for the years of experience that serves as the bedrock of accomplished performance.

### *Accelerating Orthopedic Expertise*

Kumta, Tsang, Hung, and Cheng (2003) evaluated the benefits of scenario-based Internet tutorials for senior-year medical students completing a three-week rotation in orthopedics. One hundred and sixty-three medical students were randomly assigned to complete the traditional three-week program, consisting of formal lectures, bed-side tutorials, and outpatient clinics, or to a test program that included the traditional program plus eight computer-based clinical case simulations. The scenarios required learners to comment on radiographs, interpret clinical and diagnostic test results, and provide logical reasoning to justify their clinical decisions. The test groups met with facilitators three times a week to discuss their responses to the simulations.

At the end of the three weeks, students were assessed with a multiple-choice computer-based test, a structured clinical examination test, and a clinical examination with ward patients. The students in the test group scored significantly higher than those in the control group. The research team concluded that well-designed web-based tutorials may foster better clinical and critical thinking skills in medical students. "Such multimedia-rich pedagogically sound environments may allow physicians to engage in complex problem solving tasks without endangering patient safety" (p. 273).

Note that, in this research, the test group received most of the same learning opportunities in the form of bedside tutorials and outpatient clinics as the control group. In addition, they received eight online cases to analyze, coupled with faculty debriefs. Therefore, it's not surprising that additional carefully selected learning opportunities led to more learning.

### Accelerating Electronic Troubleshooting Expertise

Lesgold and associates (1992, 1993) tested a scenario-based troubleshooting simulation called Sherlock, designed to build expertise in electronic troubleshooting of the F-15 test station. Sherlock provides learners with simulated test station failures to resolve, along with tutorial help. Thirty-two airmen with some electronics background experience were divided into two groups. One group completed twenty-five hours of training with the Sherlock simulated environment, while the other sixteen served as a comparison group. All participants were evaluated through pre- and post-tests that required them to solve simulated test station diagnosis problems—problems that were different from those included in the training. In addition to the thirty-two apprentice airmen, technicians with more than ten years of experience were also tested as a comparison group. As you can see in Figure 10.6, the average skill level of those in the trained group was equivalent to that of the advanced technicians. The 1993 report concluded that "the bottom line is that twenty to twenty-five hours of Sherlock practice time produced average improvements that were, in many respects, equivalent to the effects of ten years on the job" (p. 54).

In this experiment we see that expertise was accelerated by a relatively short amount of time spent in a troubleshooting simulation coupled with online coaching. Note, however, that the learners already had some background experience. Also note that, in this study, a group that was trained with Sherlock was compared to a group that did not receive any special training. It would be interesting to compare a Sherlock-trained group with an equivalent group that received twenty-five hours of traditional tutorial training.

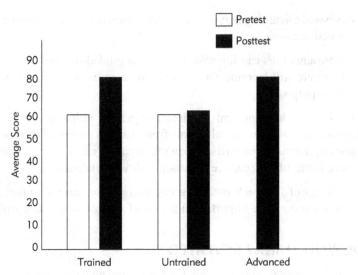

**FIGURE 10.6.** *Acceleration of Expertise Using Sherlock Troubleshooting Simulation Trainer.*
Based on data from Lesgold, Eggan, Katz, and Rao (1993).

The research I have reviewed here offers promise that scenario-based learning can accelerate expertise. However, we need more studies that include groups that receive the same number of hours of traditional training in order to conclude that scenario-based designs can accelerate expertise more effectively than traditional designs do.

## RESEARCH ON SCENARIO-BASED e-LEARNING —THE BOTTOM LINE

In summary, I make the following generalizations based on evidence to date on scenario-based e-learning and related guided discovery learning environments:

A.  Effective implementations of scenario-based e-learning must impose guidance and structure.

B.  Unguided problem solving can result in deeper learning in learners with appropriate background knowledge if followed by direct instruction.

C.  Different types of guidance and structure may be effective depending on your context. Some alternatives being researched include collaboration, self-explanation questions, provision of domain-specific information, and methods to make the environment easy to use.

D.  Scenario-based e-learning may help learners build deeper understandings that transfer to different problem situations in the domain, as shown in the Excel research.

E.   Scenario-based e-learning may improve motivation and lead to higher enrollment and completion rates.

F.   Visual representations can improve learning in guided-discovery environments, although we are still learning which types of representations are most effective for different purposes.

G.   Scenario-based e-learning can accelerate expertise, although we have limited comparisons of expertise acceleration from various forms of instruction. The strongest arguments for expertise acceleration can be made in situations in which alternative forms of job practice are unsafe, slow, or impractical.

H.   Specific forms of feedback including comparisons of learner's misconceptions with expert solutions are important elements of scenario-based e-learning.

## WHAT DO YOU THINK? REVISITED

Previously in the chapter you evaluated several statements about scenario-based e-learning. Here are my thoughts.

❑   A. Scenario-based e-learning can lead to better job transfer than traditional course designs.

❑   B. Learning is better when scenarios are presented in video or animation rather than in text.

❑   C. Overall discovery learning has proven ineffective.

❑   D. Scenario-based e-learning has been proven to accelerate expertise.

❑   E. Learners are more motivated by a scenario-based e-learning lesson than by a traditional lesson.

Based on my review of the evidence accumulated to date, I would vote for Option C as having the most research support. A meta-analysis of more than five hundred studies showed learning was better from either traditional directive or guided-discovery lessons than from discovery versions.

Regarding Option A, there is limited evidence (mostly involving learning of Excel) that a scenario-based approach can enable learners to apply Excel to different problems than those presented during training.

Option B may be true when (1) visual cues are important to the analysis and solution of the case or (2) learner engagement is prompted by the emotional qualities of video, for example. We need more evidence on representations of scenarios.

Regarding Option D, I don't see sufficient evidence to show that scenario-based e-learning can accelerate expertise, although it makes sense that for tasks that cannot be practiced in a real-world environment, a form of guided discovery—be it online simulation or scenario-based—would offer unique opportunities to compress expertise.

As to motivation (Option E), medical students do report problem-based learning as more motivational. However, medical students are a unique population and you will need to evaluate how your learners might respond.

## COMING NEXT

As you have seen, the design and development of guided-discovery learning environments can be resource-intensive. When your focus is on thinking skills, it is critical that you define expert heuristics in specific and behavioral terms during your job analysis. In some situations knowledge and skills are tacit and thus cannot be readily articulated by your subject-matter experts. In the next chapter I review cognitive task analysis techniques you can use to surface and validate the knowledge and skills that underpin expertise.

## ADDITIONAL RESOURCES

Alfieri, L., Brooks, P.J., Aldrich, N.J., & Tanenbaum, H.R. (2011). Does discovery-based instruction enhance learning? *Journal of Educational Psychology, 103,* 1–18.
A technical report with a great deal of data. Worth reading on an important issue if you can invest the time.

Clark, R.C., & Lyons, C. (2011). *Graphics for learning.* San Francisco: Pfeiffer.
Our book that summarizes evidence and best design practices for effective visuals in various media.

Kapur, M.. & Rummel, N. (2012). Productive failure in learning from generation and invention activities. *Instructional Science, 40,* 645–650.
This special issue of *Instructional Science* includes several papers reporting research on problem solving first followed by directive instruction. This article overviews the issue.

Loyens, S.M.M., & Rikers, R.M.J.P. (2011). Instruction based on inquiry. In R.E. Mayer & P.A. Alexander (Eds.), *Handbook of research on learning and instruction.* New York: Routledge.
A useful review of research that focuses on different types of inquiry learning.

Mayer, R.E. (2004). Should there be a three-strikes rule against pure discovery learning: The case for guided methods of instruction. *American Psychologist, 59,* 14–19.
A classic article that should be in every advanced practitioner's file.

## SCENARIO-BASED e-LEARNING AND YOU: EVIDENCE-BASED DECISIONS

Before you move forward with scenario-based e-learning, consider whether the evidence accumulated to date supports your investment by reflecting on the following questions:

☐ Will scenario-based e-learning offer opportunities to accelerate expertise in knowledge and skills that are not easily or practically acquired by your learners in their job roles?

☐ Will your learners find a scenario-based e-learning approach more relevant than the current approaches your organization is using?

☐ Do you have a need for transfer of learning from the tasks presented in training to tasks relying on the same skills but in different contexts?

☐ Do you have the resources to design successful scenario-based e-learning environments with sufficient guidance for your particular learners to minimize the flounder factor?

☐ Does problem solving in your domain rely on interpretation of visual cues? Would a more emotive visual environment increase learner engagement? These are the two central issues to consider regarding modes used to represent your scenarios.

# CHAPTER

## 11

# ELICITING CRITICAL THINKING SKILLS FOR SCENARIO-BASED e-LEARNING

When doing a task analysis, have you ever asked the subject-matter expert questions such as: "Why did you do that?" or "What made you think of that?" and get responses such as: "Well—you just know" or "It's kind of intuitive" or "You can't really teach that—it's just something you have to get a feeling for." Your expert is not trying to be obtuse. It's just that he or she has a lot of tacit knowledge—knowledge that cannot be readily articulated. Experts literally can't tell you what they know. Your challenge—especially when planning courses based on ill-structured problems—is to use special elicitation techniques that help experts reveal what they know.

As you've seen throughout the book, designing and developing scenario-based e-learning can be resource-intensive, especially compared to receptive or even directive designs. However, the resources you invest in preparing scenario-based e-learning lessons or courses will be largely wasted unless the knowledge and skills you incorporate are valid. By valid I mean that the specific behaviors illustrated and behavioral responses elicited in your scenarios mirror best practices linked to operational goals. Of course, this is true for any form of organizational training. However, scenario-based e-learning is more likely than traditional training to focus on critical thinking skills—knowledge and skills that cannot be readily observed by you or described by your subject-matter experts.

Scenario-based e-learning has the potential to accelerate expertise so that the actions and decisions of your most senior and effective performers can be emulated by more junior staff. But unless time is devoted to eliciting those behaviors and the knowledge that underpins them, you may end up with a multimedia training package that is engaging and popular but only gives an illusion of building expertise.

## WHAT IS KNOWLEDGE ELICITATION?

The basic premise of knowledge elicitation is that tacit knowledge and skills must be drawn out indirectly from expert experience. When you directly ask experts how or why they resolve particular situations, they can often provide only limited information. To get the real story, you need to dig into their brains by using inductive task analysis methods. Rather than ask them to describe the principles, rationale, or methods they use, you will obtain better data by having them talk about what they are doing—either while they are doing it or by describing past real situations. By carefully recording, probing, and analyzing what several experts say and do in a target problem situation, you can define their actions and also identify the behind-the-scenes knowledge that led to those actions.

## WHAT DO YOU THINK?

As you consider the what, when, and how of knowledge elicitation for your projects, check the options below that you think are true. You will find the answers by reading through this chapter, or skip to the end, where I summarize my thoughts.

❑    A. It's usually a good idea to conduct knowledge-elicitation interviews as the basis for scenario-based e-learning.

❑    B. Talking aloud while solving a problem is the best method for knowledge elicitation.

❑    C. Knowledge-elicitation interviews are efficient substitutes for traditional task analysis techniques.

❑    D. Cues embedded in problem scenarios are an important element of critical thinking skills.

## THREE APPROACHES TO KNOWLEDGE ELICITATION

In this chapter I describe three approaches to knowledge elicitation that you can adapt to your own context. All three techniques involve a two-to-three-hour recorded interview of an expert, a transcription of the interview, and an analysis of the transcription to identify critical thinking skills. The three approaches are (1) concurrent verbalization, (2) after-the-fact stories, and (3) reflection on recorded behaviors. In Table 11.1, I summarize each of these approaches. Keep in mind that they are not mutually exclusive and you might benefit from combinations of the three.

### Concurrent Verbalization

In concurrent verbalization, you ask the expert to perform a task or solve a problem aligned to the class of problems that is the focus of your lessons. The problem may be a "real" work task the expert performs on the job or may be a simulated problem. As they are working on the problem, they verbalize aloud all of their thoughts. In Figure 11.1 you can review typical directions given to experts asking them to verbalize while problem solving. The actions and verbalizations are recorded for later analysis. Occasionally, an expert might become absorbed in the problem and forget to talk aloud. Whenever the expert is silent for more than three to five seconds the interviewer gives her a gentle reminder to continue talking.

You can probably immediately think of some work contexts that would not lend themselves to concurrent verbalization. If the work situation involves interpersonal communication—for example, overcoming objections as part of a sales cycle or interviewing for a hiring position—it will not be possible for the expert to do a secondary verbalization. Therefore, concurrent verbalization will only apply to problems that do not require talking during performance. Secondly, some problems will not lend

**TABLE 11.1.** **Three Approaches to Knowledge Elicitation**

| Approach | Description |
| --- | --- |
| Concurrent Verbalization | The performer verbalizes her thoughts aloud as she resolves a problem or performs a task related to the training goal. |
| After-the-Fact Stories | The performer thinks back on tasks performed or problems solved in the past that are relevant to the training goals. |
| Reflection on Recorded Behaviors | The performer verbalizes her thoughts aloud as she reviews a recording of her performance. Recordings could include video, audio, keystroke, or eye tracking. |

> As you work through this XXXXXX task, voice aloud all of your thoughts. Don't edit yourself; please verbalize everything that comes to mind as you solve the problem without thinking about or judging your statements.

**FIGURE 11.1.** *Typical Directions for Concurrent Verbalization.*

themselves to this method because of privacy concerns (e.g., financial consulting), hazardous situations (e.g., military operations), or scarce problem occurrences (e.g., emergency responses to unusual events).

Sometimes you can set up a simulation that is close enough to the real-world situation that you could use concurrent verbalization. For example, for troubleshooting infrequent failures in specific equipment, the failure could be replicated in samples of the equipment, which could then be used as a model problem for experts to resolve. Likewise, in some settings, realistic simulators are already in place that could be programmed to emulate the types of problems that are the focus of your training. For example, realistic simulators are common training devices in medical settings, computer networking, military operations, aircraft piloting, and power plant control operations, to name a few.

### After-the-Fact Stories

If concurrent verbalization is not feasible, consider harvesting expert tacit knowledge and skills through stories of past experiences. The stories should be descriptions of actual problems faced and solved by expert performers. There are several approaches to finding useful stories and I will summarize two.

Crandall, Klein, and Hoffman (2006) describe in detail the "critical decision method" for eliciting and extracting knowledge from expert descriptions of past experience. The interview process involves five main phases: (1) helping the expert to identify a past experience that will incorporate the knowledge and skills relevant to the instructional goal, (2) eliciting a high-level overview of the problem and how it was resolved, (3) recording and verifying a timeline or sequence of events of the problem solution, (4) reviewing the story in depth with frequent probing and amplifying questions from the interviewer, and (5) making a final pass with "what-if" questions. In total, the interview can require one or two hours and, as with all knowledge elicitation, it must be recorded and transcribed for later analysis. In Figure 11.2 I summarize some typical directions given to experts at the start of the interview. Further in the chapter are some examples from a critical decision method interview.

A second approach to getting after-the fact stories described by Van Gog, Sluijsmans, Joosten-ten Brinke, and Prins (2010) involves prework assignments to a small team of three to six experts, followed by synchronous collaborative team discussions on the completed assignments. First, ask each team member to work alone

> Recall a time when your skills were particularly challenged as you resolved a problem dealing with XXXX. Think of a time when your knowledge and expertise made a difference to how the situation turned out. We want to find an incident that required more than the typical knowledge and routine steps of a more junior worker.
>
> Start by giving a brief account of the situation from start to finish.

**FIGURE 11.2.** *Typical Directions to Initiate the Critical Decision Method.*

and write down three incidents that he or she faced in the problem domain. Ask the experts to write about a situation that was relatively simple to resolve, a second situation of moderate difficulty, and a third that was quite challenging. In Figure 11.3 I include directions for team members that you could adapt for your context. Ask each expert to bring a typed copy of the three situations to a meeting of approximately two or three hours. Begin the group discussion with the problems that each expert classified as relatively simple. Ask each expert to read his description in turn. Alternatively, make copies of each scenario and ask experts to read them. After hearing or reading each sample, ask the team for consensus that the problem indeed would qualify as relatively simple (or moderately challenging or very challenging). Then, using all the scenario samples of a given level as a resource, ask the team to identify the key features that characterize situations and solutions at that level. Use a wall chart, whiteboard, or projected slides to record features in three columns of simple, moderate, and complex.

Several aspects of this method appeal to me. First, it offers a useful approach to identifying the features that distinguish easier and more difficult scenarios, as well as a repository of actual scenarios to be adapted for the training. Since scenario-based e-learning courses should incorporate a range of complexity among a given class of problems, the features that distinguish simple from complex will inform your problem progression. In addition, basing the analysis on problems derived from actual experiences will be more valid than simply asking experts: "What makes a problem more complex?"

Second, the prework assignment will save time. Third, the collaboration of a team of experts will ensure a less idiosyncratic knowledge base compared to stories based on a single expert. Fourth, from the common guidelines derived from the various solutions, you can define the outcome deliverables of your scenarios. On the downside, you may not obtain the depth of knowledge compared to the critical decision method. However, you could follow up this initial round of work with individual interviews that dive into greater depth on the stories that seem the most appropriate for training purposes.

---

Please think back to several times that you solved a problem dealing with XXXX. As you review your past experiences, identify a situation that you resolved that you consider basic – the kind of situation that a junior person should be able to handle. Next think of a situation that was very challenging – a situation that would probably exceed the knowledge and skills of a junior person. Finally, think of a situation that you would classify as intermediate.

As you think of each situation, please type out an account of the incident – each on a separate piece of paper. Include the events that led up to the situation, along with a description of how the situation played out (what you did, why you did it, and what happened). Use the template provided to summarize each situation.

---

**FIGURE 11.3.**  *Sample Directions for Identifying Past Scenarios.*

### Reflections on Recorded Behaviors

One potential disadvantage to after-the-fact stories is the reliance on memory. As experts think back on past experiences, especially experiences they will share in a group of peers, they may omit or edit important details or events—especially mistakes. Alternatively, they may embellish elements that, upon reflection, seem more important. Finally, they may distort details simply due to memory failure. One approach to making reflections more accurate and detailed involves asking an expert to comment on recorded episodes of problem solutions. For example, a teacher might make video recordings of his classroom activities. Alternatively, customer service representatives are routinely audio-recorded during customer interactions. Later, you can review the recordings with the expert and use probing questions to elicit details, such as why he took a particular action or made a specific statement.

Naturally, this method relies on the feasibility of recording events. A video recording would be useful for situations that involve movement; engagement with artifacts, such as troubleshooting a vehicle failure; and interpersonal exchanges, such as those involved in teaching, sales, giving presentations, and so forth. For tasks that can be completed on a computer, you could record on-screen actions as well as focus of attention via eye-tracking methodologies. A replay would superimpose the eye-tracking data onto screen changes and/or a review of keystrokes. If you are unable to record real-world events, you might be able to set up model problem situations realistic enough to elicit authentic behaviors from expert performers. For example, in a pharmaceutical setting, doctor consultants could engage in recorded role plays with experienced account agents. Or equipment problem failures could be re-created for experts to identify and repair.

## WHICH ELICITATION METHOD SHOULD YOU USE?

First, you need to decide if and where to use these resource-intensive knowledge elicitation methods. I would recommend blending one or more of these approaches with a traditional job analysis. Using traditional job analysis methods, identify the more critical tasks that will be the focus of problem-centered learning—the tasks that make a difference to operational outcomes. Next, isolate the tasks or task segments that involve knowledge and skills that are likely to reside as tacit knowledge in expert memory. For example, if during a task analysis interview you are hearing comments like: "Well, it's just intuitive" or descriptions of actions that are very generalized and/ or vague, you might bookmark that task as a candidate. Third, consider the volatility of the tasks. If the critical thinking skills underlying given problems are likely to change substantially and relatively quickly, you have to decide whether the investment required to elicit detailed knowledge and skills is worth it.

Once you have identified some tasks or classes of problems that are good candidates for knowledge elicitation, decide which method is best. Often, your context will dictate that decision for you. As I mentioned previously, in many situations concurrent verbalization won't be a viable option. If not, consider whether there is a way to record problem-solving episodes in a real-world or simulated situation and ask experts to view the recordings and reflect on them. If reflection on recorded behaviors is not practical, then you will have to rely on after-the-fact stories by adapting one of the methods I described previously.

### Evidence on Knowledge Elicitation Methods

Van Gog, Paas, van Merrienboer, and Witte (2005) compared the effectiveness of the three methods I've discussed in this chapter. In their experiment, they asked twenty-six college students to solve computer-simulated electrical circuits troubleshooting problems. Each individual solved two different problems using each of the three methods. For example, an individual would solve a problem and voice his thoughts as he worked (concurrent verbalization). Next, the same individual would solve a different problem silently and, after completing the problem, describe what he did and why (after-the-fact stories). Finally, the same individual would solve a third problem in silence while his keystrokes and eye fixations were recorded. These records were played back while the individual described what he did and why he did what he did (reflections on recorded behaviors).

The team reviewed all of the verbalizations, classifying them into four types of information: actions taken, rationale for actions, rules of thumb, and monitoring thoughts (more on monitoring coming up in this chapter). In Figure 11.4 you can see the results of their comparison. Overall, the concurrent verbalization technique yielded the most information. After-the-fact stories yielded the least amount of

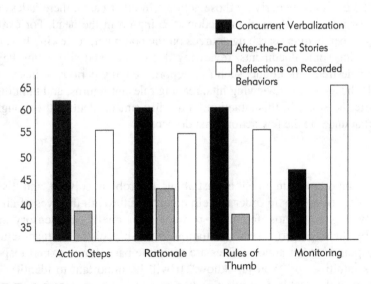

**FIGURE 11.4.** *Amount of Knowledge Elicited by Three Methods.*
Adapted from Van Gog, Pass, Van Merrienboer, and Witte (2005).

information. However, as the research team pointed out, in the after-the-fact verbalizations, the interviewer did not ask additional probing questions, thus potentially
limiting the amount of information that would normally surface with this method. In
addition in the recorded condition, the problem solver viewed the recording in real
time and did not have an opportunity to pause or replay episodes. Future research
should give us more detailed guidance on when each method might yield the best
results. In fact, some methods might be better for some types of problems, contexts,
and type of knowledge desired.

## TYPES OF KNOWLEDGE AND SKILL TO ELICIT

As you decide if and how to conduct knowledge elicitation and as you analyze the
transcripts of your interviews, you need to define the categories of knowledge and
skills most important to your instructional goals. In Table 11.2 I summarize six common general categories of knowledge to consider and illustrate each category with an
example from an interview with an emergency room physician. The six types are (1)
actions taken, (2) decisions made, (3) cues used, (4) rationale, (5) rules of thumb, and
(6) monitoring.

### Actions and Decisions

In just about all knowledge elicitation involving problem solving, you will want to
identify a combination of actions and decisions. In some situations, such as the ER
physician example shown in Table 11.2, there are many actions and you will need to
probe for the decisions underlying those actions. In other cases, there is less observable behavior involved. More of the action is going on in the head. For example, a
news analyst spends time searching sources on the computer, reviewing hits, refining
searches, saving some documents, reviewing documents, and abstracting key information for a desired end-product such as a report. Lengthy periods of inactivity may
occur while the analyst is reviewing hits, reading relevant returns, and thinking about
how to write the story. In this situation, you will want to identify the thoughts and
decisions that underlie the few actions that do occur.

### Cues

Cues are an important component of just about all problem solving, and it's important to identify those cues in order to help others see through the eyes of an expert.
Cues involve sights, sounds, feelings—perhaps even smells—all sensory information used by the expert to assess a situation, make a decision or take action, and
monitor responses to her actions. Cues are often the basis for an expert response of
"Well—it's intuitive" or "You just know." It will be important to identify specific
cues relevant to the problem solution and to reproduce those cues in your training
scenarios.

## TABLE 11.2.  Six Types of Knowledge to Elicit

| Knowledge Type | Description | Example from ER Physician Interview |
|---|---|---|
| Actions Taken | Observable behaviors exhibited during problem solution | In two minutes' time we did several things simultaneously—we put him on the bed, started oxygen, and called the respiratory therapist. |
| Decisions Made | Mental choices that drove actions | Before we intubated him, I spoke with his wife because I needed to be sure that he would want to be put on a ventilator. |
| Cues Used | Physical signs that led to a decision or an action | He was cyanotic. He was breathing, but the area above his collar bones was pulling in. |
| Rationale | Underlying principles or reasoning for a decision or action | The critical part was determining the cause of his respiratory distress. He had a history of emphysema and asthma and he was near a wood stove, which in the past had kicked off an attack. |
| Rules of Thumb | Underlying heuristics commonly used by expert performers to resolve specific classes of problems | When pulmonary edema causes respiratory distress, the breathing usually sounds wet. His respirations did not sound gurgling. |
| Monitoring | Monitoring and assessment of a situation leading to potential adjustments in actions or decisions | I was pretty certain of my diagnosis and I wanted an X-ray to confirm it. I was not going to wait for the X-ray to decide. I was going to treat him and review the X-ray to confirm. |

Thanks to Gary Klein for data from the emergency room physician interview.

### Rationale and Rules of Thumb

Rationale and rules of thumb are closely related, and you may want to collapse them into a single category. Rationale refers to the reasons behind decisions made and actions taken. Rationale is often based on an interpretation of cues in light of prior experience and domain-specific knowledge. Rationale may involve knowledge components such as facts, concepts, processes, or other domain knowledge.

Rules of thumb are commonly held guidelines or principles that experts use when making decisions or taking actions. Rules of thumb, also called heuristics, tend to be cause-and-effect relationships and are often based on past experience. To identify rules of thumb, look for statements such as "Well—when I see XYZ I generally consider ABC first" or "The fact that XYZ happened tells me that most likely ABC would follow if we did not do D because . . ." or "More often than not, when faced with XYZ, we consider either ABC or FWQ."

### *Monitoring*

Monitoring involves mental activity used to (1) assess a given situation (based on cues, experience, and knowledge), (2) set goals for optimal outcomes, (3) note situation changes, and (4) adjust activities or decisions based on scenario progress. Psychologists refer to these skills as metacognition, and these types of skills often distinguish expert from junior performance. For example, Schoenfeld (1987) asked graduate mathematics students and expert mathematicians to talk aloud as they solved a challenging problem. He analyzed their monitoring or metacognitive statements and created the graph shown in Figure 11.5. The novices tended to start down a solution path and stick with it no matter what. In contrast, the expert moved more frequently among the problem-solving stages. This pattern of problem-solving behaviors of experts reflected greater monitoring skills. Based on this analysis, Schoenfeld emphasized metacognitive thinking in his practice sessions. For example, as student teams worked on problems, he encouraged metacognitive thinking by asking: "What are you doing now? Why are you doing that? What other course of action have you considered? How is your current course of action working?"

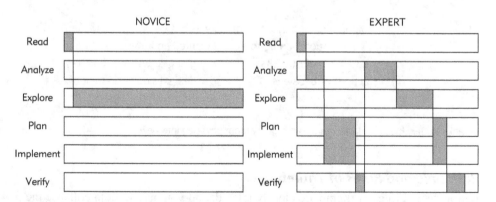

**FIGURE 11.5.** *A Comparison of Problem-Solving Patterns Between Novices and Expert Mathematicians.*
From Schoenfeld (1987).

### Questions to Elicit Knowledge Needed During the Interview

Having in mind specific categories of knowledge and skills you need for your scenarios will help you ask productive probing questions during the interview and to identify specific examples of those categories for coding of the transcript. In Table 11.3 I list some common questions that will help elicit each type of information.

## TABLE 11.3. Sample Questions to Elicit Knowledge Types

| Knowledge Type | Sample Questions |
| --- | --- |
| Actions Taken | What did you do? What other alternatives did you consider? What might someone with less experience have done differently? |
| Decisions Made | What decisions did you make before taking the action? What part of this decision led to a desired outcome? What might someone with less experience have decided? Why did you make that decision at this point? |
| Cues Used | What did you hear, see, smell, or feel that indicated this situation was challenging? What did you hear, see, smell, or feel that led you to make this decision or take that action? What would have looked, sounded, smelled, or felt differently that would have led to a different action or decision? What did you hear, see, smell, or feel that told you that your action or decision was leading to a desired outcome? What did you hear, see, smell, or feel that someone with less expertise might have missed? |
| Rationale | Why did you take that action or make that decision? What was your rationale? What concepts or facts did you apply at this stage? What did you consider that someone with less experience might not have known or thought of? |
| Rules of Thumb | What general rules of thumb do you use in these situations? What general principles did you apply? What specific techniques made a difference to the outcomes? What would other experts like yourself consider when faced with this type of problem? In what ways is this situation similar to or different from others you have solved? |
| Monitoring | What were your initial goals? What did you look for after you took action X? Describe what you looked for that told you the situation was headed in the desired direction. What alternative actions did you consider? On what basis did you rule them out? What might have caused you to change your path of action? What did you notice as the situation played out that a more novice individual might have missed? |

You would use probing questions such as these only during after-the-fact stories or reflection on recorded behaviors, as you do not want to interrupt the expert with questions during concurrent verbalization.

## INCORPORATING CRITICAL THINKING SKILLS INTO YOUR LESSONS

Now that you have elicited and identified some key critical thinking skills, how will you incorporate them into your design model? In Table 11.4 I summarize some suggestions and will illustrate with some examples to follow.

### Use of Actions Taken

The actions taken should reveal the work flow or the basic paths experts take to progress through a scenario. You will use the workflow to specify response options aligned to the task-deliverable stage of your design plan, as well as in guidance resources, feedback, and reflection. For example, in a branched scenario design, action steps from the cat anesthetic lesson (Figure 1.5) can be selected. In a menu-driven interface, you may use the main workflow stages as menu tabs, as in the bank loan analysis scenario (Figure 5.1). Identify and create not only correct response options but also the erroneous or less efficient actions that reflect misconceptions common to the target audience.

### Use of Decisions Made

If task success relies heavily on the decisions behind actions, incorporate mechanisms for learners to make decisions explicit during problem solving as well as an emphasis on decisions in guidance resources, feedback, and reflection. For example, when selecting a given action in a branched scenario, the learner could be asked to also select a rationale or principle supporting the choice. As you can see in Figure 11.6, after prioritizing the evidence supporting a diagnosis, the learner can compare her priorities with those of an expert and type in lessons learned or additional questions.

### Use of Cues Identified

Important cues can guide your trigger event, the responses to learner actions or decisions during the scenario, the scenario data, guidance, and intrinsic as well as instructional feedback. In other words, all of the major design elements may incorporate critical cues. In Figure 1.5 from the anesthetics lesson, vital signs are critical cues and summarized in the left-hand chart. In a dynamic simulation for treatment of blood loss in dogs (Figure 1.4), an EKG provides ongoing cues that fluctuate with treatment decisions. In Bioworld, the learner is required to select specific relevant patient signs and symptoms that are stored in the evidence table. In the automotive troubleshooting scenario, after an incorrect action is tried, the symptom still appears as an example of the use of cues as intrinsic feedback (see Figure 3.3). Overall, cue recognition and interpretation are key distinguishing features of expert performance, and the integration

## TABLE 11.4.  How to Use Knowledge Types in Scenario-Based e-Learning

| Knowledge Type | Some Ways to Apply to Design Model |
| --- | --- |
| Actions Taken | Integrate into task deliverable to design selection options of actions to take or avoid during problem solving. Actions are the basis for response options (links, buttons, etc.) that learners select to research and resolve the problem. In addition, actions taken can be the basis for guidance (advisors, examples, etc.) as well as feedback. |
| Decisions Made | Integrate into task deliverable to provide decision options to take or avoid. In branched-scenario designs, include expert decision options as well as potential suboptimal decisions that a more junior performer might make as alternatives. Provide scaffolding for decisions, such as worked examples or worksheets. |
| Cues Used | Incorporate important cues in the trigger event, in case data, as well as in intrinsic feedback, to actions selected or decisions made. Cues can also be presented in guidance and feedback. If actions or decisions rely heavily on cue identification, incorporate realistic rendering of those cues into the interface. |
| Rationale | Make the reasoning behind actions and decisions explicit in worked examples of expert solutions, as well as in the feedback to actions taken or decisions made. Add response options in the interface that require learners to explicitly identify rationale behind decisions made or actions taken. |
| Rules of Thumb | Make the rules of thumb that support actions and decisions explicit in guidance, such as worked examples of expert solutions or virtual advisors. Interactions in the program ask learners to identify rules of thumb as they progress through a scenario. Instructional feedback can make rules of thumb explicit. |
| Monitoring | Identify junctures in the scenario when monitoring events occurred. Include explicit examples of expert monitoring questions and responses in worked examples. Incorporate monitoring reminders or choices in learner response options. Virtual experts and advisors model monitoring events, and monitoring is prompted during the reflection phases. |

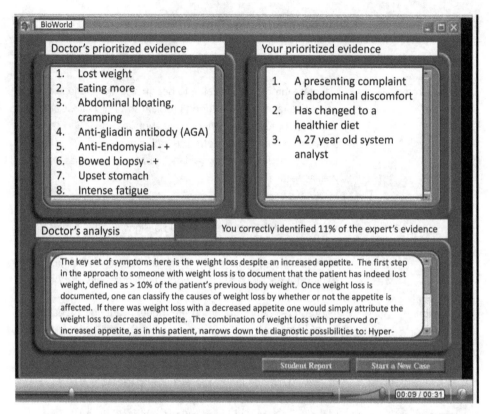

**FIGURE 11.6.** *Learners Compare Their Prioritized Evidence (Right) with Expert Priorities (Left).*
With permission of Susanne Lajoie, McGill University.

of important cues throughout your scenario is a hallmark of effective scenario-based e-learning.

Use the type and salience of cues also to select your scenario display modes. If decisions rely heavily on interpretation of visual and auditory cues, realistic visuals may be essential to an authentic representation of the scenario.

### Use of Rationale and Rules of Thumb

Rationale and rules of thumb may be some of the most important elements of your training. You will want to illustrate these in your guidance resources, including problem-solution demonstrations. You may also ask learners to make them explicit during problem solution. As the learner gathers data in Bioworld, she selects a hypothesis and prioritizes evidence to support her hypothesis, eventually comparing her priorities with those of an expert. In this way, not only the solution, that is, the diagnosis, but also the rationale for the solution is made explicit. In the automotive troubleshooting lesson, the only test that can be selected initially is verify the problem. All other test options are inactive. This is a form of guidance to ensure application of the rule of thumb that all failures should be verified as a first step.

### Teaching Monitoring Skills in Your Scenario-Based e-Learning

Problems offer a great opportunity to illustrate and to ask learners to practice monitoring skills. As shown in Figure 7.4, during a demonstration, the learner hears the expert respond to the doctor, but also sees a thought bubble that illustrates a situation-monitoring statement. Adding thought bubbles to demonstrations is a powerful technique to make expert rationale and monitoring explicit. Periodically during problem resolution, learners can be asked to monitor their progress by responding to questions asking them to assess whether they are moving toward their goal and what other actions they might consider. During reflection, the learners can describe what they might have done differently.

## GUIDELINES FOR SUCCESS

If you have decided to conduct some form of knowledge elicitation, here are a few caveats:

### 1. Take Care in Selecting Experts

Since the experts you are interviewing will provide the basis for knowledge and skills potentially disseminated to hundreds of staff, take care in selection of those experts. In some situations, I've had specific experts assigned to my project because their absence would not adversely affect productivity. A different individual would have provided better expertise, but he or she was already overcommitted.

Also consider the level of expertise you need. If your course is for more junior staff, journeyman-level experts might articulate more appropriate scenarios or solutions than would those at the highest level of expertise.

Third, I always feel more comfortable when I am able to draw on several experts. A single expert may have some idiosyncratic approaches to resolving problems. Comparing the approaches of several experts to a similar scenario will help you define common knowledge elements shared by the community of practice. Also look for balance in your experts. In one project I conducted, my organizational liaison was an Army staffer. Even though the organization included civilians and four different military branches, 90 percent of my experts were Army. As I collected data, I felt certain that it was not representative of the work of the broader community of practice. In retrospect, I should have requested a cross-functional committee to nominate individuals with expertise for given classes of problems.

### 2. Don't Over-Extend

Any of the knowledge-elicitation methods I've mentioned will be resource-intensive. The time of experts, interviewers, transcribers, and analysts can add up quickly. Be realistic about what you can accomplish with your resources. Narrow down to problems or problem phases that rely heavily on tacit knowledge that cannot be readily identified in more direct ways.

### 3. Work in a Team

Not only do you need balance in expertise, but it is also helpful to have a diverse team conducting interviews and helping with the analysis. Your analysis team should include subject-matter experts who can ask probing technical questions and interpret responses.

## WHAT DO YOU THINK? REVISITED

Now that we have reviewed knowledge-elicitation techniques, let's revisit the questions. Keep in mind that your context may justify a different answer than mine.

- ❑   A. It's always a good idea to conduct knowledge-elicitation interviews as the basis for scenario-based e-learning.

- ❑   B. Talking aloud while solving a problem is the best method for knowledge elicitation.

- ❑   C. Knowledge-elicitation interviews are efficient substitutes for traditional task analysis techniques.

- ❑   D. Cues in problem scenarios are an important element of critical thinking skills.

I consider Option A to be false. In some situations you can identify much of the important content from traditional job analysis methods, including work observations and traditional interviews. Some scenario domains, such as tradeoffs or situations that involve highly structured problems, can often be built based on documentation, interviews, and observations.

Option B is both true and false. In their research, Van Gog, Paas, Van Merrienboer, and Witte (2005) obtained the best data from concurrent verbalization. However, they did constrain the other methods, which may have yielded more complete data otherwise. In addition, there are many situations that will not lend themselves to verbalization during problems solving as discussed in this chapter.

Option C I consider false. Knowledge elicitation is resource-intensive and should be reserved for important tasks that cannot be validly identified in more efficient ways.

Option D is true. The ability to identify, act on, and interpret cues such as sounds, visuals, or patterns found in text documentation often distinguishes expert problem solving from problem solving by less experienced staff. Cues are often stored in memory as tacit knowledge, and experts may not readily articulate them in traditional interviews.

## COMING NEXT

Throughout the first eleven chapters of this book, I have summarized the what, when, why, and how of scenario-based e-learning. However, even the best design possible will fall short in a poorly executed project. In the last chapter I review some guidelines unique to scenario-based e-learning projects to help you sell, plan, develop, and implement your course.

## ADDITIONAL RESOURCES

Crandall, B., Klein, G., & Hoffman, R.B. (2006). *Working minds: A practitioner's guide to cognitive task analysis.* Cambridge, MA: MIT Press.
I find this book very practical, with real-world examples, and it's one of my training Bibles.

Van Gog, T., Paas, F., van Merrienboer, J.J.G., & Witte, P. (2005). Uncovering the problem-solving process: Cued retrospective reporting versus concurrent and retrospective reporting. *Journal of Experimental Psychology: Applied, 11,* 237–244.
This is a technical report that I summarized in this chapter. I think it's a good example of the type of research that will be helpful to practitioners who want to take an evidence-based approach to cognitive task analysis.

## SCENARIO-BASED e-LEARNING AND YOU: ELICITING TACIT KNOWLEDGE

Answer the questions below to decide whether, where, and how to include knowledge elicitation as part of your job analysis.

1. Should you conduct knowledge elicitation analysis?

   ☐ The standard job and task analysis methods such as observations and interviews will not reveal sufficient critical thinking skills underlying expert problem solutions.

   ☐ You will have access to appropriate experts who can participate in the interviews.

   ☐ You can narrow the focus of the analysis to tasks and decisions that are manageable given your resources.

   ☐ The validity of your training is likely to be improved substantially by identifying and incorporating critical thinking skills surfaced via elicitation interviews.

   ☐ The critical thinking skills underlying performance are sufficiently important and stable to warrant the effort invested.

   ☐ You have resources to conduct interviews and analyze interview data.

2. Should you use concurrent verbalization?

   ☐ Verbalization is not required to complete the target tasks.

   ☐ Appropriate problems or problem simulations are available, sufficiently brief, and practical to allow concurrent verbalization.

   ☐ Privacy policies will not be violated.

   ☐ Pilot trials indicate that experts will provide appropriate critical thinking knowledge and skills through concurrent verbalization.

3. Should you use after-the-fact stories?

   ☐ Concurrent verbalization is not feasible.

   ☐ You need critical thinking details such as cues, rationale, and rules of thumb that did not surface during concurrent verbalization or traditional interviews.

   ☐ You need to identify features that distinguish simpler from more complex scenarios.

   ☐ You need a repository of scenarios that can be adapted to your instructional goals.

4. Should you use reflection on recorded behaviors?

☐ You did not obtain sufficient critical thinking details from other methods.

☐ It is likely that experts describing past experiences will be subject to forgetting or distorting events.

☐ You have practical ways to record problem-solving performance using tools such as video, eye tracking, and keystroke recording.

☐ Privacy policies will not be violated.

5. Can you identify critical tacit knowledge needed from transcripts?

☐ Decisions that underpin the actions they took.

☐ The cues that influenced actions and other mental events.

☐ Rationale and rules of thumb.

☐ Monitoring events such as situation assessment, goals set, progress assessed, and changes made.

6. Does your team have a workable process to ensure the success of cognitive task analysis?

☐ Identification of specific knowledge types such as cues, domain concepts, rationale, or monitoring likely to distinguish expert from sub-expert performance.

☐ Narrowing to several high-impact tasks or task segments that rely on critical thinking skills.

☐ Construction of a number of specific probing questions to be used during knowledge-elicitation interviews.

☐ Opportunities to collaboratively practice coding transcripts to assure consistency in analysis.

☐ Access to SMEs with sufficient and adequate expertise.

# CHAPTER

## 12

# IMPLEMENTING SCENARIO-BASED e-LEARNING

In previous chapters we've reviewed the analysis, design, development, and evaluation of scenario-based e-learning. But I would be remiss not to acknowledge the importance of the context in which your scenario-based e-learning courses are proposed, approved, created, and deployed. You can adopt a low- or a high-profile road to your project. A low-profile approach involves planning, creating, and deploying a scenario-based e-learning lesson or course with a minimum of fanfare, typically using your tried-and-true processes for e-learning projects. You may even decide *not to give* any special name or attention to the project. A low-profile approach is the "*better to ask forgiveness than to ask for permission*" path. It might be the wiser path to design and test your first projects, buying you time to learn and improve subsequent efforts.

However, if you are planning a scenario-based e-learning course that will consume more resources than normal or will otherwise draw attention, or if it is a course that you would like to use as a showcase piece for your organization, it's a good idea to do some high-profile prework to obtain and maintain stakeholder support. In this chapter I summarize four steps to a successful project—steps that you can implement informally and quietly with a small team or that you can deploy in a formal and visible project process.

## WHAT DO YOU THINK?

As prework for you, put a checkmark next to statements that you believe or have found to be true in your training projects:

❑   Project implementation from planning to deployment can be more important than the actual training itself.

❑   Projects such as scenario-based e-learning should be preceded by a business case.

❑   A prototype lesson is more important in scenario-based e-learning than in other types of e-learning.

❑   Generally, scenario-based e-learning will yield good return on investment.

## FOUR STEPS TO PROJECT SUCCESS

Let's take a look at some steps you can adapt to your own context that will increase the probability of getting your scenario-based e-learning off the ground and minimize the turbulence of a new design and development effort.

## STEP ONE: PRESENT A STRONG BUSINESS CASE

In many situations, you will need to "sell" your scenario-based e-learning project—especially if it will require substantial resources or will be uniquely visible to your client as an approach quite different from status quo courseware. In the following sections I provide suggestions, along with some sample resource data based on recommendations from experienced scenario-based e-learning practitioners.

### Visualize Scenario-Based e-Learning for Stakeholders

Chances are your stakeholders won't know what you mean by scenario-based e-learning or whatever term you decide to use. I recommend that you start your kickoff meeting with a demonstration. It could be a rough prototype of the course you are planning or some samples of external courses that effectively illustrate the key design features of scenario-based e-learning. When selling scenario-based e-learning, a few pictures really are worth a thousand words. Starting the conversation with an effective, concrete example gets attention and generates immediate interest. Depending on your audience, you may even want to contrast scenario-based e-learning with a more traditional directive or receptive lesson to stimulate a discussion of the differences between them.

### Determine the Magnitude of the Performance Gap

I assume that you have completed a performance analysis and determined that a knowledge and skill gap is one barrier to achieving organizational goals. At this point, get an estimate of the costs of the skill gap. The costs of ineffective performance can help you position the potential gains from an investment in scenario-based e-learning.

Take your first clues from a review of performance data linked to operational goals such as sales, customer complaints, scrap, audits, fines, and so forth, supplemented by staff interviews and observations at field sites. Some typical comments or data from management might allude to dollars lost due to waste, lost sales, employee attrition, or customer dissatisfaction. Ask questions such as: "In an ideal world, if everyone is performing close to the level of our most productive workers, what percentage improvement or dollar gain is it reasonable to expect?"

During the performance analysis, identify the workers, worker teams, job roles, and tasks that most contribute to the organizational goals, along with the specific knowledge and skills that distinguish high from low performers. Document the main knowledge and skills, such as those listed in Table 2.1, as well as the predominant scenario learning domains listed in Table 2.2. For example, suppose that data and management interviews point to electrical troubleshooting as a major task category leading to performance gaps, such as disappointed customers or too much time wasted in inefficient problem solving. Close observations may show that more proficient performers follow a logical troubleshooting process, review schematics early in the problem-solving stages, and also draw on a mental bank of heuristics related to electrical troubleshooting. Your analysis suggests that building expertise around electrical troubleshooting will reduce the performance gap.

### Incident-Driven Training

In some situations your training may be driven by an incident or problem that was sufficiently costly to mandate training as a remediation. In these cases, join the investigation team (or form your own team) to identify the reasons for the incident, and stress to anyone who will listen that training alone is rarely the solution to problems of this type. Often stakeholders will mandate training as a fix-all solution to an incident and assume the problem is now resolved, neglecting other critical performance factors, such as work standards, feedback, and incentives, for example. In other words, take a broad performance perspective. At the same time, no doubt training will be one of the solutions. To mine maximum value for the training effort, conduct interviews about the incident from those involved as well as from other experts to identify the core knowledge and skill gaps, as well as to identify the most relevant scenario domains.

### Compliance Training

Compliance training is often a mandated event required by internal or external regulatory bodies. The training is organized by compliance topic or content, such as information security, ethical conduct, or workplace discrimination. Some lessons simply present the principles—often in terminology written by legal staff. Others include some examples and non-examples and may even add a few interactions. The workforce typically dreads the annual compliance ritual and invests minimal mental effort. The learning management system (LMS) tracks "completions" of these courses, and the "training requirement" box has been checked.

Unfortunately, topic-centered lessons on compliance regulations have a small chance of being translated into work behaviors that will minimize the adverse effects of violations. If any of the previous description sounds familiar, it might be time to treat compliance like any other important knowledge and skill topic and integrate it into task-centered training, performance support, and other critical performance factors, such as specific goals, regular and specific feedback, incentives, reminders, and so on. This does not necessarily mean you need to use a scenario-based e-learning design, although it does offer a solution to make compliance training interactive and job-centered.

## Identify Tradeoffs to Diverse Solution Options

Consider the different ways that your training has been or could be delivered to achieve the performance goals. For example, to build automotive troubleshooting expertise, training could be delivered via (1) on-the-job training (OJT) using coaching during actual shop operations, (2) instructor-led classes using either real or mocked equipment with simulated failures, or (3) a scenario-based e-learning self-paced lab similar to the one I have shown in this book.

There are several drawbacks to an OJT approach. First, in an actual shop, auto failures will not present themselves in a balanced or optimal sequence for learning. Second, the learning environment will be inconsistent, depending on the coach and the particular failures that surface. Third, each shop will have to allocate the time of an experienced worker for coaching purposes. Last, learning time will be equivalent to real elapsed time needed to resolve a failure. On the positive side, no additional time is needed to develop instructional materials, so actual work can be accomplished during the training cycle.

A well-planned instructor-led lab using real equipment with actual or simulated failures has the advantage of consistency and a logical learning progression. Likewise, it makes efficient use of expertise by assigning one or two expert instructors to a group of learners. In addition, the high social presence among instructors and students in a classroom or laboratory setting can add instructional value. On the downside, learners will incur travel costs getting to and residing near centralized training centers. Secondly, although time to perform repairs will be more efficient than in an OJT setting, it will still be longer than in a simulated multimedia environment.

In contrast, if using a scenario-based e-learning self-paced lab, similar to the instructor-led class, the sequence of failures can be organized to provide a consistent and optimal learning experience. Also, with the scenario-based e-learning, you will accrue savings in travel expenses and learning time will be compressed. Depending on the size of your current and anticipated learning audience, these savings could be considerable. On the downside, a scenario-based e-learning development project may require a larger up-front investment than a face-to-face class and may also cost more to update, depending on (1) what media you use, for example, video versus animation, as well as (2) the volatility of your content. Therefore, you will need to estimate costs incurred and saved to present a balanced argument.

As you can see, each delivery option has advantages and disadvantages. This is the reason that a recent U.S. Department of Education Report (2010) found best learning from blended solutions that made use of the best features of a combination of in-person and digital training. For example, novice technicians could start training with a prework self-study program that oriented them to basic terminology and troubleshooting methods. Next, a two- or three-week instructor-led session would consist primarily of hands-on troubleshooting in a laboratory setting. Third, after some time back on the job, scenario-based e-learning could be used to accelerate expertise of apprentice technicians.

### Delivery Media Tradeoff Analysis for Automotive Troubleshooting

Automotive service industry experts estimate that a typical entry-level technician may require exposure to about one hundred successful diagnostic experiences (that is, one hundred work orders) in order to achieve baseline troubleshooting competencies in a particular class of failures such as brakes, transmission, engine, etc. In Table 12.1 I summarize the amount of time needed to complete the one hundred work orders in the three delivery environments summarized above. As you can see, the scenario-based e-learning requires only about 16 percent of the training time needed in an OJT environment to achieve minimal competency. You will need to translate that time savings into dollars to determine whether the savings justify the expense to design and develop scenarios.

To apply this process to your own context, list your delivery alternatives with advantages and disadvantages to each. Determine the number of current and future projected learners. Evaluate the volatility of your content. Ask experienced supervisors or managers for estimates of the approximate number of situations or cases needed to achieve target levels of competency, and contrast the time and other costs to achieve those levels. See Table 12.2 for a checklist summary.

**TABLE 12.1.**  **Time to Reach Automotive Troubleshooting Competency in Three Learning Environments**

| Learning Environment | Time/Work Order | Time to Complete 100 Work Orders |
| --- | --- | --- |
| In Dealership: OJT | 2 to 6 hours | 200+ hours |
| Instructor-Led | 1 hour | 100 hours |
| Scenario-Based e-Learning | 20 to 40 minutes | 33 to 66 hours |

## TABLE 12.2.   Steps to Compare Training Delivery Alternatives

❑ Determine the costs of doing nothing to close the performance gap:

  ❑ Lost sales

  ❑ Disappointed customers

  ❑ Scrap

  ❑ Turnover

  ❑ Fines

  ❑ Other:

❑ Identify key job roles linked to the performance gap.

❑ Document the knowledge and skills linked to those roles (see Table 2.1).

❑ Obtain estimates of the amount of experience (number of cases) to reach competency on targeted knowledge and skills.

❑ Obtain data and estimates regarding the number and prior knowledge of current and future learners.

❑ Estimate the volatility of your content.

❑ List your training delivery options.

❑ Identify tradeoffs for training delivery options:

  ❑ Learning time to build expertise

  ❑ Practicality/safety to practice in real environment

  ❑ Effectiveness of learning environment

  ❑ Travel costs

  ❑ Instructor time/costs

  ❑ Benefits of social presence

  ❑ Costs to design and develop learning environment

  ❑ Technology infrastructure

  ❑ Need to update content

❑ Propose scenario-based e-learning for tasks, learners, and delivery media with reasonable cost-benefit.

❑ Consider blends of instructor-led and self-paced digital training to optimize synergy among delivery alternatives.

### Highlight Opportunities to Build Expertise That Are Unavailable or Impractical in Workplace

In many settings on-the-job training may simply not be an option because skills cannot be practiced in an operational setting. Tasks with safety consequences, such as leading a combat mission or making anesthesia decisions, offer two examples. Even if OJT is possible, learning on the job may lead to customer dissatisfaction—or simply may take too long. For example, a long-term sales engagement may require weeks or months to play out, whereas in a virtual world that time can be compressed. In Chapter 2 I summarized a number of tasks that are not feasible to practice in an actual work setting and thus are good candidates for scenario-based e-learning.

### Leverage the Motivational Potential of Scenario-Based e-Learning

Because the trigger event of a scenario-based e-learning lesson situates the learner as an actor to resolve a work-related problem, learning can be both highly engaging and immediately relevant. Research evidence and anecdotal comments suggest that, compared to traditional approaches to learning such as lectures, scenario-based e-learning is more popular with students. Particularly for content that is potentially boring—compliance courses filled with policies and legal mandates, for example—a scenario-based e-learning approach may lead to higher ratings as well as deeper mental engagement that translates into desired behavioral changes. Consider building a short prototype lesson in PowerPoint and testing it out with a small group from your target audience to confirm that the design will be positively received.

### Present Evidence on the Benefits of Scenario-Based e-Learning

In Chapter 10 I summarized research evidence that compared learning from scenario-based e-learning to learning from alternative lesson designs *or* that compared learning from different versions of scenario-based e-learning. Although limited, we do have evidence that a scenario-based e-learning design can generate more effective transfer of learning than other designs and can accelerate expertise through compressed experience. If your stakeholders are likely to be interested in evidence, show some of the research findings I summarized in Chapter 10.

### Estimate Your Production Costs

No doubt some of your stakeholders will be impressed by your demonstrations and discussions of acceleration of expertise with scenario-based e-learning. Still they will ask: "That's all well and good—but how much is this going to cost?" I recommend you incorporate not only the potential cost savings but also production costs as part of your presentation.

As an experienced e-learning developer, you might have data from your previous projects in the form of costs to produce an hour of multimedia learning. Typical estimates range from seventy-five to two hundred hours of analysis, design, and development time per hour of instruction for a receptive or a directive approach to software training. Analysis, design, and production times and resources are often higher for scenario-based e-learning—especially for initial scenarios. Some major factors that will determine your scenario-based e-learning costs include (1) complexity of your design, (2) the navigational structure you plan to use, (3) the media you might include, such as video, audio, computer animations, or still visuals, (4) what, if any, cognitive task analysis is needed, (5) the extent to which you can reuse lesson templates for multiple scenarios, and (6) what expertise and authoring resources you will need for design and development.

In Table 12.3 I summarize the time and costs estimates for three different scenario-based e-learning treatments for a troubleshooting lesson: branched, menu-driven, and whole-screen active object. The resources are estimated as total hours per simulation and costs per scenario. I was surprised to see that the branching template was the most time-consuming, not only for the first scenario but also for subsequent scenarios. In contrast, the whole-screen design required four to five hundred hours for the first simulation; but with the basic graphics, programming, and design completed, subsequent simulations were much less expensive. Once the simulations for the on-screen objects were programmed in Flash, the data was imported to XML making it easy to repurpose to new scenario problems.

Keep in mind that this data is based on scenarios that are relatively complex, requiring access to multiple sources of case data and tracking of the learner's choices during solution. Other domains that require less case data will show different cost patterns. An important point is to consider not only the cost of the initial scenario but how those costs might differ for subsequent scenarios.

## STEP TWO: PLAN YOUR PROJECT

Having gained approval for a scenario-based e-learning course, consider the time and resources needed for the major analysis, design, development, and evaluation activities.

### Plan and Secure Your Resources

As you scope out your project, identify the critical resources you will need, including SME time, graphics, instructional design, and programming expertise. If you are new to scenario-based e-learning and plan a project of medium to high complexity, I recommend you work with an experienced development firm for your initial project. More often than not, the investment in their expertise pays off in fewer pitfalls, sidesteps, and outright project failures. With or without consultant support, you will need SME time. If you are targeting critical thinking skills and will need cognitive task analysis to elicit tacit knowledge, that time could be considerable. Don't forget to also specify the quality of the SME's expertise. Some managers will make their less proficient SMEs available because they can most afford to lose their input to ongoing projects.

Over-estimate your needed SME resources (time and quality) and negotiate those resources with your stakeholders before you commit to the project. Inappropriate or insufficient SME availability is a common cause of projects that either fail or fall far

**TABLE 12.3.** Hours and Cost Comparisons for One Troubleshooting Scenario for Menu, Branched, and Whole-Screen Designs

| Resources | Menu | | Whole-Screen | | Branching | |
|---|---|---|---|---|---|---|
| | Initial Scenario | Subsequent Scenarios | Initial Scenario | Subsequent Scenarios | Initial Scenario | Subsequent Scenarios |
| SME | 75 | 75 | 75 | 70 | 125 | 125 |
| ISD | 75 | 75 | 75 | 10 | 125 | 125 |
| Graphics | 100 | 100 | 150 | 10 | 250 | 250 |
| Programming | 50 | 50 | 100 | 10 | 250 | 150 |
| Total Hours per 30 to 45 min. Scenario | 300 to 400 | 300 to 350 | 400 to 500 | 100 to 125 | 750 to 800 | 650 to 700 |
| Cost @ $50/hr | $15,000 | $15,000 | $20,000 | $5,000 | $37,500 | $32,000 |

Hours based on review of industry averages.

short of potential. Remember the critical elements of your course, such as what scenarios to use, what distinguishes an easier from a more challenging scenario, the work flow, the sources and interpretation of case data, the rationale and heuristics for problem solution, the feedback—all ultimately come from your SMEs. Better to pass up on a scenario-based e-learning approach than to proceed with suboptimal SME input.

### Define and Classify the Target Knowledge and Skills

Depending on the scope of your project, defining and classifying the knowledge and skills to be incorporated into your scenarios may well consume a major segment of overall project time. But it's time well spent. Although the outcomes may be readily specified, breaking these into classes of specific behaviors with associated knowledge and arranging those classes in an optimal sequence of scenarios for learning is a major design task. In Chapter 11, I summarized some techniques you can use to elicit tacit knowledge from experts and to identify what features distinguish simpler from more complex tasks.

As you identify the outcomes and associated knowledge, define domains and tasks within those domains. In domains that involve a problem-solving process—domains such as diagnosis and repair, research, or design—document the work flow of an expert performer. For example, in automotive troubleshooting of an electronic failure, the expert follows six steps to isolate and repair the problem. For domains that require application of policies and procedures, identify the correct policies for each scenario class. For tradeoff domains, identify main sources of diverse expertise and find ways to embed virtual advice into your program.

As you identify the main tasks associated with the work flows or policies, translate them into learning objectives. For example, the automotive troubleshooting course would fall primarily into the diagnostic domain, and critical tasks might include troubleshooting of electronic failures, hydraulic failures, and mechanical failures. A sample learning objective is: "Given a work order with XXX symptoms, the learner will select and interpret appropriate tests and identify the correct failure in the most efficient manner." Recall from Chapter 4 that your design will require a translation of these high-level objectives into more detailed statements that specify the behaviors learners can perform online to record the actions and decisions they make during scenario resolution. For example, the general troubleshooting learning objective may be translated to: "Given a work order specifying XZY, the learner will click on an optimal sequence of on-screen tests and select the correct failure from a list of fifteen failures."

### Consider Your Evaluation Strategy and Secure Resources

Yes, I know it's early in the project and you are busy getting it off the ground. However, an effective evaluation requires planning from the start of your project. Do you need to measure both learner satisfaction and learning? Will you have to develop reliable and valid tests to assess learning? Will you have to conduct a formal validation of any tests used for certification purposes? Is there an opportunity to measure transfer to the job and/or bottom-line benefits of your course? All of these tasks require time and resources that are best factored into the original project plan.

## STEP THREE: DESIGN YOUR APPROACH

### *Template Your Scenario to Align to the Workflow or Design Model*

Take a look at Figures 12.1, 12.2, and 12.3 to review models of templates for the whole-screen, menu, and branched scenario designs. Note that for the automotive troubleshooting lesson using the whole-screen design (Figure 12.1), five core screens serve as the basic template for all scenarios. For a branched scenario template, first map out the critical path, that is, the series of choices that lead to the specified outcome, and then add diversion loops along different stages of the path. Base diversion loops on plausible misconceptions that could lead to suboptimal choices. If using a menu navigation, menu options could reflect the main stages of the workflow or they could be structured to lead to the main design components, such as case data, guidance and

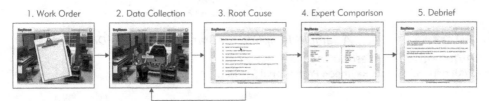

FIGURE 12.1. *A Sample Template for Whole-Screen Automotive Troubleshooting.*
With permission from Raytheon Professional Services.

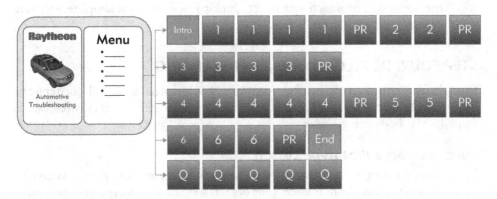

FIGURE 12.2. *A Sample Template for Menu Design of Automotive Troubleshooting.*
With permission from Raytheon Professional Services.

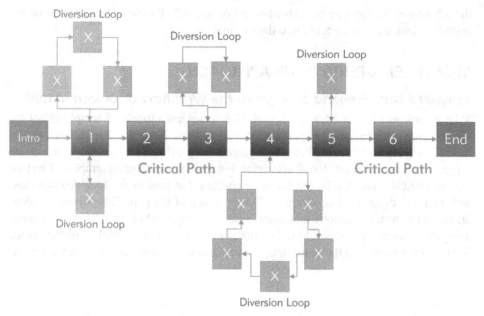

**FIGURE 12.3.** *A Sample Template for Branched Scenario Design of Automotive Troubleshooting.*
With permission from Raytheon Professional Services.

instructional resources, outcome deliverables, and so forth. You can contrast the menu structure for the bank underwriter lesson (Figure 5.1) with that for Bridezilla (Figure 6.6). The bank menu tabs primarily reflect the workflow, whereas the Bridezilla menu tabs primarily link to guidance and instructional elements.

Whatever design approach you select, thinking in terms of a template will save you time and resources in later lessons.

## STEP FOUR: DEVELOP YOUR FIRST SCENARIO

Many books have been written on e-learning development, so I will not replicate their guidance here. However I do recommend a couple of steps especially relevant to scenario-based e-learning

### *Build and Test a Prototype Lesson*

I mentioned previously that as part of your business case, you show your stakeholders either an actual lesson from outside your organization or a prototype you have built. However, as you complete the design activities, you now have a much clearer idea of the content and the learning objectives and have made some decisions about the screen layouts and navigation. You may routinely build prototypes as part of your e-learning development process. If not, it's a good idea to develop a simple operational proto-type of your first scenario. Test the prototype with a few SMEs not involved in the design to glean technical input, and also test with a few learners typical of the target audience to identify problems such as missing content or lack of guidance. If you have developed a learning test, use it now to identify gaps in the instructional support in your lesson.

### Build a Lesson Orientation

If your organization and staff are new to scenario-based e-learning, I strongly recommend a student orientation. Learners used to listening to online lectures or working within the structure of a directive learning design risk disorientation by a learning goal that puts them at the center of the action. Some may feel lost or confused. I recommend you prepare a succinct but meaningful introduction that explains the rationale expectations and main features of the course. Figure 12.4 shows an example from the Bridezilla course.

### Plan Course Launch

We all know that, just because we build it, they won't necessarily come. Or if they have to come, they may not really be there. Apple Computer devotes a great deal of time,

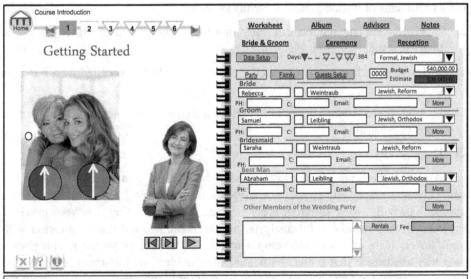

**FIGURE 12.4.** *Part of the Introduction to the Bridezilla Course.*

attention, and energy to new product advertising, packaging, and announcements. How effectively has your team deployed new e-learning products in the past? Were multiple channels used to announce the courses or did they simply show up one day as a new link in your LMS? Was social media used to announce, review, and rate the courseware? If your previous implementations have been suboptimal, use the scenario-based e-learning course as an excuse to plan a better rollout strategy.

### Document "Lessons Learned"

No project flows as we first anticipate. The end product is likely different from your initial vision. Unanticipated outcomes—both negative and positive—emerge along your path. To maximize value from your first efforts, elicit and document lessons learned. Collect data from a variety of sources, including a project manager's journal, input from SMEs, your design and development team, managers, and learners, formal data collected from evaluation tools, spreadsheets, and so forth. Synthesize your data into a report that can inform your next projects to promote a cycle of continuous improvement.

## WHAT DO YOU THINK? REVISITED

We started the chapter with some statements for you to consider, based on your previous experiments or instincts. Below are my opinions.

❏ A. Project implementation from planning to deployment can be more important than the actual training itself.

❏ B. Projects such as scenario-based e-learning should be preceded by a business case.

❏ C. A prototype lesson is more important in scenario-based e-learning than in other types of e-learning.

❏ D. Generally, scenario-based e-learning will yield good return on investment.

Although there are always exceptions, I believe the first three statements are generally true. Especially if your scenario-based training project is a relatively new approach or will involve different processes and/or more funding than your previous projects, I recommend careful analysis, project planning, and communication with your stakeholders and design/development team. I think a prototype lesson goes a long way to advance your project by helping stakeholders, subject-matter experts, and staff understand the approach and also to pinpoint missing requirements early in the process.

Regarding D, I believe that scenario-based e-learning has some potential opportunities for good ROI, but certainly not in all situations. I recommend it be used as one resource in your toolkit of performance solutions used to help your organization achieve bottom-line objectives.

## COMING NEXT: YOUR SCENARIO-BASED e-LEARNING PROJECT

This chapter concludes this book, which I hope has given you a useful overview and solid introduction to the major features and applications of scenario-based e-learning. Like all learning approaches, scenario-based e-learning is not suitable for every performance gap and every training need. My hope is that the guidelines and examples in this book will help you pinpoint optimal opportunities and adapt these ideas to your own organizational needs. It's always helpful to hear from you with suggestions, success stories, and lessons learned. Please contact me at Ruth@Clarktraining.com.

## ADDITIONAL RESOURCES

Cross, J., & Dublin, L. (2002). *Implementing e-learning.* Alexandria, VA: ASTD Press.

Phillips, J.J., & Phillips, P.P. (2007). *The value of learning: How organizations capture value and ROI and translate it into support, improvement, and funds.* San Francisco: Pfeiffer.

There are many excellent resources on training implementation. I recommend you supplement this list with a search using terms such as implementing training, implementing e-learning, training project management, and so on to find resources related to the topics of this chapter.

## SCENARIO-BASED e-LEARNING AND YOU:
## PLANNING YOUR IMPLEMENTATION

Throughout the book I've provided detailed checklists for you to adapt to your own context as you tackle each stage of a scenario-based e-learning design. In this final checklist, I summarize the important elements to consider as you propose, sell, plan, and implement your project. Feel free to add steps that you already use for your e-learning projects.

**A Project Checklist**

A. Plan a "sales" presentation with rationale relevant to your stakeholders. Choose and add to the following topics:

- What is scenario-based e-learning: Start with demonstrations.

    - ☐ Use a demonstration borrowed from an outside source.

    - ☐ Use a demonstration from a vendor you will work with.

    - ☐ Construct a short demonstration using your own content.

    - ☐ Compare a scenario-based e-learning demonstration with traditional approaches in your organization.

- What are the current costs of the organization's performance gaps?

- What is the tradeoff costs among alternative delivery approaches?

- How can the advantages of different delivery options be optimized in a blended solution?

- How much time could be saved with acceleration of expertise?

    - ☐ How many cases or hours are needed to build acceptable levels of competency in tasks related to the performance gaps?

    - ☐ How many hours will be needed to deliver sufficient cases in diverse delivery environments?

- What is the feasibility of building expertise on the job (OJT)?

    - ☐ Safety concerns

    - ☐ Time concerns

    - ☐ Adverse impact concerns

    - ☐ Consistency concerns

    - ☐ Practical concerns such as cost

- What is the motivational potential among your learners of a scenario-based e-learning approach?

- What is the evidence of the effectiveness of scenario-based e-learning?

- What are the cost estimates for development of scenario-based e-learning?

- What is an estimate of the costs and benefits of a scenario-based e-learning approach along with a summary of the resources (don't forget SME resources) you will need to design and produce an effective product?

- Other:

B. Plan Your Project
- Secure the resources you will need for the project.
  - ☐ SME expertise
  - ☐ Graphic design, instructional designers, writers, programmers
  - ☐ Budget to hire external contractor
  - ☐ Authoring system(s)

- Define critical work tasks to be trained linked to the performance gap.
  - ☐ Specify high-level tasks that distinguish expert from novice performance.
  - ☐ Identify the key knowledge and skills and domains for those tasks.
  - ☐ Write higher- and lower-level learning objectives for the scenarios.
- Plan the evaluation.
  - ☐ Learner reaction (rating sheets, focus groups, course completions)
  - ☐ Learning (tests)
  - ☐ Transfer (job metrics)
  - ☐ Bottom line (improvement in the performance gap minus training costs)

C. Design Your Project
- ☐ Identify classes of scenarios.
- ☐ Identify criteria for easier and more challenging scenarios.
- ☐ Identify tacit knowledge underlying critical decision making of experts.
- ☐ Define the screen design and navigational template.
- ☐ Complete and evolve the design plan presented in this book.

D. Develop Your Project
- ☐ Build and test a working prototype for one scenario.
- ☐ Build a lesson orientation.
- ☐ Plan course implementation.
- ☐ Identify and store reusable elements of your lessons.

E. Roll Out Your Course
- ☐ Marketing
- ☐ Promotion through social media

F. Document and Apply Lessons Learned
- ☐ What elements of the process were smoother and more effective than others?

☐ Where did unanticipated barriers arise?

☐ How could these be avoided in future projects?

☐ What did you learn from evaluation data?

☐ What are the strengths/weaknesses of your initial courses?

☐ How can future processes and products be improved?

# APPENDIX

# AN INTRODUCTION TO THE SCENARIO-BASED e-LEARNING EXAMPLES

Throughout the book I include screen shots from diverse scenario-based e-learning courses to illustrate the concepts and guidelines of each chapter. Some screen shots are from actual courses, and others were designed specifically for this book. To provide you with context, in this section I summarize background information on the seven main lessons I have used, accompanied by a screen shot. I introduce the lessons in the order in which they appear in the book.

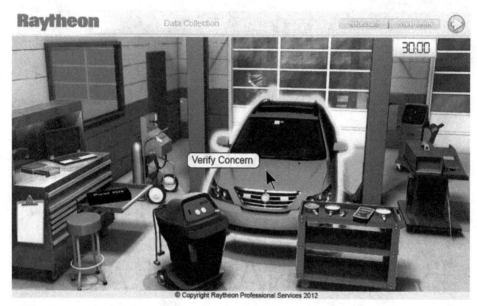

**FIGURE A.1.** *A Virtual Automotive Shop.*
With permission from Raytheon Professional Services.

## COURSE 1: AUTOMOTIVE TROUBLESHOOTING

*Major Features*

| | |
|---|---|
| Goal | To build skills in troubleshooting of automotive failures |
| Audience | Apprentice automotive technicians |
| Reason for scenario-based e-learning design | Troubleshooting in the service center takes more time than online; some failures are relatively infrequent and failures do not occur in a logical learning sequence. |
| Knowledge and skills involved | Facts, concepts, mental models, analysis, rules of thumb, monitor progress |
| Learning domains | Diagnosis and repair |
| Objectives | Given work orders, the learner will use a logical sequence to apply tests and interpret data to diagnose failure in most efficient manner |

The whole-screen design includes simulated diagnostic testing objects in the service bay, which, when selected, will display testing data appropriate to the failure.

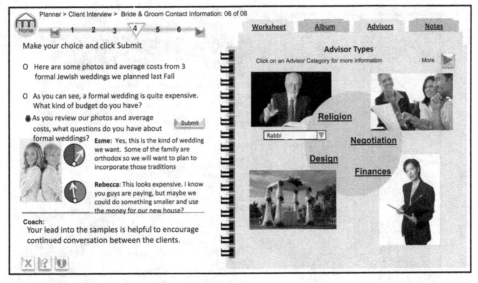

**FIGURE A.2.** *The Learner Can Access Virtual Advisors for Wedding Planning.*

## COURSE 2: BRIDEZILLA

### *Major Features*

| | |
|---|---|
| Goal | To train the knowledge and skills associated with wedding planning |
| Audience | Newly hired wedding planners |
| Reason for scenario-based e-learning approach | The task requires critical thinking and specialized knowledge domains; opportunity to accelerate expertise |
| Knowledge and skills involved | Facts, concepts, procedure, analysis, rules of thumb, create a product |
| Learning domains | Interpersonal skills, tradeoffs, design |
| Objectives | Given client inquiries, the learner will interview client, identify needs and constraints, and select optimum wedding features that balance needs and constraints |

The left side of the screen uses a branched scenario for the client interview. Tabs on the right side lead to worksheets for planning the wedding, examples under the album tab, domain-specific information under the advisors tabs, and notes.

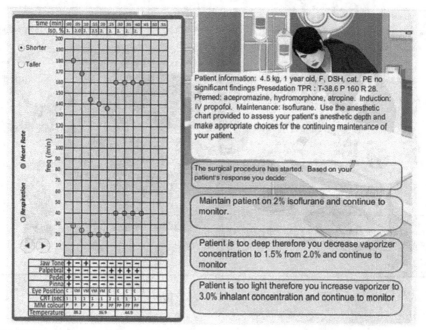

**FIGURE A.3.** *A Branched Scenario Can Be Based on Links in Presentation Software.*
With permission from Veterinary Information Network.

## COURSE 3: ANIMAL ANESTHESIA

*Major Features*

| | |
|---|---|
| Goal | To train the adjustment of anesthetic dosage based on physical signs of the animal and the surgical stage |
| Audience | Anesthetic technicians, veterinarians |
| Reason for scenario-based e-learning design | The task has high safety consequences and is best practiced in a simulated or multimedia setting. Some surgical events may be infrequent and scenario-based e-learning offers an opportunity to learn/refresh unusual events. |
| Knowledge and skills involved | Facts, concepts, mental models, analysis, rules of thumb, monitoring |
| Learning domains | Diagnosis and repair |
| Objectives | Given physical signs and surgical progress, learner will select the correct anesthetic dosage to maintain optimal anesthetic depth |

This branched scenario design allows the learner to make anesthetic adjustments based on physical signs shown in a left-hand chart, as well as surgical process summarized on the right side of the screen.

**FIGURE A.4.** *The Learner Has the Opportunity to Make Better Decisions to Avoid This Failed Situation.*
With permission from Will Interactive.

## COURSE 4: GATOR 6

*Major Features*

| | |
|---|---|
| Goal | To train new combat officers in effective leadership and decision-making skills |
| Audience | Army officers |
| Reason for scenario-based e-learning design | The task has high-risk safety consequences; combat situations are not routine and scenario-based e-learning offers a safe opportunity to apply decision-making skills |
| Knowledge and skills involved | Facts, concepts, mental models, analysis, rules of thumb, monitoring |
| Learning domains | Interpersonal skills, compliance, analysis and rationale, tradeoffs, team coordination |
| Objectives | Given multiple demands, learners will select actions most likely to optimize combat outcomes |

After an introductory battle scenario in which lives are lost unnecessarily, the learner is assigned the role of the commander and has the opportunity to go back in time and make decisions that will result in a better outcome.

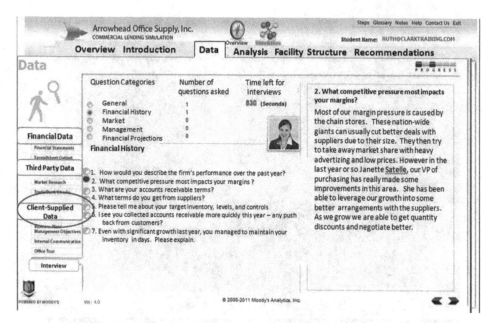

**FIGURE A.5.** *To Interview Client Managers, the Learner Must Select from a List of Questions in a Limited Time Frame.*
With permission from Moody's Analytics.

## COURSE 5: BANK UNDERWRITER TRAINING

*Major Features*

| | |
|---|---|
| Goal | To train the process and decisions involved in commercial loan underwriting |
| Audience | Apprentice underwriters |
| Reason for scenario-based e-learning design | The task requires critical thinking and specialized knowledge domains; opportunity to accelerate expertise; some loan scenarios are infrequent and the process can be accelerated online |
| Knowledge and skills involved | Facts, concepts, mental models, analysis, rules of thumb, create a product, monitoring |
| Learning domains | Compliance, research, analysis, and rationale |
| Objectives | Given loan applicants, the learner will identify and interpret relevant case data and make and justify a loan recommendation with acceptable risk |

In analysis and design cases, gathering and analyzing case data is a central feature. Here, the learner can collect financial, third-party, and client-supplied data. On this screen the learner has limited time to select the most productive questions to ask the client.

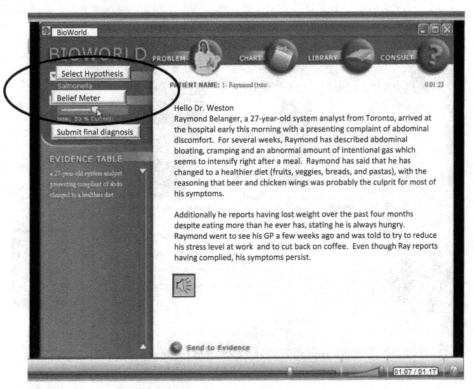

**FIGURE A.6.**  *Learners Indicate Confidence in Their Hypotheses with the Belief Meter Slider Bar (Upper Left Corner).*
With permission from Susanne Lajoie, McGill University.

## COURSE 6: BIOWORLD

### *Major Features*

| | |
|---|---|
| Goal | To train science and medical students in critical thinking skills linked to medical diagnosis |
| Audience | College students |
| Reason for scenario-based e-learning design | The task requires critical thinking and specialized knowledge domains; scenario-based e-learning can prompt the learners to make their thinking process explicit |
| Knowledge and skills involved | Facts, concepts, mental models, analysis, rules of thumb, monitoring |
| Learning domains | Diagnosis and repair |
| Objectives | Given patient cases, learners will identify, prioritize, and interpret relevant data to select a diagnosis |

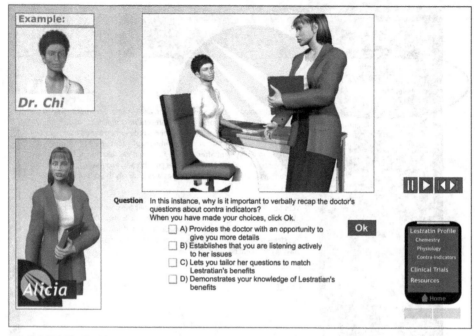

**FIGURE A.7.** *Following a Video Example of Responding to Objections, Questions Are Used to Promote Engagement with the Example.*

## COURSE 7: PHARMACEUTICAL ACCOUNT REPRESENTATIVE TRAINING

*Major Features*

| | |
|---|---|
| Goal | To train pharmaceutical account representatives how to present and overcome objections to a new drug |
| Audience | Apprentice and experienced pharmaceutical account representatives |
| Reason for scenario-based e-learning design | The task has high adverse consequences of poor performance; some clinical situations may be infrequent; scenario-based e-learning provides an opportunity to accelerate expertise; learning product knowledge in a sales context should promote transfer to the workplace |
| Knowledge and skills involved | Facts, concepts, mental models, analysis, rules of thumb, monitoring |

Learning domains          Interpersonal skills, research, analysis, rationale
Objectives                Given physician visits, learners will present new drug features and benefits and respond effectively to questions or objections

In the pharmaceutical course, an avatar models best practices in presenting features and benefits of a new drug and responding to physician questions. This type of lesson would be a useful prerequisite to an instructor-led role-play session for newer representatives and would likely suffice on its own for experienced representatives.

# APPENDIX

# B

# REPEATED FIGURES

The format of a book constrains the number of figures that can easily be displayed in conjunction with the text describing the figures. Therefore, some figures are referenced in several places throughout the book. All figures are online at www.pfeiffer.com/go/scenario,

**FIGURE 1.1.** *A Virtual Automotive Shop.*
With permission from Raytheon Professional Services.

but I have also placed figures referenced in multiple chapters here for easy access while reading the book. You might put a bookmark on this section for ease of access.

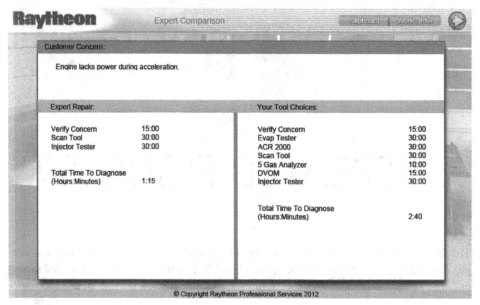

**FIGURE 1.2.**  *Learner Actions (on Right) Compared with Expert Actions (on Left).*
With permission from Raytheon Professional Services.

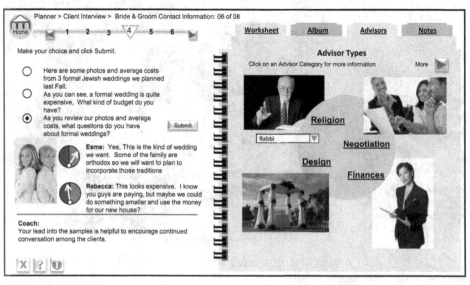

**FIGURE 1.3.**  *The Learner Can Access Virtual Advisors for Wedding Planning.*

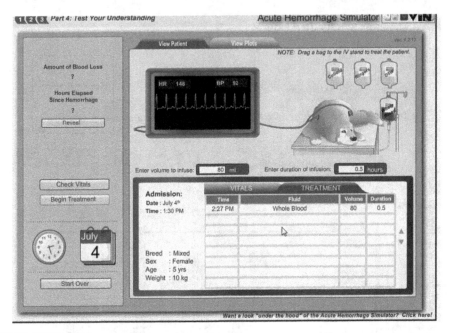

FIGURE 1.4. *A Scenario-Based e-Learning Simulation of Treatment of a Dog for Blood Loss.*
With permission from Veterinary Information Network.

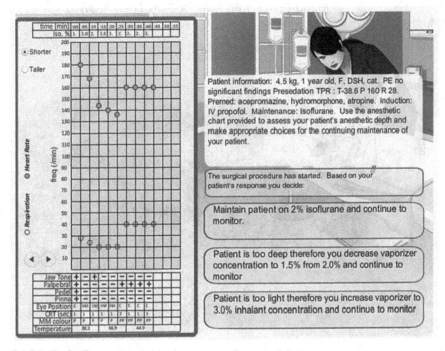

FIGURE 1.5. *A Branched Scenario Can Be Based on Links in Presentation Software.*
With permission from Veterinary Information Network.

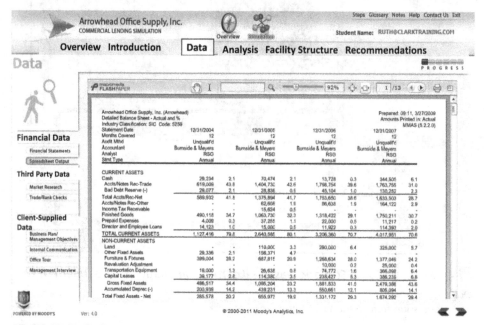

**FIGURE 2.3.** *A Menu-Driven Interface for Bank Loan Analysis.*
With permission from Moody's Analytics.

**FIGURE 3.3.** *Persistent Failure Symptoms Provide Intrinsic Feedback to Selection of an Incorrect Failure Cause.*
With permission from Raytheon Professional Services.

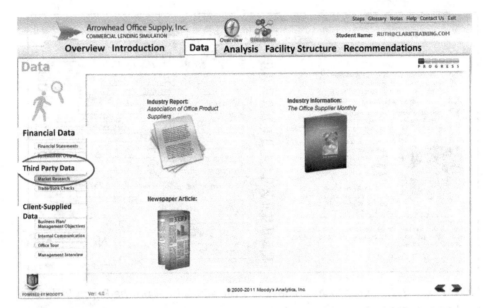

**FIGURE 5.1.** *The Upper Tabs and Left Menu Links Link to Scenario Data.*
With permission from Moody's Analytics.

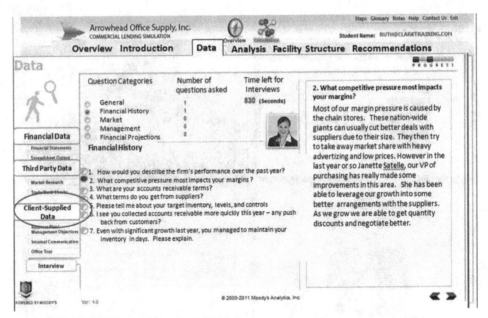

**FIGURE 5.2.** *To Interview Client Managers, the Learner Must Select Relevant Questions in a Limited Time Frame.*
With permission from Moody's Analytics.

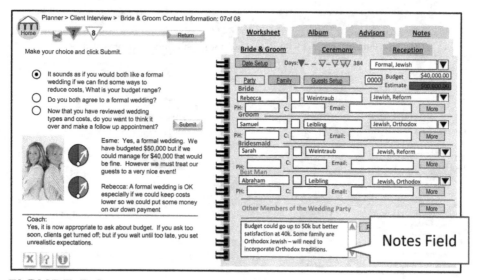

**FIGURE 5.3.** *Client Data Is Saved in the Worksheet on the Right, Including the Lower-Right Notes Field.*

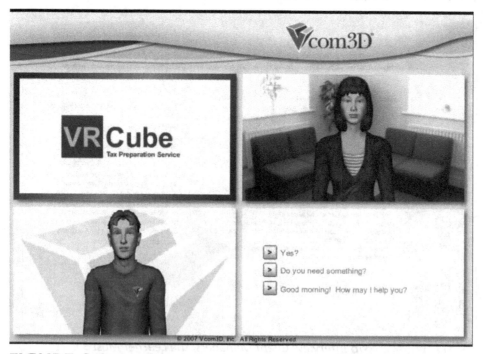

**FIGURE 6.1.** *A Customer Service Scenario-Based e-Lesson.*
With permission from Vcom 3D.

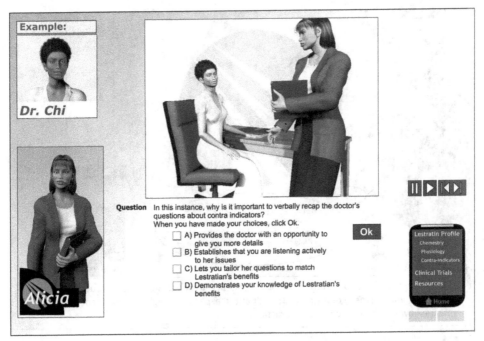

**FIGURE 6.4.** *Following a Video Example of Responding to Objections, Questions Are Used to Promote Engagement with the Example.*

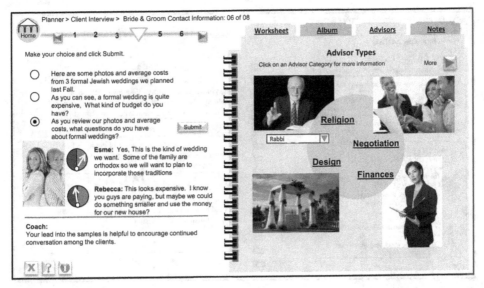

**FIGURE 6.6.** *The Album and Advisor Tabs (Upper Right) Link to Guidance in the Bridezilla Lesson.*

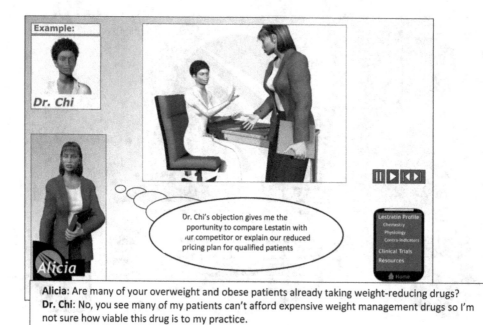

**FIGURE 7.4.** *A Cognitive Modeling Example Illustrates Not Only the How But Also the Why.*

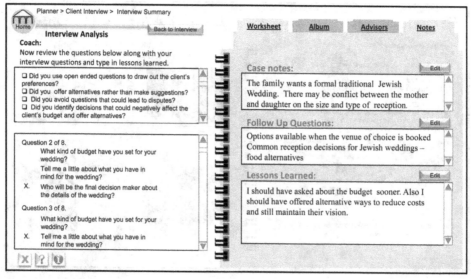

**FIGURE 8.2.** *Response Windows (on the Right Side of the Screen) Encourage Learners to Reflect on Feedback.*

# APPENDIX

# RELIABILITY AND VALIDITY FOR LEARNING MEASURES FOR SCENARIO-BASED e-LEARNING

In Chapter 9 I review different paths to evaluate the outcomes of your scenario-based e-learning project. If you plan to evaluate learning outcomes, you will need to construct tests that are reliable and valid. This appendix reviews the basics of reliability and validity. Read it if you plan to measure learning outcomes and if you need a refresher. For detailed information, I recommend *Criterion-Referenced Test Development* by Shrock and Coscarelli (2007).

## ENSURE TEST RELIABILITY

A test will never be valid unless it's reliable. One of your first tasks is to prepare enough test items to support reliability. Basically a reliable test is one that gives consistent results. There are three forms of reliability, any of which you might need to evaluate learning from scenario-based e-learning. These are equivalence, test-retest, and inter-rater reliability.

## Equivalence Reliability

Equivalence among different forms of a test means that test Version A will give more or less the same results as test Version B. Equivalence would be important if you plan a pretest-posttest comparison of learning. It would also be important if learners must reach a set criterion on the test to demonstrate competency. For those who fail the test on their first attempt, after some remediation, they will take a second test, which must be equivalent to the first but should not be identical to the first. As an example of reliability, Test A with twenty items and Test B with twenty different items would yield similar scores when taken by the same individuals (assuming no changes in those individuals). A person who scores 60 percent on Version A, will score close to 60 percent on Version B of an equivalent test.

## Test-Retest Reliability

A second form of reliability is called test-retest reliability. Test-retest reliability means that the same person who took the test today and the same test tomorrow, without any additional learning, would score more or less the same both times. Test-retest reliability is a measure of the consistency of any given test over time.

## Inter-Rater Reliability

Inter-rater reliability is the third type to consider. You may need to include open-ended test questions such as *respond in a role play* or *draw a circuit* to evaluate some of the strategic or critical thinking outcomes of scenario-based e-learning. Open-ended tests such as a role play will typically have multiple correct solutions. Therefore, you will need raters to evaluate responses, and it will be important that the raters be consistent in their scoring. If you use a single rater, it will be important for that individual to score each product in a consistent manner. If you use multiple raters, it will be additionally important that the group of raters be consistent in how they assess the same product.

For example, if a test involves a role play or requires the learner to create a product such as a drawing to illustrate a deeper understanding of principles, a human must review and "score" the product or performance. Consistency among your raters is called inter-rater reliability. As an aside, using raters on a large scale to evaluate outcomes is a labor-intensive activity. Therefore, you may want to use raters during pilot stages of scenario-based e-learning evaluation or in high-stakes situations in which individual performance is critical enough to warrant the investment and when other more efficient testing methods such as multiple-choice questions would lack sufficient sensitivity or validity to assess knowledge and skill competency.

## Build Reliable Tests

How do you ensure your test is reliable? In general, longer tests are more reliable, although the exact length will depend on several factors, including knowledge and skill scope and task criticality. How broad is the span of knowledge and skills that you are measuring? A reliable test for an entire course or unit must include more items than a reliable test for a single lesson. How critical are the skills being assessed? More critical skills warrant longer tests and higher reliability correlations. There are no absolute answers but, in general, your test should include from five to twenty-five questions, depending on span and criticality.

There are statistical equations to calculate the reliability of your test. A perfect correlation between the scores of two forms of a test or two raters, for example, would be 1.00. Two tests with items that are completely unrelated would have a correlation of 0. You should obtain professional guidance on an acceptable correlation, but as a general figure it should be above +.85 for critical competencies and above +.70 for important competencies (Shrock & Coscarelli, 2007).

## ENSURE TEST VALIDITY

A valid test is one that measures what it is supposed to measure. Remember your driving test? Most likely you completed a written test that evaluated your knowledge of the facts and concepts associated with driving. A high score on a written test, however, would not be a valid indicator of a competent driver. For that, you needed to take the dreaded behind-the-wheel examination—a performance test in which the examiner (hopefully) used a rating scale to assess driving skill and asked you to perform a reasonable sampling of common driving maneuvers.

### Items to Measure Knowledge Topics

As illustrated in Figure C.1, test validity rests on a solid link from the job analysis to the learning objectives and, finally, to the test items. That's why learning objectives are as important in scenario-based e-learning as in any form of training. Many scenario-based e-learning lessons may include learning objectives that focus on knowledge. For example, the Bridezilla course may include an objective requiring learners to identify key terms and practices of different religious or ethnic marriage traditions. For facts and concepts you can use multiple-choice test items such as the one in Figure C.2.

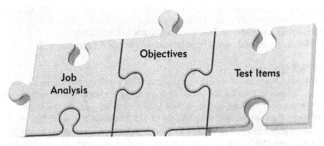

**FIGURE C.1.**  *A Valid Test Links Test Questions to Job Knowledge and Skills via Learning Objectives.*

> For the Jewish wedding ceremony, which of the following should be available under the Chuppah:
>
> A. A plate
> B. A small bowl of water
> C. Two glasses of wine
> D. A loaf of challah bread

**FIGURE C.2.** *A Sample Multiple-Choice Item to Measure Facts or Concepts.*

## Items to Measure Problem-Solving Skills

In addition to facts and concepts, scenario-based e-learning typically has some form of problem-solving objective. To evaluate problem-solving skills, your test will require learners to solve problems similar to those faced in the workplace and practiced in the training. While you could evaluate problem-solving ability on the job, it may not be easy to assess worker competence in the job setting. For many reasons, such as safety, expense, and time, some skills cannot easily be evaluated on the job. Instead, construct tests that come as close to real-world problem solving as practical. A simulation or scenario-driven test might be your best option. Your test scenarios may be quite similar to those presented during the training. These types of tests are called near transfer because the skill demonstrated is quite similar to the skills practiced in the training.

To evaluate learning transfer, you might include items that require the learner to apply new skills to somewhat different problems. These types of items are called far transfer because the learners will need to adapt what they learned to different situations than those practiced in the training. For example, in Figure C.3 are two potential simulation test questions for the Bridezilla course. The first item is quite similar to the kinds of scenarios included in the training. The second question focuses on an anniversary celebration with a number of potential differences from a wedding ceremony. Since none of the lesson scenarios focused on an anniversary, learners will need to adapt what they learned to a new situation.

> **A. Near Transfer Skill Question**
> Based on the following case notes, complete the reception worksheet in the planning database: The bride and groom are paying for their wedding with contributions from both parents. Although the bride prefers a formal wedding, after reviewing costs the couple compromised on a semiformal non-denominational Christian event. The ceremony costs will be approximately $8,000, including attire, church flowers, music and fees. The total budget cannot exceed $22,000.
>
> **B. Far Transfer Skill Question**
> Mr. and Mrs. Wilbanks have asked for help planning a 30th wedding anniversary event to include a renewal of wedding vows at their local Methodist church and a dinner reception with open bar for about seventy-five guests. However, as they review your cost estimates, shown in the online planning worksheets, they realize that their budget of $15,000 may not be sufficient. Revise the ceremony and/or reception worksheets in the database, selecting alternatives appropriate to their event that will also meet their budget. Refer to the client interview notes in the planner to make selections aligned to their preferences.

**FIGURE C.3.** *A Knowledge Question for the Bridezilla Course.*

### *Items to Measure Open-Ended Outcomes*

In some cases, your learning objective will require the learner to produce a product or demonstrate performance that is sufficiently nuanced and open-ended that you will need human raters to assess the accuracy or quality. A role play and design of a website that incorporates both functional and aesthetic features are two examples. Of course, using raters to assess performance or products of each learner is resource-intensive so you may want to do so only when there is no other practical way to evaluate competency and when the criticality of the skill warrants the investment. The behind-the-wheel driving test is one good example.

It is important to conduct formal validation of any test that will be used for any learning assessment that will be recorded or reported for individual learners. For example, a competency test may be required for certification, which in turn leads to promotions or specific work assignment eligibility. High-stakes evaluations such as these require a formal validation process. You can take a couple of approaches for formal validation, and I recommend you collaborate with your legal department and/or psychometrician to decide whether you need a formal validation and how best to go about it. For more details, refer to Shrock and Coscarelli (2007).

# LIST OF FIGURES
# AND TABLES

# GLOSSARY

**After-the-fact stories**  A knowledge elicitation technique in which experts describe a previous incident that required critical thinking skills.

**Behaviorist learning psychology**  An instructional theory based on stimulus-response that supports a rule-example-practice-feedback approach to learning. The psychological basis for directive learning designs.

**Bloom's taxonomy**  A well-known categorization of knowledge and skills for instructional purposes. The original version specified three main categories of skills: cognitive, affective, and psychomotor, each with a number of sub-skills.

**Branched scenario**  A type of scenario-based e-learning interface and navigation scheme in which most screens present a short scenario segment followed by three or four response options. Selection of an option leads to another screen showing the consequences of that option or providing additional choices. *See Figure 1.5.*

**Case data**  A component of a scenario-based e-learning design that includes information needed to make a decision or take action in the scenario. Case data plays a prominent role in diagnostic or research scenarios. Common forms of case data include quantitative metrics, interviews, and documents.

**Cognitive task analysis**  A type of job analysis that attempts to elicit tacit knowledge from experts. *See Chapter 11 for details.*

**Collaborative learning**  A process in which two or more learners work together to resolve a problem or respond to a scenario. Recent research indicates that collaboration is especially effective for more challenging scenarios.

**Concurrent verbalization**  A method of knowledge elicitation in which an expert talks aloud as he or she performs a task. Used to identify tacit knowledge that experts can't readily articulate.

**Critical decision method**  A method of knowledge elicitation in which an expert describes a past situation that was challenging and the interviewer asks probing questions to elicit tacit knowledge.

**Critical thinking skills**  Skills that are strategic in nature and underpin non-routine problem solving. Includes the use of heuristics or rules of thumb as well as progress monitoring experts use to solve challenging problems.

**Cutoff scores**  A test score that designates whether an individual passes or fails an assessment.

**Delivery media**  The carriers of instruction to include computers, smart phones, books, and instructors.

**Delivery mode**  The use of text, visuals, or audio to present instructional materials.

**Directive learning environments**  Traditional training that breaks work into small tasks and teaches each in a hierarchical sequence. Typical lessons present content, give examples, assign practice, and provide immediate feedback. A common design used in software training.

**Discovery learning**  An instructional approach that emphasizes inductive learning with little guidance. By exploring the learning environment or experiencing a simulated event, the content is learned. Research has shown discovery learning to be generally ineffective and inefficient.

**Domain-specific skills**  Skills that are unique and specific to a professional or work specialty, for example, preparing a brief for a lawyer or prescribing a treatment for a specific condition for a doctor.

| | |
|---|---|
| **Effect size** | A statistical measure of the overall impact of an instructional method or approach. The effect size indicates the proportion of a standard deviation difference between one instructional approach and a comparison instructional approach. Typically, an effect size of .5 or more indicates practical significance. |
| **Fading** | An instructional strategy in which initial lessons offer high levels of guidance, which is gradually removed or faded as the learner progresses. |
| **Feedback** | Knowledge of results in an instructional program. May directly inform the learners about the accuracy of their responses or may show how the learners' actions affect outcomes to the scenario. |
| **Full-screen active object** | A screen/navigational design for scenario-based e-learning in which a number of active objects are displayed on the screen. The on-screen objects are the main path to collect data, obtain guidance, and resolve the scenario. *See Figure 1.1 as an example.* |
| **Game** | A competitive activity with a challenge to achieve a goal, a set of rules and constraints, and a specific context. |
| **Guidance** | A component of a scenario-based e-learning design that minimizes the flounder factor by providing structure, examples, help, and other supportive elements. |
| **Guided discovery learning** | An instructional approach that emphasizes learner activity but provides structure and support as the learner progresses. Scenario-based e-learning is one form of guided discovery learning. Project-based learning and inquiry learning are other examples. |
| **Flounder factor** | An indication of the degree to which a learner becomes lost in a learning environment. Discovery learning environments often lead to a high flounder factor. |
| **Immersive learning** | An instructional environment that is highly learner-centered. Could refer to scenario-based e-learning or to virtual world learning environments. The term tends not to be used consistently. |
| **Inductive learning** | Learning from examples or experience rather than being told knowledge and skills. Scenario-based e-learning is a form of guided inductive learning. |
| **Instructional feedback** | An instructional response to a learner action or decision that informs the learner whether he or she is correct and provides an explanation. |
| **Instructive learning** | A traditional instructional approach in which learners are directly told knowledge and skills rather than inducing them from examples or experiences. Also called directive instructional designs. |
| **Interface response options** | Any of a number of ways learners can engage with the screen in e-learning, including clicking on objects, typing, or dragging and dropping objects |
| **Intrinsic feedback** | The response of the environment to a learner action or decision that reflects a likely real-world consequence. For example, if the learner makes a rude comment, the customer's responses will be negative. |
| **Knowledge elicitation** | Any of several techniques used to mine tacit expert knowledge. Also known as cognitive task analysis. *See Chapter 11.* |
| **Learning-focused feedback** | Knowledge of knowledge or skill gaps based on how the learner has responded to a scenario. May include specific topics and resources for additional study. |
| **Media** | How instruction is delivered, such as through a book, a computer, or a job card. |
| **Menu-driven** | A scenario-based e-learning interface and navigation scheme in which the learner accesses different components of the scenario through menus. Menu labels may reflect a workflow and/or lead to design components such as guidance. *See Figures 1.3 or 5.1 for examples.* |
| **Meta-analysis** | A research technique in which the results of multiple experiments about a common question or issue are synthesized. The meta-analysis combines the effect sizes of many individual studies to report median effect sizes. |

| | |
|---|---|
| **Meta-cognition** | A process of setting goals, mindfully selecting solution steps, monitoring progress, and adjusting actions as needed during problem resolution. |
| **Modes** | How content is presented in an instructional environment, such as with text, graphics, or audio. |
| **Murphy's Law introduction** | A type of trigger event in which everything goes wrong. After viewing the introduction, the learner has the opportunity to revisit the situation in order to take actions that mitigate the negative outcomes shown in the trigger event. |
| **Part-task learning** | Another term for directive learning. |
| **Performance analysis** | A process in which the work environment is reviewed to identify gaps that sub-optimize operational outcomes. |
| **Problem-based learning** | A form of guided discovery learning initiated in medical education in the 1970s in which groups of learners review a case scenario, discuss and research learning issues, and resolve the case. |
| **Procedural task** | A task that is completed step-by-step in more or less the same manner each time. Procedures are often good candidates for a directive instructional design. |
| **Receptive learning environments** | An instructional environment in which learners remain relatively passive while exposed to information. Many non-interactive lectures are examples of receptive learning environments. |
| **Reflection** | A component of a scenario-based e-learning design that prompts learners to review the decisions made and actions taken to resolve a scenario, consider the outcomes, and draw some conclusions about lessons learned. |
| **Reflection on recorded behaviors** | A knowledge-elicitation technique in which expert activities are captured as they perform a task. After task completion, the expert reviews the recordings and describes knowledge and skills used. |
| **Rubric** | A checklist typically used for scoring an open-ended assessment. The rubric provides guidance for graders to assess the accuracy of learner responses. *See Figure 9.2 for an example.* |
| **Scaffolding** | An instructional design feature that adds guidance to a learning environment. There are many types of scaffolding, but the goal of any of them is to minimize the flounder factor. *See Chapters 6 and 7 for examples.* |
| **Scenario-based e-learning** | An instructional environment in which the learner assumes a role to make decisions or take actions to resolve a work-related situation. *See Chapter 1 for a detailed definition.* |
| **Scenario data** | A component of a scenario-based e-learning lesson that involves quantitative or qualitative information about the scenario essential to resolving it. Scenario data typically play a large role in diagnostic or research scenarios. |
| **Simulation** | A dynamic model of a real-world system that responds in a realistic manner to learner actions. Usually based on a mathematical algorithm. *See Figure 1.4 for an example.* |
| **Social presence** | The degree to which a learner experiences or contacts others in a learning environment. A classroom training session should have high social presence compared to an asynchronous self-study multimedia lesson. |
| **Solution-focused feedback** | Knowledge of results regarding the solution (decisions, actions) made to resolve a scenario. |
| **Strategic tasks** | Tasks that are based on guidelines and typically require experience-based judgment and critical thinking skills to complete. |
| **Structured argumentation** | A type of collaboration in which learner teams research and present opposite (or different) aspects of a problem followed by a synthesis of viewpoints. |

| | |
|---|---|
| **Synchronous e-learning** | Online classes that are instructor-led and attended at the same time but in different geographic areas. Also known as virtual classrooms. |
| **Task deliverable** | A component of a scenario-based e-learning design that specifies the actions or decisions a learner makes to resolve a scenario. Should correspond to the learning objective. |
| **Task-process focused feedback** | Knowledge of results about the solution path the learner takes to research and/or resolve a scenario. |
| **Test reliability** | The extent to which a test will yield consistent results. |
| **Test validity** | The extent to which a test measures what it claims to measure. |
| **Training wheels** | A type of scaffolding in which part of the on-screen environment is disabled to minimize the flounder factor. |
| **Transfer of learning** | The extent to which knowledge and skills acquired during training are applied to the job. Also the extent to which a skill learned in training can be applied to a slightly different task after training. |
| **Trigger event** | A component of a scenario-based e-learning design that specifies how the scenario will kick off. Scenario-based e-learning should immerse the learner quickly into the scene and the trigger event specifies how this will appear or occur in the lesson. |
| **Value added** | An experimental approach in which various versions of a specific learning environment are tested. For example, learning is measured from a game with and without examples. |
| **Virtual advisors** | Online experts who can offer advice relevant to scenario resolution. *See Figure 6.6 for an example.* |
| **Virtual classroom** | See *Synchronous e-learning.* |
| **Virtual worlds** | Three-dimensional digital interfaces in which individuals assume an avatar persona and can move and interact with objects in the environment, including other avatars. Second Life is one well-known virtual world interface. |
| **Whole-task learning** | Another term for scenario-based e-learning. Contrast with part-task learning. |
| **Worked examples** | Demonstrations of how to perform a task or make a decision. A useful form of scaffolding in scenario-based e-learning. |

# REFERENCES

Adams, D.M., Mayer, R.E., MacNamara, A., Koenig, A., & Wainess, R. (2012). Narrative games for learning: Testing the discovery and narrative hypotheses. *Journal of Educational Psychology, 104,* 235–249.

Albanese, M.A. (2010). Problem-based learning. In W.B. Jeffries & K.N. Huggett (Eds.), *An introduction to medical teaching.* New York: Springer.

Alfieri, L., Brooks, P.J., Aldrich, N.J., & Tenenbaum, H.R. (2011). Does discovery-based instruction enhance learning? *Journal of Educational Psychology,* 103, 1–18.

Anderson, L.W., Krathwohl, D.R., Airasian, P.W., Cruikshank, K.A., Mayer, R.E., Pintrich, P.R., Raths, J., & Wittrock, M.C. (2001). *A taxonomy for learning, teaching, and assessing: A revision of Bloom's taxonomy of educational objectives.* New York: Longman.

Ayres, P., Marcus, N., Chan, C., & Qian, N. (2009). Learning hand manipulative tasks: When instructional animations are superior to equivalent static representation. *Computers in Human Behavior, 25,* 348–353.

Basarab, D.J. (1991). Evaluation of sales training on the bottom line. *Performance & Instruction,* pp. 35–40.

Clark, R.C. (2010). *Evidence-based training methods.* Alexandria, VA: ASTD Press.

Clark, R.C., & Lyons, C. (2011). *Graphics for learning.* San Francisco: Pfeiffer.

Clark, R.C. & Mayer, R.E. (2011). *e-Learning and the science of instruction* (3rd ed.). San Francisco: Pfeiffer.

Crandall, B., Klein, G., & Hoffman, R.R. (2006). *Working minds.* Cambridge, MA: MIT Press.

Cross, J., & Dublin, L. (2002). *Implementing e-learning,* Alexandria, VA: ASTD Press.

Lazonder, A.W., Hagemans, J.G., & de Jong. T. (2010). Offering and discovering domain information in simulation-based inquiry learning. *Learning and Instruction, 20*(6), 511–520.

de Jong, T. (2011). Instruction based on computer simulations. In R.E. Mayer & P.A. Alexander (Eds.), *Handbook of research on learning and instruction.* New York: Routledge.

Ericsson, K.A. (2006). The influence of experience and deliberate practice on the development of superior expert performance. In K.A. Ericsson, N. Charness, P.J. Feltovich, & R.R. Hoffman (Eds.), *The Cambridge handbook of expertise and expert performance.* New York: Cambridge University Press.

Ericsson, K.A. (2009). Enhancing the development of professional performance: Implications from the study of deliberate practice. In K.A. Ericsson (Ed.), *Development of professional expertise.* New York: Cambridge University Press.

Fiorella, L., & Mayer, R.E. (2012, April 9). Paper-based aids for learning with a computer game. *Journal of Educational Psychology.*

Gadgil, S., Nokes-Malach, T.J., & Chi, M.T.H. (2012). Effectiveness of holistic mental model confrontation in driving conceptual change. *Learning and Instruction, 22,* 47–61.

Gerjets, P., ImHof, B., Kuhl, T., Pfeiffer, V., Scheiter, K., & Gemballa, S. (2010). Using static and dynamic visualizations to support the comprehension of complex dynamic phenomena in the nature sciences. In L. Verschaffel, E. De Corte, T. de Jong, & J. Elen (Eds.), *Use of representations in reasoning and problem solving.* New York: Routledge.

Goldstone, R.L., & Son, J.Y. (2005). The transfer of scientific principles using concrete and idealized simulations. *Journal of the Learning Sciences, 14*, 69–110.

Green, M.C., Strange, J.J., & Brock, T.C. (2002). *Narrative impact: Social and cognitive foundations.* Mahwah, NJ: Lawrence Erlbaum Associates.

Hartley, D.E. (2001). *Selling e-learning.* Alexandria, VA: ASTD Press.

Hattie, J. (2009). *Visible learning: A synthesis of over 800 meta-analyses relating to achievement.* New York: Routledge.

Hattie, J., & Gan, M. (2011). Instruction based on feedback. In R.E. Mayer & P.A. Alexander (Eds.), *Handbook of research on learning and instruction.* New York: Routledge.

Holzinger, A., Kickmeier-Rust, M., Wassentheurer, S., & Hessinger, M. (2009). Learning performance with interactive simulations in medical education: Lessons learned from results of learning complex physiological models with the Haemodynamics Simulator. *Computers & Education, 52*, 292–301.

Horton, W. (2006). *e-Learning by design.* San Francisco: Pfeiffer.

Hung, W. (2011). Theory to reality: A few issues in implementing problem-based learning. *Educational Technology Research and Development, 59*, 529–552.

Jonassen, D.H. (2004). *Learning to solve problems.* San Francisco: Pfeiffer.

Kalyuga, S., Rikers, R., & Paas, F. (2012). Educational implications of the expertise reversal effects in learning and performance of complex cognitive and sensorimotor skills. *Educational Psychology Review, 24*, 313–337.

Kapp, K.M., & O'Driscoll, T. (2010). *Learning in 3D.* San Francisco: Pfeiffer.

Kapur, M. (2012). Productive failure in learning the concept of variance. *Instructional Science, 40,* 651–672.

Kapur, M., & Rummel, N. (2012). Productive failure in learning from generation and invention activities. *Instructional Science, 40*, 645–650.

Kirschner, F., Paas, F., Kirschner, P.A., & Janssen, J. (2011). Differential effects of problem-solving demands on individual and collaborative learning outcomes. *Learning and Instruction, 21*, 587–599.

Kluger, A.N., & DeNisi, A. (1996). The effects of feedback interventions on performance: A historical review, a meta-analysis, and a preliminary feedback intervention theory. *Psychological Bulletin, 119*, 254–284.

Kumta. S.M., Tsang, P.L., Hung, L.K., & Cheng, J.C.Y. (2003). Fostering critical thinking skills through a web-based tutorial programme for final-year medical students: A randomized controlled study. *Journal of Educational Multimedia and Hypermedia, 12*, 267–73.

Lazonder, A.W., Hagemans, M.G., & de Jong, T. (2010). Offering and discovering domain information in simulation-based inquiry learning. *Learning and Instruction, 20*, 511–520.

Lee, H., Plass, J.L., & Homer, B.C. (2006). Optimizing cognitive load for learning from computer-based science simulations. *Journal of Educational Psychology, 98*, 902–913.

Leighton, J.P. (2011). A cognitive model for the assessment of higher order thinking in students. In G. Shaw & D.R. Robinson (Eds.), *Assessment of higher order thinking skills.* Charlotte, NC: Information Age Publishing.

Lesgold, A. Eggan, G., Katz, S., & Rao, G. (1993). Possibilities for assessment using computer-based apprenticeship environments. In M. Rabinowitz (Ed.), *Cognitive science foundations of instruction.* Mahwah, NJ: Lawrence Erlbaum Associates.

Lesgold, A., Lajoie, S., Bunzo, M., & Eggan, G. (1992). SHERLOCK: A coached practice environment for an electronic troubleshooting job. In J.H. Larkin & R.W. Chabay (Eds.), *Computer-assisted instruction and intelligent tutoring systems: Shared goals and complementary approaches* (pp. 201–239). Mahwah, NJ: Lawrence Erlbaum Associates.

Lim, J., Reiser, R.E., & Olina, Z. (2009). The effects of part-task and whole-task instructional approaches on acquisition and transfer of a complex cognitive skill. *Educational Technology Research & Development, 57,* 61–77.

Loyens, S.M.M., & Rikers, R.J.J.P. (2011). Instruction based on inquiry. In R.E. Mayer & P.A. Alexander (Eds.), *Handbook of research on learning and instruction.* New York: Routledge.

Mayer, R.E. (2004). Should there be a three-strikes rule against pure discovery learning: The case for guided methods of instruction. *American Psychologist, 59,* 14–19.

Mayer, R.E. (2011). Multimedia learning and games. In S. Tobias & D. Fletcher (Eds.), *Computer games and instruction* (pp. 281–305). Greenwich, CT: Information Age Publishers.

Mayer, R.E., & Alexander, P.A. (Eds.). (2011). *Handbook of research on learning and instruction.* New York: Routledge.

Mayer, R.E., Hegarty, M., Mayer, S., & Campbell, J. (2005). When static media promote active learning: Annotated illustrations versus narrated animations in multimedia instruction. *Journal of Experimental Psychology: Applied, 11,* 256–265.

Mayer, R.E., & Johnson, C.I. (2010). Adding instructional features that promote learning in a game-like environment. *Journal of Educational Psychology: Applied, 8,* 147–154.

Merrill, M.D. (2012). *First principles of instruction.* San Francisco: Pfeiffer.

Moreno, R., & Mayer, R.E. (2005). Role of guidance, reflection, and interactivity in an agent-based multimedia game. *Journal of Educational Psychology, 97,* 117–128.

Moreno, R., & Ortegano-Layne, L. (2008). Using cases as thinking tools in teacher education: The role of representation format. *Educational Technology Research and Development, 56,* 449–465.

Moreno, R., Ozogul, G., & Reisslein, M. (2011). Teaching with concrete and abstract visual representations: Effects on students' problem solving, problem representations, and learning perceptions. *Journal of Educational Psychology, 103,* 33–47.

Phillips, J.J. (2007). Measuring the ROI of a coaching intervention, part 2. *Performance Improvement, 46,* 10–23.

Phillips, J.J., & Phillips, P.P. (2007). *The value of learning: How organizations capture value and ROI and translate it into support, improvement, and funds.* San Francisco: Pfeiffer.

Renkl, A. (2011). Instruction based on examples. In R.E. Mayer & P.A. Alexander (Eds.), *Handbook of research on learning and instruction.* New York: Routledge.

Schoenfeld, A.H. (1987). What's all the fuss about metacognition? In A. Schoenfeld (Ed.), *Cognitive science and mathematics education.* Mahwah, NJ: Lawrence Erlbaum Associates.

Schank, R.C., & German, T.R. (2002). The pervasive role of stories in knowledge and action. In M.C. Green, J.J. Strange, & T.C. Brock (Eds.), *Narrative impact: Social and cognitive foundations.* Mahwah, NJ: Lawrence Erlbaum Associates.

Schraw, G., & Robinson, D.R. (Eds.). (2011). *Assessment of higher order thinking skills.* Charlotte, NC: Information Age Publishing.

Shrock, S.A., & Coscarelli, W.C. (2007). *Criterion-referenced test development* (3rd ed.). San Francisco: Pfeiffer.

Shute, V.J. (2008). Focus on formative feedback. *Review of Educational Research, 78*(1), 153–189.

Shute, V.J., & Glaser, R. (1990). A large-scale evaluation of an intelligent discovery world: Smithtown. *Interactive Learning Environments, 1,* 51–77.

Sitzmann, T., Brown, K.G., Casper, W.J., Ely, K., & Zimmerman, R.D. (2008). A review and meta-analysis of the nomological network of trainee reactions. *Journal of Applied Psychology, 93,* 280–295.

Stark, R., Kopp, V., & Fischer, M.R. (2011). Case-based learning with worked examples in complex domains: Two experimental studies in undergraduate medical education. *Learning and Instruction, 21*, 22–33.

U.S. Department of Education, Office of Planning, Evaluation, and Policy Development. (2010). *Evaluation of evidence-based practices in online learning: A meta-analysis and review of online learning studies.* Washington, DC: Author.

Van Gog, T., Paas, F., van Merrienboer, J.J.G., & Witte, P. (2005). Uncovering the problem-solving process: Cued retrospective reporting versus concurrent and retrospective reporting. *Journal of Experimental Psychology: Applied, 11*, 237–244

Van Gog, T., Sluijsmans, D.M.A., Joosten-ten Brinke, D., & Prins, F.J. (2010). Formative assessment in an online learning environment to support flexible on-the job learning in complex professional domains. *Educational Technology Research and Development, 58*, 311–324.

Van der Meij, J., & de Jong, T. (2011). The effects of directive self-explanation prompts to support active processing of multiple representations in a simulation-based learning environment. *Journal of Computer Assisted Learning, 27*, 411–423.

Van Merrienboer, J.J.G., & Kirschner, P.A. (2007). *Ten steps to complex learning.* New York: Routledge.

Wiedmann, M., Leach, R.C., Rummel, N., & Wiley, J. (2012). Does group composition affect learning by invention? *Instructional Science, 40*, 711–730.

Wong, A., Marcus, N., Ayers, P., Smith, L., Cooper, G.A., Paas, F.G.W.C., & Sweller, J. (2009). Instructional animations can be superior to statics when learning human motor skills. *Computer in Human Behavior, 25*, 339–347.

Zacharia, Z.C., & Olympiou, G. (2011). Physical versus virtual manipulative experimentation in physics learning. *Learning and Instruction, 21*, 317–331.

# ABOUT THE AUTHOR

**Ruth Colvin Clark, Ed.D.,** has focused her professional efforts on bridging the gap between academic research on instructional methods and application of that research by training and performance support professionals in corporate and government organizations. Dr. Clark has developed a number of seminars and has written seven books, including *e-Learning and the Science of Instruction, Building Expertise,* and *Evidence-Based Training Methods,* that translate important research findings into practitioner guidelines.

A science undergraduate, she completed her doctorate in instructional psychology/educational technology in 1988 at the University of Southern California. Dr. Clark is a past president of the International Society of Performance Improvement and a member of the American Educational Research Association. She was honored with the 2006 Thomas F. Gilbert Distinguished Professional Achievement Award by the International Society for Performance Improvement and was an invited *Training Legend* Speaker at the ASTD 2006 International Conference. Dr. Clark is currently a dual resident of Southwest Colorado and Phoenix, Arizona, and divides her professional time among speaking, teaching, and writing. For more information, consult her website at www.clarktraining.com.

# INDEX

Page references followed by *fig* indicate an illustrated figure; followed by *t* indicate a table.